MIRACLE IN BUFFALO

MIRACLE IN BUFFALO

How the Dream of Baseball
Revived a City

ANTHONY VIOLANTI

St. Martin's Press
New York

To my wife, Andrea, and daughter, Heather,
whose support, encouragement, and love have helped me
overcome every obstacle.

Design by Dawn Niles

Library of Congress Cataloging-in-Publication Data

Violanti, Anthony.
    Miracle in Buffalo : how the dream of baseball revived a city / Anthony Violanti.
        p.   cm.
    ISBN 0-312-04878-5
    1. Buffalo Bisons (Baseball team—History. 2. Buffalo (N.Y.)—
History.   I. Title.
GV875.B8V56   1991
796.357'64'0974797—dc20

                                                                90-27374
                                                                CIP

First Edition: May 1991

10 9 8 7 6 5 4 3 2 1

CONTENTS

ACKNOWLEDGMENTS

Writing this book has been an arduous, grueling, and exhilarating process. There are many people who contributed; without them the book would not have been possible.

Joe Overfield, Buffalo's baseball historian, offered invaluable assistance with editing, research, and encouragement. His book, *The 100 Seasons of Buffalo Baseball,* was my main reference tool. I must also acknowledge Joe's wife, Clara Overfield, for her inspiration.

Gene Krzyzynski also played a crucial role in my finishing this project. He spent countless hours helping me with writing, editing, and organization. He also kept my spirits up through the tough times and never stopped believing in me or this project. His wife, Arlene, also played a role in this book, through her faith, courage, and living example of hope.

I want to thank my fellow members of the Buffalo Baseball Hall of Fame Committee, who have given their lives to baseball in Buffalo: Vince McNamara, Chairman; Joe Alli; George Daddario; Ralph Hubbell; Cy Kritzer; Joe Overfield; Pete Weber; Cy Williams; and the late Phil Ranallo. The committee's secretary is Gerri Kozlowski.

I want to thank Peter Ciotta, Director of Publications for the Buffalo Bisons.

Bisons General Manager Mike Billoni was always ready to help when needed. So were Jon Dandes, Vice President of the team; and Marta Hiczewski, Assistant General Manager, Mike Buczkowski, the team's Public Relations Director; John Isherwood, Public Relations Assistant; and Ken Lehner, the Operations Manager, also helped. The entire Bisons organization, from Bob and Mindy Rich on down, was cooperative and made this chore a little bit easier.

I want to also thank Scott Brown, former Buffalo television reporter, for his help with the Robert Redford interview.

I used files of *The Buffalo News* as a research tool, and wish to express my thanks to Sally Schlaerth, librarian at the *News,* and her staff, and my colleagues at the *News.*

Likewise, I must thank Ken Goldfarb for his help with the story of Mario Cuomo's baseball days. I used his story on Cuomo, published in the *Schenectady Gazette* on August 19, 1988, as a research tool. The book, *Mario Cuomo, A Biography,* by Robert S. McEl-vaine, was also used as a research tool.

I want to thank Sheila Murphy for helping me to arrange an interview with Governor Cuomo.

I want to thank Pete Weber, voice of the Bisons, for his invaluable help in my research.

I want to also thank George Witte, for his help and encouragement at St. Martin's Press.

Others who helped make this book possible include Sally Violanti, Alice Pyle, Ben Gardon, Walter Gardon, Ed Gardon, Sr., Bob Gardon, Dorothea and Gene Nischik, Betty Leising, Dutch Leising, Debbie Nischik, Pam, Werner, Greg and Chris Gstattenbauer, Tom Gaffney, John Keller, John Nowak, David Cahn, Charles Monteleone, Pat and Ivan Moore, Jerry Reo, Jeff Morrison, Greg Brown, Clip Smith, Doug Smith, Carol Jasen, Irv Weinstein, Kevin Lester, Fred A. Luongo, Sr., Modesto Argenio, Paula Voell, Dick Bradley, Jeff Simon, Dick Wich, Dick Hirsch, Jim Schrader, Terry Doran, Herm Trotter, J. W. Lennon, Wayne Jones, Charley Young, Joan Danzig, Bob Schreiber, Dick Johnston, Jimmy Bell, Judy Maurer, Mark Goldman, Nelson Hughes, John Colazzi, Herb Hodge, Andrew Yusick, Dr. Elizabeth O'Neil, Pete Siedlecki, John Masterson, Sister Margaret Irr, Father Roy Herberger, Yvonne Greatwood, Helen Wagner, and John Wojtowicz.

And, most of all, I want to thank the baseball fans of Buffalo, who never stopped believing in miracles.

INTRODUCTION

The silver-haired hero is wearing a white baseball uniform with red lettering. The sun is setting as he leaves the dugout and steps onto the field. His gait is slow yet elegant, his figure slightly bent. Even in an unfamiliar uniform, his classic visage is instantly recognizable. In the warm twilight of June 1989, Joe DiMaggio appears right at home in Buffalo. This stadium—Pilot Field, with its neoclassical design, shimmering emerald grass, and nostalgic ambiance—is a throwback to the stadiums of DiMaggio's best years. But to the nearly 20,000 people who have filled this intimate ballpark, and to baseball fans across America, he will always be the Yankee Clipper, and he is accorded a standing ovation. DiMaggio's blue eyes glisten. He removes his red cap, and his hair bristles against the breeze. DiMaggio holds up the cap and majestically waves to the crowd. Instantly, the ballpark is engulfed by a thunderous roar of appreciation. Later DiMaggio will say, "I think it's a great stadium. It fits."

IN BUFFALO, PILOT FIELD—like baseball itself—has become a refuge from the congestion, rush, and tension of urban life. It is a place to gather and share a sense of community. Moreover, this ballpark, located in the heart of downtown and consistent with baseball's best architectural traditions, is a place where people can dream about the future without losing sight of the past.

"This is a special place," says Hank Aaron, baseball's all-time home-run king. "It reminds me, in a way, of Wrigley Field. It's the kind of park a ballplayer comes to, and wants to play in."

Since it opened in April 1988, more than 3 million fans have come to Pilot Field, an unprecedented feat for minor-league baseball. The ballpark has been integral to the game's rebirth in Buffalo and to the spiritual renewal of a city weary of economic hardship, bad-weather jokes, and a tarnished national image.

In 1970 professional baseball left Buffalo. It was gone for nearly a decade. And even when it returned, it was no more than a shadow of its former self.

It wasn't until almost twenty years after baseball had left that the modern ballpark with the old-time look arose as a symbol of a new era in Buffalo—the departure of Rust Belt defeatism and the arrival of a self-image that was decidedly big-league.

The keeper of the flame was a mayor named Jimmy Griffin, who brought baseball back to a beleaguered community whose proud baseball heritage included names such as Marse Joe McCarthy and Warren Spahn.

It all had to do with dreams—dreams of immigrants and their children, and the dreams of those same children after they'd grown.

For Jimmy Griffin, that dream was twofold: a downtown stadium and a big-league team. This dream would be shared by a community, and it would be fortified by unlikely dreamers from afar: Robert Redford for one, Mario Cuomo for another. As they played their roles in resurrecting the game in Buffalo, the city itself was being revived. Baseball was making it happen.

Through his city's years of self-doubt, Jimmy Griffin's faith in his dream remained unshaken. It finally began to happen when Bob Rich, Jr., bought a bankrupt Double-A ball club that played in rundown War Memorial Stadium, nicknamed the Old Rockpile. It was a dramatic move by the scion of a family long devoted to Buffalo but never associated with baseball.

Seven years and one new stadium later, Bob Rich, Jr., and his wife, Mindy, as champions of that dream, led Buffalo to the threshold of the major leagues.

"Pilot Field," says Bob Rich, Jr., "was designed for a city. I look at this stadium and the growth and comeback of our community, and it seems like a miracle in Buffalo. But it's a miracle that happened because we all believed in Buffalo."

Part One

"*Un*-believable."
"It's more than that; it's perfect."

—*Field of Dreams*

1

RISING FROM THE DEAD

Bob Rich, Jr., sat in his sunlit suite on the third floor of Cleveland's Stouffer Tower City Plaza Hotel, preparing for the most important news conference of his life. It was nearly nine on Thursday morning, June 14, 1990. Outside, on Public Square, the humid center of downtown was beginning to bake in temperatures that would reach 82 degrees. Rich, owner of the Buffalo Bisons baseball team, had awakened at six and then eaten scrambled eggs for breakfast. He now leaned back in an easy chair, holding a cup of coffee. On his lap was a folder full of papers; he still had homework to do.

Nearby, facing Rich, sat Peter Fleischer and Doug Petkus of Hill & Knowlton in New York City, one of the largest public relations firms in the world. They were preparing to pepper Rich with questions in a mock news conference. At Rich's side was his wife, Mindy, the Bisons' executive vice president. Mike Billoni, vice president and general manager of the team, nervously paced the floor. Also rushing back and forth were Mike Buczkowski, public relations director of the Bisons, and Ken Lehner, the team's youthful operations manager.

The hotel was abuzz with reporters and other interested parties who had come to Cleveland to learn what ground rules the major-league baseball owners would establish for the addition of two franchises in the National League. Rich had been anticipating this day for seven and a half years. It all began in 1983, when he purchased the insolvent Double-A Bisons, who played their Eastern League games in Buffalo's decrepit War Memorial Stadium. Since then, he had poured time, energy, and millions of dollars into building a top-flight baseball operation. Now, it was time to reach for new heights. He soon would learn the criteria for selecting the two expansion franchises that would begin play in 1993. Architects of the most successful franchise in minor-league history, Rich and his staff had reason to be optimistic that one of the franchises would be awarded to Buffalo.

Suddenly, there was a knock on the door. The suite, which had been filled with loud chatter just a minute before, turned silent. Two men wearing serious expressions and tailored, navy blue business suits stood in the doorway.

Somewhat startled, Rich and the rest of his entourage stared at the somber pair, who quickly flashed badges identifying them as agents of the Secret Service. Affixed to their ears were tiny devices for receiving instant communications from the agent in charge. The waists of their jackets showed telltale bulges of what appeared to be firearms.

Immediately, the agents got to the point: They had heard that a group of about two hundred people from the Buffalo area was going to demonstrate around the hotel, and the Secret Service was concerned. The agents were here to protect George W. Bush, son of the U.S. president, who also happened to be a part owner of the Texas Rangers baseball team. He, too, was in this hotel for the meetings, and the Secret Service would not leave anything to chance; threats to the president's family could turn up anywhere. "We're concerned," one of the agents said, "about security problems the demonstration might cause."

A background check on the group wouldn't be much help; it was only two weeks old. The name was R.B.I.—Rally Buffalo's Interests—and its members had filled four buses in Buffalo that morning for "The Stampede to Cleveland." That's exactly what these agents were worried about: the stampede. For a bodyguard, there's no greater nightmare than chaos.

"Really," Rich told the agents with the trace of a smile, "these people mean no harm. They're not going to cause any problems or trouble. They're respected members of the community—in business, government—and all of them are baseball fans. They don't work for the Bisons, and we have no connection to them, but I can vouch for all of them. They're good people who just love baseball and want to make their voices known."

Rich and the Bisons' staff explained that the demonstrators

would not enter the hotel, but only march around the outside, near Public Square. After all, these people from all walks of life were lobbyists in the best sense, with an overridingly positive message: VOTE BUFFALO, MAJOR LEAGUE. They carried T-shirts, buttons, posters, and pennants displaying that message. They were chasing a dream that the ever-resilient people of Buffalo had long considered impossible, and Bob Rich was their inspirational leader.

The two Secret Service agents seemed satisfied. As they prepared to leave the suite, Billoni—a front-office man known for never, *ever* missing an opportunity to spread the gospel of Buffalo baseball—offered each of them a Bisons T-shirt. The Secret Service men laughed, but as they did, the telephone rang. "Oh, no," one of the agents said, "I bet it's my boss, telling me not to take this shirt. I'm sorry, we've got to get going." And they left.

Bob Rich returned to his sheaf of papers. Buffalo's baseball hopes had never been higher than they were that day. It all seemed so surreal, much like another Thursday in another June in another hotel room twenty years earlier. But in a far different way.

THIS TIME, JOE ALLI could not play the role of tough reporter. It was Thursday evening, June 4, 1970, and he had just witnessed the demise of a ninety-three-year-old baseball franchise. There were tears in his eyes. He sat in front of his typewriter in a New York City hotel room and struggled to keep his composure. Nervously, he took a cigar out of his mouth and put it in an ashtray. He grabbed a handkerchief from his pocket and gently wiped the moisture from his rimless glasses, then rubbed his eyes. Alli was no softy, though; his roots were in Sicily and on Buffalo's West Side, and he was a Marine combat correspondent in the Pacific during World War II. He had seen his share of horror, on the bloody island of Peleliu, for instance. But he had never cried over a story. Until now. Slowly and painfully, he finally typed the first paragraph: "The baseball Bisons are dead!"

Nearby, sprawled on a chair and staring at the floor, was Don Labbruzzo, general manager of the Bisons. He, too, was sobbing. Heartsick, he compared losing the baseball team to losing his father or his mother. A few hours earlier, Labbruzzo had tried to make a case for Buffalo baseball during a meeting of the International

League board of directors. He had pleaded, cajoled, and begged. It had not been enough.

While Labbruzzo was inside the meeting room, Alli had paced the floor outside the door. He was on an early deadline for the *Buffalo Courier-Express*. Alli began working at the morning paper in 1937 and had covered a wide range of local sports that included boxing, both amateur and pro. Alli, now fifty-three years old, had been on the baseball beat for nearly two decades, including the days when International League road trips even included Havana. Only five feet five inches tall, he had qualified for the Marines by a fraction of an inch, and he would set his war buddies straight on the pronunciation of his name by saying he was "one of the Allies—you know, Great Britain, France, the U.S. . . . and me." As a newsman, he seemed right out of central casting: sort of an Oscar Madison, with the stub of an El Producto cigar—sometimes lit, more often not—perpetually sticking from the corner of his mouth. There was nothing fancy about Joe Alli's prose; like him, it was tough and succinct.

While he waited in the lobby for the meeting to end, he sensed that Buffalo baseball was in deep trouble. The meeting wasn't supposed to last long, but hours passed. Alli kept pacing and watching the clock and lighting his cigars. Occasionally, the directors came out for a break, and Alli asked what was happening. They would say nothing.

At last, the time for a vote arrived. Labbruzzo sensed that it was hopeless. He was right: The directors' vote was 6 to 2, meaning that Buffalo would have to forfeit its franchise. For the first time since 1877, its besieged but steadfast people—the descendants of immigrants from such places as Poland, Italy, Germany, and Ireland—would be without professional baseball.

"I felt like such a failure; I was dying inside, but what could I do?" says Labbruzzo, a short, stocky, owlish man who wears thick glasses and rumpled brown suits. When he is excited, Labbruzzo's eyes open wide, his hands are in motion, and he speaks in machine-gun bursts. But the sudden loss of this team stilled Labbruzzo's ever-buoyant spirit: "What could the league do? There was nothing anybody could do. They wanted me to continue, they were sympathetic, but I couldn't go on. I didn't have any more money."

Until that moment, Labbruzzo's twenty-one-year baseball career had been marked by success. Under his guidance, along with the help of his assistant, George Daddario, the Bisons drew 413,263 fans to Offermann Stadium in 1959, a record for Buffalo baseball. Labbruzzo left Buffalo in 1961 and went to Syracuse, where he revitalized a downtrodden baseball franchise.

Labbruzzo was enticed back to Buffalo in 1970 with promises of a five-year contract and community support. He was also led to believe that games would be played in Lackawanna Stadium, just south of Buffalo, or in All-High Stadium, a well-kept high school athletic field in North Buffalo.

No site change materialized, though, and Labbruzzo was forced back to decaying War Memorial Stadium in Buffalo's inner city. "I knew going back there was suicide—everybody knew it," he says. "It was the last thing I wanted to do, but we had no choice. We could win the pennant and people would not come to that stadium."

The reason was simple: fear.

War Memorial Stadium, later to be known as the Old Rockpile, was in a run-down section of Buffalo's East Side. In June 1967 the neighborhood was rocked by race riots. Baseball fans were afraid to go there. Even the Bisons' locker room was vandalized. For the next three years, many home games were switched to Hyde Park Stadium in Niagara Falls. But attendance continued to dwindle.

Labbruzzo mortgaged everything he owned to keep the ball club going. "I lost my home, and I went broke," he remembers sadly, and it cost much more than money. "It also cost me years off my life. You know the song 'I Left My Heart in San Francisco'? Well, I lost my heart in Buffalo."

When he went to New York for the directors' meeting, Labbruzzo did not expect it to last long. He hadn't bothered to make a hotel reservation and had nowhere to stay. Alli offered to share his room with Labbruzzo, so the two men went back there and Labbruzzo watched as Alli typed page after page of his story. It was one of those emotional moments a reporter never forgets—something that seemed straight out of a movie. But Alli knew that it was all too real.

Somehow, Alli could not even think of his city without its baseball team. "It was like losing an old friend," he recalls. "You always thought baseball was something that you had forever."

Cy Kritzer shared that feeling. He had been a sportswriter at the *Buffalo Evening News* since 1929 and had covered the baseball beat since 1939. On the day baseball died in Buffalo, he sat in front of a typewriter in his paper's sports department, but with mixed feelings.

"What killed baseball was that park in that neighborhood," Kritzer says. "It wasn't the fault of the people who lived there, but the city did nothing to provide security. If you don't feel safe, you're not going to go to a ball game. Everybody knew this was a good baseball town, but we were relieved when that team folded. It hurt like hell to lose our franchise, but you could see it was going to happen."

Buffalo would lose more than a baseball franchise in the 1970s. The once-booming steel mills and other heavy industries suffered economic downturns. The downtown area deteriorated to the point where one joker put up a billboard that read, WOULD THE LAST PERSON LEAVING BUFFALO TURN OUT THE LIGHTS? It would get much worse before it got better.

The seventies were a decade of painful transition: of blizzards, recessions, and devastating unemployment. Lake Erie was even declared dead, killed by pollution. This was a frightening experience for Buffalo, the erstwhile crown jewel of the Great Lakes—the Queen City—that had played such an important role in the growth of America.

A portent of this economic and emotional free-fall had come two years earlier, in 1968, with a rabbit punch thrown by Major League Baseball. Buffalo had been favored to land a National League expansion franchise, and Erie County, which includes Buffalo, was making plans to build a domed stadium in the suburbs. But it never happened. At the eleventh hour, after some back-room politicking by team owners, Montreal replaced Buffalo as the eastern city that would join San Diego in expanding the National League. "We felt, on the merits, we should have been given the franchise," said lawyer Robert Swados, who headed the Buffalo baseball bid at that time. "But selling Buffalo was a tough job."

Buffalo was jilted, and the dome was never built, leading to years of political bloodletting and decades of who's-to-blame lawsuits. Political and business support for baseball eroded, and there was a loss of hope that Buffalo would be in the running for any other expansion franchise awarded in the seventies or beyond. With no big-league stadium, there would be no big-league team. Period.

The disillusioning failure in the expansion race set the tone for a series of more serious traumas in the years to come. The period between 1970 and 1982 was the most agonizing since the Depression for Buffalo's economy. The city's population dropped by nearly 23 percent, from 462,768 in 1970 to 357,900 a decade later. By 1982, the unemployment rate had nearly doubled—to 11.6 percent.

Heavy industry bore the brunt of the hard times. In 1970, there were more than 33,000 steelworkers in Buffalo. By 1982, that figure dropped to 11,000. By 1989, it was down to 4,200. More than 87 percent of the steel-industry jobs had disappeared.

Nature also played a cruel role in Buffalo's decline. In January 1977 the city was battered by a killer blizzard, its worst in memory; twenty-three people died, and the damage estimate was $300 million. Buffalo came to a virtual standstill for weeks, and the jokes from across the country were as cutting as they were relentless. It was as if everyone in Buffalo had become characters in an updated version of *The Outcasts of Poker Flat,* but there was no humor to that. This was reality, and it was tragic.

But for Buffalo, the worst times lay ahead in 1982. In that one year, three of its cornerstones collapsed. The *Courier-Express,* where Joe Alli had been a newspaperman for forty-two years, died. So did Republic Steel. And giant Bethlehem Steel drastically cut back its operations. All told, six steel plants closed in the Buffalo area that year, and four more endured temporary shutdowns.

Buffalonians, used to the cyclic nature of the automobile and steel industries, wanted to believe that this economic earthquake would not last long. But they couldn't have been more wrong. The year 1982 was the shattering aftershock to the seventies. Its reverberations would be felt for many more years.

"The seventies were a period of a realignment and the decline of the manufacturing sector in Buffalo," says George Smyntek, an economist for New York State's Department of Labor. "This time, it became reality for the community and its leaders.

"It was hitting us in the face, and we couldn't deny it anymore. Bethlehem Steel was the turning point. The attempts to try and rebuild this area as a manufacturing sector ended with the end of Bethlehem Steel."

"What happened to Buffalo in the seventies and early eighties . . . was catastrophic on all levels because it affected the way people lived," says Mark Goldman, a professor of urban studies at Empire State College in Buffalo, who has written two books on the city's history.

The loss of baseball simply made a bad situation worse, especially in terms of community morale.

"God, look at the Brooklyn Dodgers!" says Goldman. "Walter O'Malley didn't realize that he didn't just take a baseball team out of Brooklyn; he took the heart and soul of that whole borough. That was one of the greatest acts of urbacide in twentieth-century America, moving the Dodgers out of Brooklyn."

Just as the Dodgers had broken the hearts of Brooklynites thirteen years earlier, the Bisons left an aching void in the morale of the many Buffalonians who identified with baseball. The team's new home would be more than 1,300 miles away, in Winnipeg, where the national pastime is ice hockey.

"I was not surprised when the franchise folded in 1970; I was relieved," asserts Joe Overfield, Buffalo's baseball historian, who has been following the game in the city for more than six decades. "By that time, baseball had become an embarrassment to Buffalo."

The move to Canada was immediate—after only thirty-eight games. For the rest of the 1970 season and for the eight years that followed, there was no professional baseball in Buffalo. A community struggling with its self-image had suffered yet another deep wound to its collective psyche.

As the decade wore on, Overfield, like most baseball fans in town, became increasingly pessimistic. "As far as Buffalo baseball was concerned," he laments, "it seemed like a lost cause."

IN GOOD TIMES or bad—and these were the worst—baseball had been a bright thread in Buffalo's historical fabric. The game was common ground for a city forged and sustained by immigrants. All the segments of Buffalo's ethnically diverse population could unite in a common passion: baseball.

The city's first professional baseball team began play on August 3, 1877. The next season, Buffalo joined the International Association, baseball's first minor league. Overflow crowds turned out to watch the team, and in 1879 Buffalo entered the National League, where it remained for seven seasons.

In 1886, Buffalo became a member of the International League, starting a relationship that would last eighty-five years—except for two brief interruptions, in the Players League (1890) and the Western League (1899–1900), which later became the American League. Buffalo had two teams during the 1914–1915 seasons, one in the International League and one in the ill-fated Federal League, which folded after 1915.

The Bisons moved into a field at Michigan Avenue and Ferry Street in 1889. It was originally called Olympic Park, then Buffalo Baseball Park. It was rebuilt in 1924 as Bison Stadium and then became Offermann Stadium in 1935, renamed in memory of the club president, Frank J. Offermann.

Offermann Stadium's capacity was 14,000, and the cozy seating arrangement created an elbow-to-elbow cordiality as intimate as a dining room table's.

"Offermann Stadium was, to me, like Wrigley Field is in the majors," says Tommy Lasorda, who pitched there for Montreal in the International League and would eventually manage the Los Angeles Dodgers. "It was a park of togetherness."

Dallas Green, who pitched for Buffalo in 1959 and went on to manage in the big leagues with Philadelphia and the New York Yankees, also praises the park. "Offermann was one of the great minor-league ballparks of all time," he says. "The people were right on top of you, and it had that same feeling you get in Fenway. And those Buffalo fans knew their baseball."

Jim Schulz was one of those fans. He grew up in Buffalo during the 1950s and went to games with his father, a Buffalo police officer. "I remember sitting there with my dad," he recalls. "It was a perfect setting for baseball; you were so close to the players. I remember there was a door near the center-field scoreboard. I used to watch a guy go in and out of that door, and I wondered where he went. It was a great place to spend an afternoon with my father. I'll never forget it."

In Offermann Stadium, the scoreboard stood like a huge altar over a baseball shrine. It was an old-fashioned wooden marvel, with a mysterious little fellow inside, almost like the man behind the curtain in *The Wizard of Oz*. If you watched closely, you might catch him putting up freshly painted white numerals in the scoreboard's square holes to post the latest results.

The old ballpark supplied lasting emotional comfort for generations of Buffalonians. It was there that they gathered to root for the hometown heroes, including the likes of Bill Dickey, Rip Sewell, Connie Mack, Jimmy Collins, Joe McCarthy, Sal Maglie, Bucky Harris, Paul Richards, Lou Boudreau, Fred Hutchinson, Jim Bunning, Billy Pierce, Chris Short, and Bobby Wine.

Offermann's magic seemed to extend beyond its walls, touching some of those who never played there as pros—most notably a tireless left-hander who was born and reared in South Buffalo and pitched his way onto a Hall of Fame plaque in Cooperstown: Warren Spahn.

The last game in Offermann Stadium was played September 17, 1960, when Toronto defeated Buffalo, 5–3, to eliminate the Bisons in the first round of the playoffs. In 1961, the stadium was torn down, and a junior high school was built in its place. The baseball team moved to War Memorial Stadium, a gray edifice built as a WPA project during the Depression. It was designed for football and served as home of the Buffalo Bills, who in 1964 and 1965 won American Football League championships under the direction of coach Lou Saban and quarterback Jack Kemp. A year later, the Bills came within a victory of playing in the first Super Bowl.

After the Bisons moved to War Memorial Stadium in 1961, such players as Pancho Herrera, Ted Savage, Jim Frey, Don Mincher, Bud Harrelson, Ed Kranepool, Cleon Jones, Norm Sherry, Pumpsie Green, Choo Choo Coleman, Ron Swoboda, Lee May, Steve Boros, Hal McRae, and Hector Lopez played for Buffalo, as did a future Hall of Famer, Johnny Bench.

Bench was eighteen when he arrived in Buffalo on July 31, 1966. His debut was disastrous: He suffered a broken thumb in the first inning of his first game behind the plate for the Bisons. He came back in 1967 and batted .259 with 23 home runs and 68 runs batted in. "I've got a lot of good memories of Buffalo, and a soft spot in my heart for that old stadium," Bench says. "Buffalo was my final stepping stone to the major leagues."

Even Marvelous Marv Throneberry, whose exploits with Casey Stengel's Mets would make him one of baseball's more dubious legends, was a Buffalo Bison.

In all, there are sixteen former Bisons players and managers enshrined in Cooperstown. Besides Mack, Collins, Dickey, McCarthy, Boudreau, Harris, and Bench, there are Joe Tinker, Charles Radbourn, Jim O'Rourke, Dan Brouthers, Herb Pennock, Gabby Hartnett, Ray Schalk, Jim Galvin, and John Montgomery Ward.

Each name, generation by generation, evokes special memories that sparkle in the minds of longtime Buffalo fans. Two other players, though, stand at the pinnacle: Ollie Carnegie and Luke Easter. They were held in awe that bordered on reverence. Buffalo loved them.

Carnegie, a slugging outfielder, arrived in 1931 and soon became a folk hero. A gritty player, five feet seven inches, and 165 pounds, he hailed from western Pennsylvania and in 12 seasons hit 258 home runs and drove in 1,044 runs; in 1938, he hit 45 homers, which is still the Buffalo record.

Joe Overfield, in his 1985 book *The 100 Seasons of Buffalo Baseball,* remembers that when Carnegie was introduced to Easter, Big Luke marveled at the small size of his bowlegged counterpart, but Ollie quickly reminded him, "You don't have to be a big man to hit home runs. Look at Hank Aaron."

But lumbering Luke *was* big, not only in stature (six feet four and a half inches, 240 pounds), but in impact on the community. In 1956, the Bisons purchased his contract for $7,500, and Overfield describes the first baseman's three seasons in Buffalo as "contemporaneous with the heyday of Community Ownership and . . . one of the glorious chapters in the history of the team. Not only was Buffalo baseball saved from extinction (as it turned out, it was only a delaying action), but crowds turned out in record numbers, and what was more important, a new spirit, for the better, was engendered among the blacks and whites of the community."

Luke Easter made a big difference, all right. He was the first black player in a Bisons uniform and the preeminent sports personality in Buffalo during the 1950s. The boundaries of Offermann Stadium were 321 feet down the left-field line, 400 to straightaway center and 297 to right, and Big Luke exceeded those limits with regularity. His home runs were colossal. He hit 114 of them (and drove in 353 runs), and the one nobody forgot would forever be known as The Home Run. When he hit it in June of 1957, he was nearly forty-two. It was the first ball ever to clear the center-field scoreboard at Offermann (later that season, he hit the only other one)—a shot of more than five hundred feet. Before the ball finished its flight through the evening haze, it had stayed aloft for a full five seconds.

Big Luke was forty-nine when he stopped playing, and Buffalo minor-league baseball would not see a player of his esteem again.

The 1959 Bisons, for whom Dallas Green pitched, won the International League pennant. "Buffalo was one of the best experiences in my minor-league career," Green says. "I had a great start, but it was a heartbreak year. I started out winning five straight games, but then I hurt my arm and couldn't pitch for two and a half months. I finished nine and five."

Like Green, the 1959 Bisons also had problems near the end of the season and collapsed in the playoffs. Still, their attendance was the highest in the minors—more than 413,000—and set a Buffalo record that stood for twenty-seven years.

In 1960, Buffalo became a charter member of Branch Rickey's Continental League, but this attempt to form a third major league never got off the ground. In 1961, their first season in the Old Rockpile, the Bisons won the Junior World Series, but it was to be their high-water mark. Two years later, the concept of a community-owned team crumbled, and the death spiral had begun.

The seventies not only brought the death of Buffalo's team, but placed a burial shroud over its baseball spirit. In 1976, Ollie Carnegie died at seventy-seven. In 1978, Marse Joe McCarthy died at ninety; his greatness as a big-league manager had been rivaled only by his endurance as an inspiration to the hometown fans. And in 1979, a pair of robbers gunned down sixty-three-year-old Luke Easter on a Cleveland street; he died of a shotgun blast just above the heart.

If there was a dominant emotion among Buffalo's baseball fans in the seventies, it was grief.

BOB RICH, JR., knew the emotional depths to which Buffalo had fallen during the previous twenty years. That knowledge was a major reason why, as the decade of the nineties began, he traveled 200 miles to Cleveland, to deliver personally his hometown's pitch for the major leagues.

"When we started this baseball thing, we were literally at the bottom of the pits," Rich says. "People told us we can't do this, and we can't do that. Well, our success has been built on things we supposedly couldn't do."

Rich had already started his own farm system by purchasing two minor-league franchises: a Double-A team in Wichita, Kansas, and a Single-A club in Niagara Falls. He also purchased the National Baseball Congress in Wichita, home of the National Semipro Baseball Tournament. No other owner or city in the history of major-league baseball had been so well-prepared for an expansion franchise. "Unlike some cities, we're basing our talk on performance, and we've put up the numbers," Rich said. "We're like a player in the minors trying to make the big leagues. Before the player goes up, the big-league team wants to see his numbers. It's the same with a city, and we've got the numbers."

Buffalo had the numbers this time, but was Major League Baseball ready to be logical? "Baseball does nothing logical, and that's why it's such a great game, and the people in it are so great," said veteran baseball writer Hal Bodley, who was covering these meetings for *USA Today*. "When it comes to baseball, logic goes out the window."

The odds facing Buffalo and the other expansion hopefuls hadn't become clear until May 1990, when Baseball Commissioner Fay Vincent told the Senate Task Force for Baseball Expansion that this expansion would likely be baseball's last of the decade, and that the number of teams to be added wouldn't be six or four, but two. There was no margin for error among the aspiring cities—Tampa–St. Petersburg and Denver were reported to be the front-runners—and no one was more aware of that than Bob Rich.

That's why the meetings in Cleveland meant so much to him and the rest of the Buffalo organization. At that time and in that place, baseball finally would set the official rules and agenda for the last expansion of the decade, and the race would begin in earnest.

During his eight seasons as Bisons owner, Rich had earned a reputation as a late-blooming but charismatically influential baseball man in a city that had never had a surplus of bold or farsighted leadership. His father, Robert E. Rich, Sr., had created and expanded Rich Products Corporation, a frozen-foods giant with annual sales of more than $700 million. But in this high-risk pursuit of his city's baseball dream, Bob Rich, Jr., was proving to be much more than his father's son.

Rich had flown to Cleveland at about midnight and, like everyone else in the room, was tired. He did not want members of the media to know that he was in Cleveland, so he called the hotel's reservations desk to change the suite's booking name from B. Rich to Roy Hobbs, the name of the hero played by Robert Redford in the baseball movie *The Natural,* which had been filmed in Buffalo. Once inside the hotel, Rich and the other members of the Bisons' staff were too excited to sleep. They watched *Baseball Tonight* on ESPN until two A.M. and then, before turning in, flipped the channel to watch a news report on baseball expansion.

There were seven people in the two-room suite, but only six beds. Operations manager Ken Lehner lost a coin flip and slept on the floor. Lehner, in his early twenties and just two years out of Fordham University, was the youngest member of the Bisons' staff there. His association with the Bisons had begun at age fourteen when he wrote a letter to apply for a job as a bat boy. He didn't get the job, but nine years later, here he was, sleeping on the floor in Cleveland, with visions of a major-league franchise dancing in his head. "There was so much anticipation," he said, "it was like the night before Christmas."

No one slept much. By six A.M., everyone was up, and the atmosphere was immediately intense. Over a room service breakfast of oatmeal, scrambled eggs, fresh fruit, and coffee, the Bisons' "Mission Impossible" team watched *CBS This Morning.* Shortly after eight, sportscaster Greg Gumbel narrated a four-minute segment about baseball expansion, and the impact on the Buffalo group couldn't have been more positive. Gumbel stated flatly that "no one comes close to Buffalo when it comes down to the organization, groundwork, and enthusiasm already in place." Much of the report focused on the record-breaking resurgence of baseball in Buffalo and its self-styled "Field of Dreams," Pilot Field. All of a sudden, as if looking in an electronic mirror, Bob Rich, Jr., and the rest of his group saw a close-up of him telling a nationwide audience that as far as major-league baseball was concerned, Buffalo was "ready to go." The hotel suite resounded with joy.

"Seeing that report so early in the morning boosted everybody's spirits," PR man Mike Buczkowski said. "We just had a feeling we were into something good." As for Rich, he drank coffee and studied notes, immersed in preparations for the question-and-answer session with the horde of reporters. Having operated in the dark for so long, Buffalo baseball was about to have a day in the sun. In Bob Rich's steely blue eyes, there was a gunfighter's glint.

A few floors above Bob Rich's suite, twenty-six major-league owners and their representatives were meeting to determine the rules for expansion competition. The owners' meeting had begun at about nine A.M. and was dragging past eleven.

Two guards stood by the door, which was near a vestibule filled with reporters and camera crews. Every once in a while, an owner would leave the meeting for a moment, only to be confronted by a crossfire of shouted questions and high-intensity light beams. But the meeting continued, and the guards stayed at their posts. Among the throng of reporters, speculation on Buffalo's chances ranged from optimism to downright cynicism. Jerome Holtzman, the *Chicago Tribune*'s rumpled, silver-haired columnist who had written his way into the Baseball Hall of Fame, was convinced that this decision had already been made and that the meetings were nothing more than a "charade." Asked by a Buffalo writer about why baseball would undertake such an elaborate sham, Holtzman took his cigar out of his mouth, pointed a finger in the writer's chest, and growled, "Guys like you." As far as the two new franchises were concerned, Holtzman believed that Denver and Tampa–St. Petersburg were locks. On the other hand, Hal Bodley was saying that "Buffalo's got a chance; you just can't count Buffalo out. I think stability of ownership is going to be a key. They don't want owners who can't afford to be in this for the long term. With Bob Rich, Buffalo's got a real chance."

It was about eleven-thirty when the buses from Buffalo pulled up near the hotel parking ramp. Ken Lehner ran to the lobby to alert the Buffalo media. Other reporters and camera crews saw and followed. Lehner walked out the front door, leading a line of about a dozen newspeople and looking to Mike Buczkowski "like the Pied Piper." The buses began to unload, and out stepped an army of Buffalo boosters, wearing black T-shirts with the logo MAJOR LEAGUE, VOTE BUFFALO that had a bright orange check mark for the letter *V*. Near the buses was a balloon—more than twenty-five feet high—in the shape of a buffalo that was brought along by a radio station. Soon the merrymakers formed a line and marched over to Public Square, where they began to parade back and forth in front of the hotel, chanting and waving signs, as reporters and cameras followed their every move.

Prominent among the busloads was a petite, gray-haired woman whose presence might not have been expected. But there she was, in blue jeans, sneakers, sunglasses, a boost-Buffalo T-shirt, and a Bison baseball cap. People from the Buffalo area were used to seeing her dressed much more demurely, and her persona bordered on the schoolmarmish. Long prominent on the local political scene as a fiercely independent outsider-turned-insider, she was widely admired for her work ethic and no-nonsense guardianship of the public purse strings. Yes, this was Alfreda Slominski, comptroller of Erie County, of which Buffalo is the hub. She was sixty-one, having long ago become one of those rare public figures whose last name is nothing short of redundant; in Buffalo, when you refer to "Alfreda," everyone knows who you mean. But most people don't know that she is a die-hard baseball fan, not only holding Bisons season tickets, but attending major-league games throughout the Northeast. On this day, though, she was cast against type, in the unlikely role of picket, toting a huge sign with the words VOTE BUFFALO, pumping it up and down, and chanting, "Let's go, Buffalo."

"This," said Alfreda, "is fun."

Alfreda was eager to get the message across that Buffalo belonged in the big time. "As chief fiscal officer of Erie County, I'm here to say that major-league baseball will succeed in Buffalo," she said as a TV camera zoomed in for a close-up. "I've been to baseball games all over the country, and no other ballpark can match Pilot Field for the fun of watching a game. We draw a million fans every year. Bob Rich is a great owner, and everybody in Buffalo supports the team. Let's face it, Buffalo deserves big-league baseball, and we're going to get it."

Melinda Sanderson, age twenty-eight, senior sales manager of the hotel, stood near a curb watching the demonstration and considered it "wonderful." Born and educated in Buffalo, she felt a familiar tingle: "I look at this, and I know what makes Buffalo so special: It's the people. There is no doubt in my mind that the fans in Buffalo would support major-league baseball. This is the kind of day when you feel proud to say, 'I'm from Buffalo.'"

The national media seemed more than a bit puzzled by such an outpouring of loyalty by the Buffalo fans, but the phenomenon resulted in a wealth of fan-in-the-street interviews being beamed nationwide.

At nearly twelve-thirty, the owners' meeting ended. Baseball Commissioner Fay Vincent presided over a news conference in the Grand Ballroom. There, he was asked whether the demonstration by the Buffalo fans would have any effect on the bid for an expansion franchise. (No fans came to the meetings from any other contending city.) "We're certainly aware that the fans in Buffalo have been exuberantly supportive of the existing minor-league franchise," Vincent said. "We tried to make it clear to people that coming to this meeting—participating in any sense—was not going to be necessary or productive." Vincent then hesitated and smiled. "On the other hand," he said, "one can recognize that these people love baseball, they came, and we're perfectly happy to have them here."

Vincent confirmed that the National League would expand by two teams for the 1993 season. The final decision would be made no later than September 30, 1991.

The criteria included a baseball-only, open-air, natural-grass stadium with seating for a minimum of 35,000 and with sufficient parking and access to public transit and highways; fan and community support; government backing, and stability and long-term commitment by local ownership. There also was mention of location—preferably places that didn't already have reasonable access to major-league baseball—and of size and population, particularly in terms of the TV audience.

The entry fee, though not announced on this day, turned out to be $95 million, much higher than many had imagined. This was a reflection of the jackpot's enormity: A city landing a team could expect to have as much as $60 million pumped into its economy each year.

With the owers' news conference now concluded, Rich himself was ready within the hour to confront the media in the hotel's Versailles Room. As he walked to the news conference, he looked out a hotel window at the Buffalo fans—he could hear their chant of "Let's go, Buffalo; let's go, Buffalo; let's go, Buffalo"—and the sight and sound seemed to lift his spirit and harden his determination. With his longish, wavy, light-brown hair brushed back from his forehead, Rich chose a dark-brown suit to go with his ever-present cowboy boots. At age forty-nine, he appeared at least ten years younger as he strode into his own national news conference. Staring into the glow of the TV lights, there was almost an Indiana Jones–like air about him as he confronted what seemed to be a roomful of microphone-headed cobras. Reporters from across the country, perhaps fifty or more, were sizing him up: So *this* was the guy from Buffalo.

Bob Rich was quick on the draw. As if from a holster, he pulled out a blank check and began waving it for all to see. He was ready, here and now, to make a down payment.

"I'm so convinced that Buffalo is the only city in the country that is prepared right now for a major-league [expansion] ball club, I brought my check today and was hoping to sign it for any fee that was charged," Rich said, smiling as the reporters laughed. "But I guess we'll have to wait a while to see how much the check should be made out for."

Buffalo had come a long way since 1970, when it said good-bye to baseball.

"Buffalo admittedly has had its down times," Rich continued. "It's gone through economic hardship as the city redefined itself. But I think one of the greatest things we have going for us is the tremendous economic turnaround. . . . I think Buffalo represents the city whose economic hardships are behind it."

But negative perceptions about his city had long since grown into caricature, and Rich found himself defending everything from the size of Buffalo's TV market to the suitability of its weather.

There was also the question of why Rich was the only prospective big-league owner to show up in Cleveland. "Maybe it's because we're ready," Rich said. "Baseball said they were going to give the criteria, and I assume they were going to give it to people like us. So I'm here, and I'm here with a message: Buffalo is ready to go."

The other potential applicants—whether from Denver, Phoenix, Tampa–St. Pete, Miami, or Orlando—didn't seem to faze him. "I think we're in competition with the criteria. I have faith in baseball . . . that they'll make a good decision."

With those words, Bob Rich put the blank check back into his wallet. For the time being.

The news conference, which had lasted about a half-hour, was over. Mindy Rich hugged her husband, and well-wishers came up to shake his hand. He answered more questions for a huddle of reporters that surrounded him and then made his way to the hotel door. Rich stepped outside into the warm sunshine and was greeted with an ovation by the Buffalo faithful. "I'm so proud of you and what you did today," Rich told the fans. One of them yelled back, "We're proud of you, Bob." About a half-dozen fans came up to Bob and Mindy Rich, and presented them with a cake. On the cake were the words, *Buffalo: Major League.*

With that, the Buffalo pep rally was over. As Bob Rich walked back to the hotel, he encountered one of the Secret Service men who had come to his door several hours before. They exchanged knowing smiles; it had been quite a day for them both.

Jimmy Griffin surely would have enjoyed all the euphoria in Cleveland, but Buffalo's rough-and-tumble, four-term mayor was back home attending to his job. Yet he, if anyone, could be called a prophet of this baseball revival.

Twelve years earlier, after being elected mayor for the first time, Griffin had been laughed at by Buffalo's news media and citizenry alike when he came up with the idea that "we're going to get baseball in Buffalo, we're going to build a new stadium downtown, and we're going to get a major-league team."

No one was laughing at his idea now.

2

IRISH JIMMY

Boys play marbles in the cinders.
The boys' hands need washing.
The boys are glad; they fight among each other.

A plank bridge leaps the Lehigh Valley railroad.
Then acres of steel rails, freight cars, smoke,
And then . . . the blue lake shore
. . . Erie with Norse blue eyes . . . and the white sun.

—From "Slants at Buffalo, New York"
by Carl Sandburg, 1918.

The neighborhood is defined by smokestacks, railroad tracks, grain mills, taverns, and tough but warmhearted people. It is a residential-industrial island pulsating with the sweat and toil of its residents who flaunt shot-and-a-beer sensibilities along with fierce parochial pride. This is South Buffalo—the First Ward—and since the late 1820s, it has been a haven for immigrants who came to Buffalo with nothing but hope. The streets of the Ward have long been populated by hungry dogs, kids in patched-up clothing, and men struggling to make a buck. But in the Ward, there are far more important things than money: things such as self-respect, ethnic heritage, family loyalty, and communal bonds. Life was never easy here, especially during the cold, dark days of the mid-1800s, when Buffalo suffered through its growing pains.

The area was settled by Indians in 1780, and it was in South Buffalo that the log cabin of the first white settler was built. Joseph Ellicott designed the village of Buffalo for Holland Land Company late in the century, but in the War of 1812, it was burned to the ground by the British. Three years later, in 1816, Buffalo was rebuilt and incorporated into a village. A civic and business leader, Samuel Wilkeson, pushed to revamp Buffalo's harbor and persuaded New York State to locate the western terminus of the Erie Canal at Buffalo. The canal opened in 1825, providing the impetus for Buffalo's first economic boom. Buffalo was incorporated as a city in 1832, and throughout the century, it would be a magnet for European immigrants eager to find opportunity amid the Industrial Revolution.

Buffalo would become the nation's mightiest inland port, served by Lake Erie, Lake Ontario, and the Niagara River. The immigrants, mostly Irish, who settled in the First Ward were lured by the work to be found on the docks of the Erie Canal. Railroads sprang up to transport goods to and from the docks, and the Ward was enmeshed in a web of tracks. As the railroads grew, so did the factories. Workers were needed to meet the demands of Buffalo's own industrial revolution. Many came from Ireland and found themselves on the lowest rung of the immigrant ladder. The houses of the Ward were built on streets with names such as Sidway, Katherine, Tennessee, Kentucky, Alabama, and O'Connell. The borders of the Ward were the Buffalo River and Lake Erie. Catholic churches became the center of the Ward's social and spiritual life: St. Brigid's, St. Valentine's, St. Stephen's, and Our Lady of Perpetual Help, which was known in the Ward as "Pets." These churches wove the fabric of life in a community of people that the rest of the city viewed as outsiders. In the Ward, everyone was equal and believed in one another. Outside the neighborhood, though, the Irish immigrants were at once vulnerable and invisible, subject to discrimination and bigotry. A cholera epidemic and an economic decline in the 1850s added to the obstacles faced by those in the Ward.

Nonetheless, the Ward continued to grow, and each year brought more newcomers from the old country. Buffalo's first census was taken in 1850, and its population was 42,261, with more than 40 percent of those people, 17,593, foreign-born. Irish immigrants totaled 6,307, a close second to German-born Buffalonians, who numbered 6,803.

By the 1860s, shipping traffic on the Erie Canal began to decline, but the railroads boomed. Between 1890 and 1900, Buffalo was the second-largest railroad center in the United States, after Chicago. The trains carried coal, steel, iron ore, and other raw materials that fed heavy industry.

Thomas Griffin had heard stories of opportunity in America. He lived in County Clare, Ireland, but had relatives who came to the United States and settled in the Ward. In 1890, Griffin and his wife, Catherine Quinn Griffin, decided that it was time to leave their homeland. The young couple came to Buffalo and made their home in the Ward. Thomas Griffin eventually landed a job on the railroad. He was known for his hard work and dedication and eventually became a section foreman.

The part of the city where Thomas and Catherine Griffin then lived was at the very center of American commerce, dominated by ships and trains and mills that produced flour and steel. They lived in the shadows of stately grain elevators that symbolized the city's stature as the flour-milling capital of America—a tradition that companies such as General Mills would carry toward the twenty-first century with Wheaties, Cheerios, and other household staples. South Buffalo—the Ward—was rich with the smell of tanneries and breweries and the lumber yards.

In 1905, Thomas and Catherine Griffin became parents of a son, Thomas, who picked up the nickname Rocko. Like his father, young Rocko was captivated by the sights, sounds, and people in the First Ward. Rocko was in his teens when he landed a job at a hardware store owned by Beals, McCarthy & Rogers, a downtown steel manufacturer, which later moved to the Ward. For fifty years, Rocko Griffin sold hardware there.

Rocko married Helen O'Brien in 1927. She, too, had grown up in the Ward. Her father, Owen O'Brien, came from Scranton, Pennsylvania, and settled in the Ward, where he met his wife, Martha. After his wife and parents, Rocko was closest to his brother, Jimmy. The two men were virtually inseparable. Jimmy, a bachelor, worked in the grain mills, and in the evening, he and Rocko could usually be found on a baseball diamond. Rocko played third base and Jimmy was a center fielder. They became stars in the highly competitive amateur leagues in Buffalo. When the Griffin brothers weren't playing the game, they were watching the Buffalo Bisons of

the International League play at Bison Stadium, later called Offermann Stadium. In the Ward, baseball was a unifying force among
the Irish immigrants. The game was something they shared and
played without restriction. Social standing and ethnic barriers meant
nothing on the ball diamonds. Between the foul lines, all that
counted was ability.

In 1928, Rocko and Helen Griffin had their first child, Thomas
who was always called Tommy. The next year, a second son was
born, James Donald Griffin, whom no one ever called anything but
Jimmy. The two boys seemed to mirror their father and their Uncle
Jim. Not only did they have the same names, Tommy and Jimmy,
but the same personalities, and the same passion for baseball.

The game was part of the routine in the Griffin household.
Rocko worked the day shift and came home at five P.M. Little Jimmy
and Tommy, then about five and six years old, would be at the door
waiting with their baseball gloves. Helen Griffin had supper ready by
five-thirty, and the boys and their father ate quickly so they could get
to Sullivan Playground while there was still plenty of daylight. The
playground was located on Sidway Street, a few blocks from Ham-
burg Street and Elk Street, later called South Park Avenue, where
Rocko and his family lived. At six o'clock, young Jimmy and Tommy
would race out on the Sullivan Playground field and play catch. They
would use baseballs that Rocko had bought from kids who had caught
them in foul territory at Bison Stadium. At sunset, the two boys
would leave the playground with their father and uncle, buy three-
cent ice cream cones, and walk home. Once back in the door, the
little boys rushed into the bathtub and then to bed. During the spring
and summer, they followed this ritual six days a week. On weekends,
Rocko often took them to see the Bisons play.

Young Jimmy's favorite player was a slugging first baseman
named Jim Oglesby. Oglesby batted .319 and .327 during his two
seasons with Buffalo, but his claim to fame had been on the negative
side: making five errors in one game. Oglesby was a terrible fielder,
but young Jimmy didn't care. Oglesby was part of the atmosphere at
the ballpark, something Jimmy Griffin loved, just as he loved his
father, his uncle, and his brother. When it came to baseball, they were
always together. The memories have lasted a lifetime. "I just can't
forget those summer nights playing ball at Sullivan Playground,"

Jimmy Griffin says a half-century later. "It was so great just to play catch with Tommy, and my dad and my Uncle Jim would hit us fly balls. I think that's the earliest memory I have of growing up."

Times were difficult during those Depression years. Rocko Griffin was paid twice a month, on the first and the fifteenth. Bill collectors, especially from the loan companies, showed up at the Griffin front door every payday. Rocko could never afford a house or a car. He and his brother, Jim, walked everywhere to save bus fare. The Griffin family, like many others in the Ward, were renters who moved often. "We never knew we were poor; back then, everybody was in the same boat," Tommy Griffin recalls. Jimmy Griffin remembers that "my dad never had a penny for himself, but he always took care of his family."

The hardest time came at Christmas. Each year, Rocko had to wait until after work on Christmas Eve to collect his holiday bonus. "There was no Christmas until the bonus came," Jimmy says. Sometimes, even with the bonus, there wasn't enough money. If there was extra money during the holiday season, young Tommy and Jimmy would walk a couple of miles down Elk Street and buy a Christmas tree to carry home. Long before they reached home, however, the two boys would argue and fight, and sometimes even forget the tree.

Despite those occasional brotherly battles, Tommy and Jimmy Griffin were devoted to each other. "Jimmy and I are as close as any brothers could be," Tommy says. The Griffin brothers played softball together for St. Brigid's, where they attended grammar school, and the two of them were bat boys for the Ward's own softball team. "Tommy was the chief bat boy; I was his assistant," Jimmy says. "There'd be a couple thousand people watching the games down at Lanigan Field; it was really exciting. I'll never forget, after the game, the two teams would split a half a keg of beer, go over to Mike McMahon's store and get cold cuts and bread. They'd even sneak Tommy and me a beer once in a while, when no one was looking." Often, the postgame celebrations took place in one of the Ward's most popular bookie joints, in back of Charlie's Tailor Shop. When young Jimmy and Tommy were directed to the back room, run by an affable bookie named Fran Bodkin, they saw policy slips and walls with lists of horse races and other sports events.

"The whole team would go to Fran Bodkin's," Jimmy says. "A couple of guys would wait outside watching for the police. Every once in a while, one got pinched. Tommy and I just looked around and kept our mouths shut. We were just kids, ten to twelve years old; we didn't know what was going on."

At home, the financial situation remained bleak. Rocko and Helen had two more children—a son named Joe and a daughter named Donna. At age twelve, Jimmy worked part time in Mike McMahon's grocery store. He liked being on his own and decided to quit South Park High School during his sophomore year.

"We needed the money pretty bad," Jimmy says, and when he was sixteen, he went to work on the waterfront as a grain scooper. Jimmy jumped into railroad cars filled with wheat, oats, and soybeans piled to the top and used a shovel to scoop grain all day long. The work was hot, dirty, and demanding, "but the pay was great. I was making more money than my father."

Life on the docks was a challenge for a boy of sixteen. Jimmy ran with a tough crowd and had his share of fights and lesser skirmishes. Beer flowed freely in the corner bars and arguments were often settled with fists. In the Ward, fighting was a sign of manhood—nothing personal—and the language was colorfully crude. On the streets, Jimmy knew you were judged on how you walked and talked. And the genuinely tough guys in the Ward never backed down.

Jimmy Griffin was not big. When he reached manhood, he was five feet seven inches and about 160 pounds; as a teenager, his weight didn't get much above 135. But he was as tough as he needed to be, and that never changed. When you'd meet him, he'd stick his jaw in your face; his eyes would glisten, and when he was provoked, his face would flush with anger. His lips would tighten, and he'd bite his tongue. The Griffin temper was hair-trigger; in the heat of an argument, Jimmy would take on anybody, in any place, at any time. "I lost as many as I won," he says. But there was another side to him. He could be polite and soft-spoken, gently uttering a Ward dialect rich with nicknames such as Jiggsy, Muddles, Boey, and Foo Foo.

In the Ward, when you mentioned a deceased person, you always said, "God rest his soul." Jimmy Griffin, in reflective moments, softly modulated a voice brimming with the accent of the South Buffalo

Irish. Jimmy was open with his expressions of love for his family. To him, loyalty mattered most. Anything could be forgiven, except disloyalty. And if you betrayed Jimmy Griffin or hurt his family, he was finished with you. He developed into an emotionally complex man who saw the world as a basic conflict: us and them.

Jimmy Griffin desperately wanted to be somebody. There was no chance of that as a grain scooper. He decided to return to school at Our Lady of Victory High School in the city of Lackawanna, just south of Buffalo. Enrolling as a junior, he was a couple of years older than most of his classmates. The principal was Sister Marie de la Salle, and she was impressed by Jimmy's determination to go back to school. She believed in him. She told him that he could take extra classes and, if able to meet academic standards, could graduate in one year. It wasn't easy. There was still a serious need for money at home, so Jimmy took a double class load, played baseball and basketball, and still worked part time.

"Every couple of weeks, I'd go in to Sister de la Salle and tell her, 'I want to quit, I can't do it.' She'd look at me and say, 'Jimmy, there's no way I'm going to let you quit. You're going to get that diploma.' She made me stay." After graduation he was forever grateful to the nun, whom he recalls as the most influential person in his life. "I owe everything I am today to her," Griffin says now. "She didn't know me until I walked into her office and asked to go back to school. She didn't have to care about me, but she did. Thank God for Sister de la Salle."

Jimmy's skill on the baseball diamond also blossomed. "He was always a hard-nosed player," says George Hartman, who played ball against Griffin as a teenager and has known him for over forty years. "On the field, Jimmy was a tough son of a gun. He's the kind of guy you wanted on your team; you know he'd run through a brick wall and do anything he could to win." Don Colpoys, a talented amateur player who went on to play pro ball, remembers that Griffin "wasn't a power hitter, but he could spray the ball and run like hell. What a competitor! Geez, he'd *kill* you to win a game. He went all-out all the time. Jimmy had tremendous enthusiasm. He played like Enos Slaughter. You watched Jimmy play, and you knew he loved the game."

George Daddario, former public relations director for the Bisons and front-office executive with Buffalo's short-lived NBA team, the Braves, also played baseball with and against Griffin. "Jimmy was a holler guy, very competitive and a winner in every sense of the word. He hasn't changed that much—I think the way he played baseball carries over into his life, especially politics."

In February 1951, Griffin had to leave baseball and everything else behind. He was barely into his twenties when he joined the Army at the height of the Korean War. In the Ward, young men, including most of Jimmy's friends, were enlisting in droves. Jimmy saw it as his duty; if other guys were going to Korea, so would he.

"Because I had that high school diploma, I was able to go to Officer Candidate School," Griffin says. In his class at OCS, 160 candidates started and fifty-five—including Jimmy Griffin—graduated. He became a paratrooper and volunteered for Korea, where he became a first lieutenant in the infantry. Griffin saw action with the Fifth Regimental Combat Team, and served in the States with the 82nd Airborne Division. From the moment he arrived in Korea and started riding the troop trains, Jimmy Griffin was a changed man.

He had known hard times in the Ward, but nothing like the poverty and suffering he saw in Korea. Women and children were starving and dressed in rags. They lived in paper boxes. There was death and destruction everywhere.

"When you go over there and see all that, and the way those people were living and dying, it made you appreciate things back home," Griffin said years later. "It made you think about the opportunity we had back in this country to make something of ourselves."

After his combat tour in Korea, Griffin was sent to Camp Kilmer, New Jersey. The once-scrawny kid was now a muscular, rock-solid adult, and he was eager to start playing baseball again. During his basic training, Jimmy had joined the regimental team at Fort Dix, where future major-leaguer Harvey Haddix was a pitcher. In Korea, First Lieutenant Griffin played a few games but soon became a victim of Army rules: The team was restricted to enlisted men, and Jimmy was an officer. "The company commander wouldn't let me play baseball," Griffin still recalls with emotion. "It broke my heart. I was already playing on the team; I loved the game. But they told me, 'You're an officer, you've got your duties, and we can't let you play baseball.' That really hurt—believe me, that hurt."

Griffin was discharged from the Army in November 1953 and moved back into his parents' home in the Ward. He then used two years of GI Bill benefits to earn an associate degree in metallurgy from Erie County Technical Institute. He went to work in a General Motors laboratory but felt cooped up. In a few months, he quit. Afterward, he bounced around a few factory jobs before working as an engineer on the railroad. In the late fifties, politics beckoned from the other side of a bar. Griffin had passed a civil service test for a recreation instructor's post but was never called. "My name was fifth on the list," he recalls, "but they just kept passing me by." One day, he was having a beer in Kennedy's bar in the Ward, discussing the meaning of life with a bartender named Frank Hahn. "I'm sitting there, moaning and groaning to Frankie about what a tough break I got because they keep passing me over on the list. Frankie says, 'Shut up, Jimmy. Stop crying, and do something about it. Why don't you run yourself?'" So he did, and lost in the Democratic primary for supervisor of the Eighth Ward by about 150 votes. The door to political power had not yet opened, so Jimmy Griffin kept doing what came naturally: He kept knocking.

In 1961, he won the Democratic primary and general election for the Ellicott District seat on Buffalo's Common Council. During that campaign, he met William Buyers, who was running for another council seat, at a meeting of the League of Women Voters. Like Griffin, Buyers was independent, and could be temperamental and outspoken; he, too, had been a paratrooper in Korea. Buyers also played baseball with and against Griffin. "He was a heck of a ballplayer, but you could see he had a feel for politics right off the bat," Buyers says. "Jimmy plays politics like he plays baseball—for real."

Griffin soon developed a reputation for his political tenacity. The news media, other politicians, and the business power structure couldn't quite figure him out. Griffin was a maverick who seemed to want to duke it out with just about anybody. The adjective *feisty* soon became permanently fused to his name. He was Ellicott District councilman for four years. In 1965 and 1966, he tried his hand at the insurance business, but it wasn't for him. "I'm selling insurance down in the Ward and these people are taking out policies, but they didn't want to pay," Griffin remembers. "I had to go and try and collect; I couldn't stand it." In 1966, he was elected to the state Senate, where he would serve until 1977. At thirty-eight, he was a confirmed bachelor who had no intention of settling down.

But the sight of Margaret McMahon changed all that. As a state senator in 1968, he often sat in Flood's tavern down in the Ward late in the afternoon and watched Margaret coming home from work. She lived in the First Ward, too, a few blocks from Jimmy's parents. She had graduated a year after he had from Our Lady of Victory High School, "but I never really knew Jimmy, I had just seen him around."

For their first date, he invited her to attend a meeting of the St. Thomas Aquinas Holy Name Society, where he was to be the guest speaker. "I figured, what the hell, she can't say no going to a Holy Name meeting," Jimmy says now. "So I took her there. I must have bored the hell out of her."

She does acknowledge that "I may have dozed off a little bit, but I found him to be an interesting guy."

Four months later, in May 1968, they were married. "Marrying Marge," Jimmy Griffin says, "is the best thing that ever happened to me." That year, as well, he made a second—and final—attempt at business, "the gin mill," which he hung on to for five years before labeling it as "the biggest mistake of my life." An entrepreneur he wasn't, but he was, to the core, what he liked to call a "political animal." By 1977, in the aftermath of the great blizzard that paralyzed Buffalo, he found himself chafing in Albany as a state senator and decided that he was ready to run for mayor.

The way he did it would become familiar: Buck the establishment.

Joseph F. Crangle, for many years the chairman of the Erie County Democratic Party and a longtime political foe of Griffin's, was furious at Jimmy for not supporting the endorsed Democratic candidate, Les Foschio. Another candidate, State Assemblyman Arthur Eve, was trying to become Buffalo's first black mayor. In heavily Democratic Buffalo, the party line is normally tantamount to ultimate victory. But if Griffin is anything, he's unconventional. Displaying the bare-knuckles style that would become his trademark, he defied the political power structure and lost by a narrow margin to Eve in a racially charged three-way primary. By gaining the Conservative Party's backing, however, he had a line on the November ballot and polled 42 percent of the vote—compared with 32 percent for Eve and 25 percent for the Republican, John Phelan—to pull a stunning upset and become the fifty-third mayor of Buffalo, filling a job once held by Grover Cleveland.

But with so many formidable challenges facing Buffalo in the late seventies, one wondered whether the mayoralty was a prize worth winning. Economically, it had been hit as hard as any Rust Belt city. Its unemployment was rising, its population falling, its inner city decaying, and its downtown withering away. It cried for leadership: a can-do attitude. "When I was elected in 1977, people didn't know what to expect," Griffin remembers. "I didn't owe anybody anything. The bankers and most of the businesspeople were against me. The city was in a bad way, and not many people thought I could turn it around. They figured, 'Hell, he's a redneck from South Buffalo, what does he know?'"

The answer came shortly after the election when Griffin met with the city's bankers and business leaders: "That first meeting, the bankers all had a chip on their shoulders, and I had a chip on mine. But for some reason, we hit it off. . . .

"I came into office with the idea that I'd go out and work with people and meet with people, and we'd do anything to get this city moving. If not, shame on us."

He made quite an impact.

Griffin's political hero is Harry Truman, whose portrait hangs above his desk on the second floor of City Hall, overlooking Niagara Square. As a mayor, his style resembles that of the late Richard Daley, Sr., in Chicago and of Ed Koch in New York: powerful, flamboyant, outspoken, and combative.

"The people that vote for him see him as kind of a Clint Eastwood type, going out to do battle against the forces of evil in Buffalo," says Irv Weinstein, an anchorman for more than a quarter-century at WKBW-TV, an ABC affiliate. "Jimmy is seen by those voters as a rebel, an individualist, standing up to the press and everyone else. It never hurts politicians to attack the media. There's an awful lot of South Buffalo mentality in that; they see Jimmy Griffin doing what he's doing, and they say, 'He's a lot like me.'"

It wasn't long before Griffin's blood feud with the news media

became local legend. Dismissing reporters as "too negative," he re-
fuses to speak to most of them individually and generally restricts
contact to once-a-month news conferences. At times, the animosity
has even gotten physical. But in a strange way, as veteran political
observers such as Joe Crangle will tell you, even the scrapes with
the media can be a plus for Griffin:

> There's a mentality in Buffalo of "Give 'em hell,
> Jimmy." People think of Jimmy as "one of us."
> One thing about Griffin that people can see is that he
> likes his job and, just as important, that he likes people.
> Some politicians, they hate going out shaking hands at fac-
> tories or campaigning in big crowds. Not Jimmy. What
> Jimmy's got comes from the inside—the gut. That comes
> through in a campaign, and people relate to that feeling.

As Jimmy Griffin took charge of the city of his boyhood, he not
only survived but flourished, with plain talk, sometimes outrageous;
he might say that bankers have "hearts as big as caraway seeds," or
tell snowbound residents, "Stay inside, grab a six-pack."

"The way he is," Marge Griffin says of the father of her three
children, "is the way he is."

That way—Jimmy's way—meant never losing his love for baseball. The absence of a professional ball club in his hometown was an
ache that wouldn't go away. Less than five years before he took
office, the county had built an 80,000-seat stadium in the southern
suburb of Orchard Park, but it was good for only two things: football and rock concerts. From the heart of downtown, it was a drive
of about fifteen miles; for all the good it did a baseball fan, it might
as well have been 15,000 miles.

From his first day as mayor, he was determined to restore professional baseball to Buffalo: "We were pretty far down back in
those days, but I knew baseball could help this city and change the
attitude of the people. All we needed was a team." There didn't
seem to be any hope—until in 1979 a young umpire, worried about
his income taxes, made a telephone call.

3

BACK IN THE GAME

The winter of 1979 was an exhilarating time in Peter Calieri's life. He was thirty-one and had been a minor-league umpire for five years. Calieri, who lived in the Buffalo suburb of West Seneca, was ready to move a step closer to his goal of becoming a major-league umpire. He spent the 1977 and 1978 seasons working in the Double-A Eastern League. In 1979 he received word that his contract had been purchased by the Triple-A International League, just one step away from the bigs. Calieri was eager to prove himself. He decided to leave early for spring training. In early February, Calieri was packing his bags for the trip to Plant City, Florida, where he was scheduled to work at the Texas Rangers' training camp. In the middle of packing, Calieri remembered his income taxes. He had been waiting for his W-2 form from the Eastern League and wanted to finish his tax returns before he went to Florida. So he called Patrick McKernan, the Eastern League's president.

McKernan's life, like Calieri's, was intertwined with baseball. At thirty-seven, McKernan was one of the youngest minor-league presidents in the game and owned an Eastern League franchise in Pittsfield, Massachusetts. McKernan also had ties to the Buffalo area. He had grown up in Le Roy, between Buffalo and Rochester, and graduated from Niagara University before working as a newspaper reporter in Batavia. In 1964 he left the newspaper business to concentrate on baseball. He was general manager of the Batavia team in the New York–Penn League in 1964 and a year later took a similar job in Pittsfield. Early in the seventies, he became Eastern League president.

In February 1979 McKernan was scrambling to find a new city so he could keep his league at six teams. A few months earlier, a severe storm had wrecked Roosevelt Stadium in Jersey City. It was an old, decaying facility, and the storm damage was the last straw. The city condemned the stadium, and the Eastern League found itself one team short. McKernan was desperate because the season opener was just two months away. One day in February, his phone rang: Pete Calieri was calling from Buffalo. Initially, the conversation was about a W-2 form, but McKernan had more pressing issues on his mind.

"I get on the phone and start talking to Pat about my taxes," Calieri recalls. "He tells me he's going to call the league accountant and then get back to me. Well, I'm getting ready to hang up, but Pat keeps talking. In the course of the conversation, he tells me the Jersey City stadium was damaged by a hurricane and is unsuitable for league play. Pat tells me he's got five teams in a six-team league."

Pat McKernan has a unique way of talking in circles. This huge, rotund, and garrulous raconteur loves to regale visitors with baseball lore, delighting in his image as a charming rogue who's deeply devoted to the game. McKernan had learned to hustle to survive in the lower minors and had mastered the art of milking a story for everything it's worth. During his two-year association with the Eastern League, Calieri had listened to plenty of McKernan's ramblings, but this time Calieri sensed an unusual urgency in the man's voice. So the young umpire decided to offer a solution to McKernan's search for a baseball city:

"I said, tongue in cheek, 'What about Buffalo?'"

"Where are we going to play in Buffalo?"

"War Memorial Stadium—you know, the Old Rockpile."

McKernan had grown up near Buffalo and had attended football and baseball games at the stadium. "Oh, yeah," he said, "the Rockpile."

Calieri was joking, but McKernan sounded serious. "When he said that right back to me, I could tell something clicked in his brain," Calieri remembers. "I mean, here we are, two people—I'm in West Seneca, and he's in Pittsfield—and we're talking about the Rockpile. Something strange was happening."

McKernan asked Calieri whether he knew any politicians or

baseball people in Buffalo who might be interested in the franchise. Immediately, Calieri thought of Don Colpoys.

Colpoys, a Buffalo fire fighter, was one of the best-known baseball figures in Buffalo. For fourteen years he had been an outstanding player and manager for the Simon Pure team that dominated amateur baseball in the city for two and a half decades after World War II. That era of dominance ended in 1971, when the team's sponsor, the William Simon Brewery, closed forever. Buffalo had once boasted of thirty-five breweries; now it had none.

Colpoys had played for three years as a catcher in the St. Louis Cardinals' farm system, had worked as a scout, and had managed a Class A team in Niagara Falls. He also had been a successful coach in the All American Amateur Baseball Association and at the high school level. In 1976, Colpoys had been named baseball coach at Canisius College. In addition, like Calieri, Colpoys was a basketball referee in the Buffalo area, and the two men had worked many games together. But there was another reason Calieri thought about Colpoys.

"I told McKernan that Colpoys was from South Buffalo, and it's a pretty good bet that he knows the mayor," Calieri recalls. "I mean, everybody from South Buffalo knows Jimmy Griffin."

Calieri was determined to make a pitch for baseball in Buffalo:

> All I kept thinking during that conversation was, "Here's a chance for Buffalo to get a baseball team." My dream was to be able to umpire a professional baseball game in Buffalo. And here was the opportunity for me to do just that. Then I thought to myself, "No, it isn't; I'm not going to be in the Eastern League—I'm going to Triple-A." It didn't matter; I just kept thinking how great it would be to have baseball in Buffalo and that I could have something to do with it. I knew it was a long shot, but I figured, "Why not?" McKernan sounded interested.

McKernan told Calieri to telephone Don Colpoys and then to get back to him. "I called Colpoys and ran everything by him that McKernan had told me," Calieri remembers. Colpoys, then forty-four, was excited about the prospect of being general manager of a

Double-A club and bringing pro baseball back to Buffalo. Colpoys had played ball against Jimmy Griffin and had known him for most of his adult life. He was sure that the mayor would jump at the opportunity to get Buffalo back in the game. When Colpoys phoned the mayor to ask, Griffin said, "Sure."

Colpoys then called Calieri, who continued to be the middleman in the deal. "I called McKernan and said the mayor was interested," says Calieri, who at the time was still finding it hard to believe what was happening in the space of a few hours. "I mean, here I am, a Double-A umpire, setting up a deal with the mayor to bring baseball back to Buffalo. I don't even know the mayor. I'm not sure why all this is happening, but it is. To tell you the truth, I'm feeling great. I'm juiced up, and McKernan is impressed that I was able to get through to the mayor so fast."

Calieri told McKernan that Griffin wanted a team. "McKernan started giggling," Calieri remembers. "He gave me one of those giggles he always gives when he's on to something. Then he said, 'Are you serious?' I said, 'Yeah, the mayor of Buffalo is interested in bringing a baseball team here.'"

McKernan asked Calieri to set up a meeting in the mayor's office in a couple of days. Calieri then gave Colpoys's phone number to McKernan. The two men talked, and McKernan decided to call Jimmy Griffin. As Griffin remembers the conversation, it started with the possibility of bringing an Eastern League franchise to Buffalo in about a year: "I'm in my office, Pat calls and says, 'Hey, how about having a team in 1980?' I said, 'Sure.'" Fifteen minutes later, the phone rang again. "It was McKernan again. This time, he says, 'You're so enthusiastic, how about having a team this year?' I said, 'Sure.' I didn't know what the hell I was doing. I thought to myself, 'What the hell am I doing with this baseball team?' Then I thought, 'What the hell, why not?'"

Professional baseball, which Buffalo had not had for nine years, was coming back. But how? The proposed team had no money, no owner, no players, no working agreement—and what it *did* have, War Memorial Stadium, hadn't been used for pro baseball since 1970 and was in terrible condition. It wasn't much better, really, than storm-wracked Roosevelt Stadium, which was declared a lost cause. Time, too, was a drawback; if Buffalo landed the franchise, it had all of two months to prepare for Opening Day.

McKernan traveled to Buffalo for a meeting in Griffin's office and told the mayor that the first challenge was to fix up War Memorial Stadium. Griffin promised that the job would be done; it would cost about $50,000. Next came the money to operate the club. The purchase price of the Jersey City franchise was $45,000. League fees were $7,500, and an additional $3,000 was needed for player-development costs. All told, Buffalo had to raise about $100,000 just to start the season.

No individual was willing to put up that much money, so Griffin decided to appeal to the community: "I thought the best way to finance the team was to try to find about one hundred people who would each put up one thousand dollars." By Opening Day, ninety-six people had made pledges, including the mayor, his brother, his father, his uncle, and his aunt. Despite those pledges, the team needed working capital. That's when John Sikorski stepped in. Sikorski, a candy merchant who also was president of the Old World–style Broadway Market in a heavily Polish-American part of town, agreed to lend the franchise $55,000. During an afternoon meeting in the mayor's office, McKernan pointed out that the league required a $25,000 franchise deposit. Without blinking an eye, Sikorski pulled out his checkbook and wrote the check on the spot. "I like baseball," Sikorski said. "I just want to be able to go see a game in Buffalo."

Griffin was moved by Sikorski's faith in the project. "I can't say enough about what John did," the mayor recalls. "He was the catalyst of this whole thing."

Sikorksi's loan was repaid when the money was raised from individuals making $1,000 investments in the ball club.

FROM DAY ONE, it was clear that it would take much more than money to resuscitate War Memorial Stadium. New York sports columnist Jimmy Cannon likened the task to putting rouge on a corpse. The man for the job was Joseph Figliola, better known as "Joe Figs," director of the stadium and of the city's indoor sports arena, Memorial Auditorium, who eventually became a city judge. He soon gained another title: president of Buffalo Baseball Incorporated.

The Old Rockpile was a mess. Thousands of gray seats were peeling and cracking. The image was ghostly, much like a cavernous graveyard, with room for nearly 50,000 bodies. On the outside, it was cracking and rusting. Grass grew wild. The terribly scarred infield was a sea of mud. The lights didn't work, and neither did most of the toilets, sinks, and urinals. This was to be the home of a new baseball team? "It wasn't much," Figliola recalls, "but it was all we had. So we had to make the best of it."

The first time that the mayor had asked Figliola about baseball in War Memorial Stadium was at a soccer game played there in 1978. "It was a Sunday afternoon, and the game was over," Figliola says. "The mayor and I were walking across the field. The mayor looked at me and said, 'Joe, how long would it take you to build a baseball diamond in this place?' I didn't know if he was serious. 'Mayor,' I told him, 'it would take about a week.' The mayor looked me straight in the eye and said, 'Put it in.'"

The conversation then turned to professional baseball. "Joe," Griffin asked Figliola, "do you think a pro baseball team would go in this place?"

Probably not, said Figliola, "because of all the riots and troubles in the sixties."

Griffin replied, "I think it would work. A lot of things have changed since then."

Griffin was serious. "At that time," Figliola says, "I think the mayor was the only person who believed there was a future for baseball in Buffalo. There was no one else."

A year later, Figliola found himself assigned to the role of miracle worker. He could often be seen at the decrepit structure, standing on the muddy infield in his three-piece suit, raking the diamond. He led by example, tackling the thankless job with enthusiasm. "Don't worry about the stadium," he would say. "It will be all right. All it needs is some work." Griffin said the job Figliola did on the stadium was "unbelievable."

Figliola wasn't alone. Griffin provided a small army of workers through the Comprehensive Employment Training Act and the Youth Conservation Corps. He negotiated deals with the painters' and the electricians' unions to allow those young workers to help with the project. The power of the mayor's office was not to be underestimated. "I remember a couple of abandoned houses right near the Dodge Street entrance to the park," Colpoys says. "These two houses were really eyesores, and Pat and I didn't know what to do. McKernan told the mayor he was worried about those two houses. . . . The next day, we come to the park, and there's a bulldozer knocking down the two houses. McKernan tells me, 'I've never seen government work this fast in my life.'"

Still, there was one final hurdle. The Buffalo park had to be approved by the Pittsburgh Pirates organization, which would be the parent club of Buffalo's Double-A franchise. Branch B. Rickey, assistant director for Pittsburgh's minor-league teams—and grandson of the Hall of Fame baseball executive best known as the man who signed Jackie Robinson—arrived in Buffalo in the middle of February. There had been a heavy snow the night before, and the temperature was about 20 degrees. Rickey, along with Figliola, Colpoys, and McKernan, braved the rough weather to tour the stadium.

"I'll never forget that day," McKernan says. "I mean, we're walking out there in three feet of snow, stepping in holes and falling in snowdrifts. Branch is asking me what I think. I tell him, 'No problem, don't worry, it'll be fine by April.'" Rickey had doubts, but the Eastern League's need for a franchise meant more than the condition of the Old Rockpile. "We needed a place to play, and we knew Buffalo was a good baseball town," Rickey says. "That was what mattered."

By April the stadium was ready. Buffalo won its 1979 home opener on a home run by future major-leaguer Luis Salazar. Other future big-leaguers who played on that 1979 club, managed by Steve Demeter, included Tony Pena, Dave Dravecky, Rick Lancellotti, Fred Breining, Stewart Cliburn, and Matt Alexander. Lancellotti tied an Eastern League record with 41 homers, most of them over the right-field wall, about 280 feet from home plate. Despite the power, the team was short on pitching and finished in fourth place with a 72–67 record. Attendance lagged in the early months, but a turning point came on a Saturday in June, when a crowd of 13,422 turned out for a Kids Day promotion. Most of those tickets were giveaways, but the size of the crowd showed that baseball passion still burned in Buffalo—even in the Old Rockpile.

"I remember all those kids showing up and how good it was to see that many people at a baseball game in Buffalo after all those years," Griffin recalls. "I always had this feeling about baseball in Buffalo. People thought I was nuts when we went back to War Memorial. They said, 'This guy doesn't know what the hell he's doing in baseball,' and I didn't, but I knew Buffalo, and I knew the old saying: 'Where there's a will, there's a way.'"

Griffin also supplied a large force of Buffalo police on game nights. They seemed to be everywhere, both outside and inside the park. For the first time in years, baseball fans in Buffalo felt safe in War Memorial Stadium. "That neighborhood had changed since the 1960s," Griffin says. "Good people lived there; they weren't violent; they were peaceful, and they were proud of where they lived. We never had one serious incident at War Memorial. People would tell me, 'I'm not going down there; it's not safe; it's a bad place.' I'd tell them, 'Hey, why don't you come to a game and see for yourself?' Once they did, they found out it was a good place. We made the most of what we had."

With Colpoys as general manager and Jack Tracz as his assistant, the Bisons drew 133,148 fans in 1979 for Double-A ball. In 1969, Buffalo's last full season in the Triple-A International League, the team's attendance had been 77,708. After such a long drought, there finally was something, however meager, to quench Buffalo's baseball thirst. "That first year was wonderful," Colpoys recalls. "We made money, and people weren't afraid to come to the park."

McKernan wasn't surprised: "It was an uphill fight, but I had no doubts baseball would work in Buffalo. When you get so many politicians and civic-minded people working together, there was no way we wouldn't pull it off."

Baseball even served as the catalyst for rare unity in the normally rib-bruising relationship between Griffin and the Common Council. Early on, George Arthur, the council majority leader and a future challenger to Griffin in a mayoral election, said the lawmakers would not fight the mayor when it came time to approve a lease for War Memorial Stadium and the new team. For a time, at least, baseball had brought political peace.

Griffin was pleased with that first season. He viewed the Double-A franchise as the first step back in the game—toward his dream of building a baseball stadium downtown. A stadium committee was soon formed. "Getting a franchise that first year was important because it set a standard for Buffalo and baseball in the coming years," Griffin says. "We laid the foundation for the game. We had the public sector and the private sector—politicians and businessmen working together for the good of the game."

Everything seemed to fall into place that first year, but it didn't take long for tough times to return. After a fast start, the 1980 Bisons struggled to a 67–70 record, and attendance fell a bit, to 130,674. By 1981, the novelty of Double-A baseball had vanished. Another mediocre team struggled to a 56–81 mark, and 83,464 fans turned out. For the first time, the team lost money. Those losses increased in 1982, with a Bisons team that finished with a 55–84 record and drew just 77,077 fans. After the 1982 season, the Bisons were nearly $100,000 in debt.

"Unfortunately, none of us knew anything about baseball management," Griffin says. "The only guy who knew anything was Donny Colpoys, and he didn't get any help from anybody."

Colpoys's problem was simple: a lack of money. The original investors did not want to provide any more. "By the end of the fourth year, we lost a ton of money and had no way to replenish it," Colpoys says. "We were always working hand-to-mouth; we never had any working capital."

Pete Calieri also was hit with a crushing setback in 1982. In June, he suffered a devastating knee injury while umpiring an International League game in Syracuse, forcing him to retire as an umpire. He worked in broadcasting and eventually became a sales supervisor for a company in Buffalo, but he would never realize his dream of being a big-league ump. Not only that, but the baseball flame that he helped rekindle in Buffalo was flickering badly and in danger of going out.

For the second time in twelve years, it appeared that Buffalo would be saying good-bye to pro baseball. The harshness of the economic climate kept any local buyers from emerging, and the league was getting out-of-town offers for the franchise. It was January 1983, and time was running out. Griffin and Colpoys were desperate to find a local buyer for the club. Colpoys told this to a friend of his, Elmer "Torchy" Reimann, a sporting-goods-store owner who had managed the Simon Pures when Colpoys played.

"Torchy said to me, 'Did you ever think about asking Bob Rich, Jr.?'" Colpoys recalls. "Torchy said Rich was a stockholder in the Buffalo Sabres and was a young guy who was very sports-oriented." Colpoys bounced the idea off Griffin, who said he knew that the Rich family "had always been interested in sports. Bob's father was a high school football coach and a damn good athlete. He was always there and always competitive."

Bob Rich, Jr., age forty-one, who several years earlier had been named president of the family's frozen-foods empire when his father became chairman, was known around town as a hockey buff. But did he care about baseball? Anything was worth a try at this point. There was a bit of a problem, though: He and Jimmy Griffin didn't get along; they weren't even speaking to each other.

MIKE BILLONI SMELLED a story. His newspaper, the *Buffalo Courier-Express,* the place where Joe Alli spent his career, had closed in September 1982. Now, four months later, the twenty-five-year-old Billoni was an unemployed sportswriter who was working as a stringer while hoping to land a full-time job with the Rochester *Democrat & Chronicle.* The Rochester paper wanted Billoni to write an article about the baseball situation in Buffalo, so he called Vince McNamara, former president of the New York–Penn League. McNamara, in his early seventies at the time, was one of the most respected and knowledgeable baseball figures in Buffalo. "I asked him if anything was going on," Billoni recalls. "He told me, ironically enough, the fate of the Buffalo baseball club would be determined on Thursday. It was Monday morning."

At seven o'clock that Thursday evening, January 13, 1983, Don Colpoys and the Bisons' investors were to meet with Bob Rich, Jr., at the Roosevelt restaurant, a small East Side bar and grill that had a long tradition of serving common folk and power brokers alike. Most of the investors knew little about Bob Rich other than that he was now a big corporate player and that he was his father's son. McNamara urged Billoni to call Rich.

"I looked into the story and began digging deeper and deeper," Billoni remembers. "Bob Rich was the last chance. Nobody else in Buffalo was going to save a Double-A baseball team playing in War

Memorial Stadium. They all told me it was throwing good money after bad."

Billoni called Rich. He had known the businessman for years, after covering him as a handball player in the Empire State Games, a statewide amateur competition, in the early seventies. Rich asked the reporter his opinion of whether he should buy the franchise. Billoni recalls telling him "that with hard work and a lot of money, he could do pretty well with it." Rich wanted no publicity; he asked Billoni to keep everything quiet.

Fourteen months earlier, Jimmy Griffin had run virtually unopposed for a second term and captured 90 percent of the vote. If there was a quality that he embodied as mayor, it was pragmatism: "We needed somebody who could afford to run a franchise. That was the only way baseball would succeed. The Riches had the money and the business experience. We were $100,000 in debt; I didn't see any other way out."

It was hard to find two men with less in common than Jimmy Griffin, the street kid whose father sold hardware, and Bob Rich, Jr., the wealthy son of one of the most successful businessmen in America. But there was common ground: sports, and baseball in particular.

"We got a call from the mayor's office that there were two out-of-town groups looking to buy the team and move it out of Buffalo," says Rich, who was surprised at the call. "Mayor Griffin and I literally had a history of not agreeing with each other on anything. He's a very strong-willed guy and has his own agendas. And I have to admit, I'm very much the same way."

Their differences, it turned out, could be overcome.

"With baseball, we both focused on a common interest," Rich says. "And suddenly, the animosity that had existed between us evaporated. This was a friendship forged in baseball."

Rich told Griffin that he was interested in buying the team. "I felt Buffalo was too good of a sports city to lose a baseball team," Rich says. As the conversation with the mayor went on, Rich learned that there also was hope for a downtown stadium in the not-too-distant future but that any such hope probably would die without a baseball franchise. "That gave me more ammunition to get involved," Rich says. "If the Bisons left, that would have meant the death of what I considered to be a very worthwhile project for downtown Buffalo."

Billoni arrived for the Roosevelt restaurant meeting about an hour early and noticed television cameras in front of the building. He went to a pay phone and called Rich. "Come in the back entrance," Billoni said. Rich drove to the meeting in an old station wagon from his company's mail-room fleet. He parked at the back entrance and darted inside.

Once in the Roosevelt, Rich headed to a banquet room, where about one hundred stockholders were waiting. He made his pitch, telling the stockholders that he would buy the team, repay the debts, and then give them ten cents on the dollar on their original investments.

"By this time, most of them had given up on ever seeing any return on their investments, let alone seeing the team saved in Buffalo," Rich says. The response was hardly overwhelming. Rich says most of the stockholders appeared "befuddled," especially when he told them that his goal was to one day bring a major-league team to Buffalo. One person in the room asked Rich, "Do you really know what you're getting into?" Another asked, "Why in the world would you want to get involved with this?"

Rich smiled, kept his cool, and exuded optimism. The stockholders then had to vote whether to sell the team to Rich, and they asked him to leave the room. He went out to the bar and talked with Billoni.

"I don't know how it's going to go, Mike; they're voting on me now."

"Don't worry; you're a lock."

"Nothing is ever a lock in business. I had to go in there and sell myself and my family and my faith in baseball. I just don't know what they'll do. I bet you a beer I don't get it."

"You're on."

Just then, a man came out of the meeting room and asked Rich to come inside. The decision had been made. Griffin warmly shook Rich's hand, telling him, "Congratulations, Bob, you're the new owner of the Buffalo Bisons."

A few minutes later, Rich came out smiling. He walked up to

Billoni and said, "Mike, I owe you a beer; I just bought a baseball team."

When Billoni and Rich went up to the bar, they were joined by many of the stockholders. "I'll never forget that moment," Billoni says. "It was the first public appearance of Bob Rich as a baseball man. Until then, everyone knew him as 'the son of . . .' 'the president of the company . . .' or 'the guy with his name on the football stadium. . . . ' Now, he was Bob Rich the baseball man."

As for the Bisons' new owner himself, "I'd like to think it's Bob Rich the Buffalonian. No matter what I do in baseball, I'd like people here to think of me as someone whose heart is in Buffalo."

Before deciding to buy the Bisons, Bob Rich, Jr., did what was normal for him when he wanted to make a business move and needed advice: He consulted his father. Robert E. Rich, Sr., made it crystal clear, though, that the family business must come first: "I was in Florida, and Bobby called me on the phone. He asked me, 'What do you say, should we do it or not?' I told him, 'Go ahead, if you want to. My answer is yes, providing you'll give me your word that you'll only work on baseball during lunchtime, or after five o'clock.' Bobby told me, 'Dad, you got my word.'"

It was a tough promise to keep. Although Rich Products was Rich's top priority, baseball became more time-consuming with each passing day. Like the food business, selling baseball in Buffalo—especially Double-A baseball at the Old Rockpile—was hard work. "But I knew we could turn it around," said Robert Rich, Sr. "The frozen-food business is a promotional business, and you always have to have programs going, and you often have to give customers incentives. Baseball is the same way. I knew Bobby knew how to promote frozen foods, and I certainly thought he could do the same with baseball."

4

FATHER AND SON

Baseball had never been high on Robert Edward Rich's list of priorities. He had wanted to interest his first son, Bob, Jr., in amateur wrestling "because I think that's the greatest sport there is; it's a body-builder and a one-on-one contest." But the son would have no part of it. He gravitated toward football and hockey; skiing and squash, too; even surfing and polo. As for wrestling, his father says, "I could never get him interested. I think I pressed too hard."

THE RICH FAMILY had always pressed hard. Robert Rich's ancestors were farmers who had come from England in the early 1800s to settle in Massachusetts and later in upstate New York. His father, Paul J. Rich, was twenty years old in 1900 when he came to Buffalo from Cattaraugus, a rural community south of the city. Paul Rich worked as a schoolteacher for a few years and managed to save fifteen hundred dollars, which he invested in a dairy on Niagara and Maryland Streets on the city's West Side. He called the business Rich Milk Company.

Within a decade, Rich's dairy became the largest wholesale milk and cream business in Buffalo. In 1910, Paul Rich married Eleanor MacKenzie, who was born in Oak Park, Illinois, but had grown up and been educated in Buffalo. The second of their five children was Robert, who was born in 1913. The Rich dairy business was a family enterprise, and Eleanor Rich was an essential part of it. "She was an exceptional businesswoman who was completely devoted to her family," Robert Rich said of his mother. It was the beginning of a tradition for the Riches: family life and business always entwined; husbands and wives and children working closely together, at home and on the job. A few years after they were married, Paul and Eleanor Rich sold the milk business and started Rich Ice Cream Company, which became one of the largest independent producers in America's then-infant ice cream industry. Through the years, Paul Rich had many offers from larger dairy companies to buy him out, but his answer was always no; he believed strongly in the concept of an independent business that was family-oriented.

Paul Rich instilled that philosophy in his son Robert, who as a youth became fascinated with sports and shared that fascination with his father when they attended International League games together in the 1920s at Bison Stadium. You could get a ballpark hot dog for a dime back then, and a soft drink cost a nickel. The Rich company's ballpark ice cream also cost a dime. Paul Rich had box seats along the first-base line, from which father and son would cheer especially hard for the boy's favorite player, a slugging first baseman named Billy Kelly. As time passed, though, the boy discovered that the athlete in him loved wrestling—its one-on-one challenge, its honesty. There was no place to hide, and he liked that. But he knew that you couldn't wrestle all year long, so he developed a parallel passion—football, with its demands for unity, team spirit, and individual sacrifice. At Bennett High School in North Buffalo, Robert Rich was a tenacious, five-foot-ten-inch, 160-pound center. In 1931, his senior year, Bennett won the public school championship, the Harvard Cup.

Janet Webb, who was to become his wife, attended a different high school, Lafayette, across town. She didn't know him other than by his reputation in sports before they both enrolled at the University of Buffalo. He was easy to recognize: Now five feet eleven inches, and 185 pounds, he was handsome, with wavy brown hair, blue eyes, and a certain swagger. Of course, his heroics in football and wrestling also made him a big man on campus. Janet would later learn that when Robert Rich arrived on campus, there had been no wrestling program, but that in his inimitable style, he did the only thing that made sense to him: He founded one. "Right away," Janet would say later, "I knew he was a pretty capable guy."

By 1933, amid the anguish of the Depression, the two of them were midway through their college careers. Their paths had not yet crossed, but they were about to. Janet, nineteen, was a liberal arts

major and wanted to be a social worker. Her faculty adviser, however, was not optimistic about her future in that field. "Janet," he
told her, "you would be the world's worst social worker, because
you think with your heart and not your head. Why don't you get
into personnel work and take some business courses?" Janet decided to do so, although she still had hopes of being a social worker.
But the idea of learning about business made sense, because it
would help her find a job. Her father, Oliver Webb, worked for the
local electric utility and stressed the importance of steady employment. So she enrolled in Economics 101, and sitting nearby in that
class was none other than Robert Rich, twenty, star athlete and
business administration major, who at the time was pondering
whether to pursue a career in football coaching or the dairy business.

Janet found that in contrast to his intimidating presence on the
football field, the true Robert Rich was downright charming. Soon,
he asked her for a date. She accepted, and a courtship blossomed.
Before long, they decided to elope.

The University of Buffalo wrestling team, of which Robert Rich
was captain, had a match scheduled against Cornell. On a cold February night in 1934, Robert and Janet jumped into his blue 1931
Ford convertible, turned the heater up full blast and drove together
to Ithaca. Their first stop was Alden, a small village just east of
Buffalo, where they were married by a minister. They continued to
Ithaca, returned to Buffalo and were able to keep their marriage a
secret for three months.

Robert and Janet Rich, husband and wife, graduated from the
University of Buffalo in 1935, she with a degree in liberal arts, he
with one in business administration. Soon, there came an opportunity to buy a small milk business, Wilber Farms Dairy. Robert's
father offered him a $5,000 loan as a down payment, and Robert
was to pay Mrs. Wilber $20,000 over five years.

Still, Robert Rich was torn between business and sports. He
also had taken the job as football coach at Buffalo's Riverside High
School and now had to juggle two jobs. Janet also faced a career
decision. She had received an appointment as a social worker, much
to the surprise of her academic adviser. But her career in social

work was to be short-lived. Her husband urgently needed office help in his fledgling dairy business.

"Janet," Robert Rich told his young wife, "you'd really be of much more value to me if you'd let someone teach you how to run a trial balance and be my accountant." Janet took a crash course in accounting from a friend and began to handle all the bookkeeping chores for her husband. "We had no accounting department," Janet Rich remembers. "I was it."

At the beginning, business was hardly booming. Robert Rich himself drove a horse-drawn milk wagon, and there were four routes, one of which was handled by truck. Financially, he faced an additional burden of a $6,500 mortgage. But in due time, the loan was paid off, and Robert offered to repay the $5,000 to his father. "That was no loan; it was a gift," Paul Rich told his son.

Robert Rich now laughs when he thinks of his first business venture. "I call that my original leveraged buyout; I bought a company with no money down."

The mid-1930s were difficult times to start a business, but Robert and Janet Rich were young and confident. In 1934, Mrs. Wilber's dairy had had gross sales of about $50,000 and had made a profit of just over $5,000. Rich was determined to better those figures. He was also determined to prove something: "I always wanted to show my father that I could be successful."

Robert and Janet would drive all over Buffalo, talking to the owners of the small family grocery stores and selling dairy goods. From sunup till sundown, they immersed themselves in their business. "We had times where we'd strive just to make sure we'd make ends meet," Janet Rich recalls. The hours were long and the work arduous, and for Robert Rich, there was an additional high-pressure responsibility: coaching football.

Riverside High was a perennial loser, never having placed higher than eleventh in a twelve-team league. Robert Rich wanted to change that history. He was twenty-two, just a few years older than many of his players. "He was so young-looking, the first time I saw him I thought he was barely old enough to be my big brother," says Leon "Red" Moulin, co-captain of the team. "We all knew he was an outstanding player in college, but it was his manner that gained so much respect. Once you talked to him, you knew he was special." Joseph DiVincenzo, another player on the team, says Rich "had a tremendous effect on my life, as far as learning the difference between right and wrong. He taught me sportsmanship, the will to win, and doing what you had to do in order to win."

Rich's coaching strategy paid off; in 1935, his first season, Riverside improved enough to finish seventh.

Rich's dairy business also showed progress; in its first year, the profit was about $9,000. The plant had four workers and a supervisor. Rich soon added a plant manager. He paid the workers the going rate of a dollar a day and gave each married worker a quart of milk a day, which was worth six cents. Workers with children received an extra quart, and they were allowed to grow tomatoes and vegetables near plant property for their own use. There was a long waiting list of job applicants. The workers, who took home about ten dollars each payday, were on the job seven days a week. "That was the Depression," Rich recalls vividly, "and that's what everyone was doing."

For Riverside football, 1936 was a year to remember. Rich's team won the championship by going unbeaten in its six league games and finished 8–0 overall. In league play, Riverside rushed for an average of 348 yards a game. It was a rough, tough, ethnic stew of a football team, made up of just about every nationality in Buffalo. The best all-around player was Johnny Polanski, who went on to become an All-American at Wake Forest and play professionally with the Detroit Lions. But the league's other coaches did not like seeing a newcomer win the title, so they managed to do something off the field that they hadn't been able to do on it.

In 1937 Rich's team finished 6–2, but the school board then passed a rule that coaches must have physical-education degrees. Because Rich's degree was in business administration, this meant that he no longer would be allowed to coach in the league. He was devastated, since at that point he was considering whether to make coaching a career. But fate intervened, and he was forced to leave Riverside.

"That was the toughest decision in his life," Janet Rich recalls. Red Moulin remembers it as "heartbreaking; you can't describe how much he loved that job."

Robert Rich says, "There was nothing I could do. They made

the rule, and that was that. It was very tough to leave, but—you know something?—if I had become a full-time coach, it would have been the worst thing that ever happened to me. It turned out that losing my coaching job was the luckiest thing that happened to me. I was able to concentrate on business." In 1938 and 1939 Rich worked part time as a freshman football coach at the University of Buffalo, but that was to be his last stint on the sidelines.

When Robert Rich had gone into the dairy business, his goal had been to go beyond a million dollars in annual sales. By 1940, he had done so. The couple's first child, Joanne, was born in 1939. In January 1941 he and Janet welcomed their first son, Robert, Jr., whom the family called Bobby. Later there also was a second son, David.

The advent of World War II brought about dramatic changes. Robert Rich was called to Washington, where he was named a consultant to the War Food Administration. He was sent to Detroit to be milk-order administrator for Michigan. While in Detroit, he learned of successful research by the George Washington Carver Laboratories to develop a milk and cream replacement using soybean oil. Rich returned to Buffalo in 1944, determined to pursue the idea of using soybean oil to create a vegetable-based substitute for whipped cream.

A research team at Spencer Kellogg & Sons in Buffalo assisted him in developing the whippable cream from soybean oil. In 1945, Rich decided to form Rich Products Corporation to market the whipped topping. The company's first big test would be to present the whipped topping in New York City to a major distributor and his sales force. Robert Rich approached the presentation the same way he did a football game or a wrestling match: by going all-out and pressing hard.

To those who knew him best, his willingness to battle for his company and his intense desire to succeed came as no surprise. "If you didn't have the enthusiasm Robert Rich had, you wouldn't have been with him, because he separated those who wanted to go and those who didn't want to go very quickly," said Herb Kusche, one of the original employees of Rich Products who still works with Robert Rich. Since the early days, these two men have shared the same philosophy: "Give your life to the company; this is our life," says Kusche, now an executive vice president of the corporation.

Janet Rich was confident of the outcome of her husband's meeting with those New York sales executives. "It never crossed my mind that he wouldn't be successful."

Rich boarded a train for the ride to New York on a Friday evening, having packed the whipped topping in dry ice to keep it fresh. The train ride lasted all night.

"In the ice cream business, you always used dry ice," Rich says. "When you use dry ice to keep a product cold, you always wrap it real well, which I had done." But he was in for a shock when he arrived in New York the next morning. He had used too much dry ice, and the product was frozen solid. When he arrived for his Saturday morning demonstration, about twenty salesmen were waiting to confront him. "They were there to see the gold from the soil—my miracle cream," Rich says, "and they don't know it, but it's frozen solid. I had been in the dairy business ten years, and I knew once you freeze heavy cream, it'll never whip. But there was nothing else I could do but take a one-in-a-hundred chance that this stuff would whip. I borrowed a knife from one of the salesmen and kind of cut it up. I'm up there telling corny jokes, doing a soft shoe, trying to kill time. These New York salesmen are getting impatient. Finally, I take the knife and start whipping. I don't know if it's going to thaw and whip, but I'm hoping. All of a sudden, it starts coming up and whipping beautifully—geez, am I relieved!"

Within a few months, Robert Rich was a part of America's embryonic frozen-food industry, whose worldwide market would prove to be almost limitless. That first year, his company did a modest $28,000 worth of business, but before long, it was booming.

In two years, Rich's Whip Topping was being sold in thirty-nine states and around the world. In 1961, Rich's was marketing another innovation: Coffee Rich, a frozen nondairy liquid creamer. By the mid-1960s, Rich Products' sales exceeded $30 million.

Robert Rich is a tenacious, shrewd businessman who if provoked can be brass-knuckles tough. That's what happened when Coffee Rich hit the market and began hitting the competing dairy companies right in the wallet. In several states, dairy lobbies brought court actions to inhibit or restrict the marketing of Rich's nondairy products. Rich did not back off. He fought the lawsuits and, over the years, won more than forty of them, paying millions of dollars in legal fees to keep his products on store shelves.

The company expanded its products and acquired bakery plants worldwide. In 1975 Rich Products sales surpassed $100 million for the first time. Another research breakthrough came in 1977, when Rich Products was awarded a patent for Freeze Flo, a process that allows frozen foods to stay soft, eliminating the need to thaw. It was introduced to the public in 1980, and led to another boom in sales, which in 1985 were more than $545 million and which went on to exceed $700 million.

Yet while amassing a fortune that has been estimated at more than $400 million, Robert Rich and his family never have lost sight of their community roots.

During Buffalo's economic hard times of the 1970s, while other businesses left town or cut back, Rich Products swam against the tide and expanded, acquiring numerous properties in what once was a run-down section of the West Side. The company spent $17 million to acquire and renovate an eyesore warehouse and make it headquarters for the company's research facility.

The members of the Rich family have shown strong interest in the arts, and their eclectic collection of hundreds of works—by artists ranging from Henry Moore to Robert Rauschenberg to Andy Warhol—enlivens the walls of all their business locations.

On the personal side, the family has been deeply involved in community service, charity work, and cultural projects. It all stems from Robert Rich's heartfelt loyalty to his city: "This is a friendly city, and it has been a part of me and my family all my life. I owe a lot to this city. Buffalo is where I was born. Buffalo is where I started in business—and Buffalo will always be the home of Rich Products."

BY 1978 ROBERT RICH was approaching sixty-five, and he decided to step down as president of Rich Products and become chairman. In August of that year, Bob, Jr., then barely thirty-seven, was named president of the company.

Although Robert Rich had long before seen to it that his elder son was introduced to the family business, Bob's future had been far from certain.

"There were times, when he was young, that it looked like Bobby would never go into the business or work as hard as his father," Janet Rich says, "but after he grew up, things changed."

George Ostendorf, now a sales executive, tells of how "Bobby and I kind of grew up together" as close friends in North Buffalo during the 1940s and how

> when Bob was growing up, it wasn't always easy. I think Bob felt strongly that he wanted to live up to what his dad did. There was a kind of competition, but that ended a long time ago.
> I think Mr. Rich, Sr., and his son both realized that Bobby really was something special, and he could do it in business or sports, just like his father. In fact, there's a lot of his father in Bobby. They're both strong on relationships, community responsibility, and hard work. And they're loyal to their family and friends.

Robert Rich, thinking back to the relationship he had had with his own father, insisted that Bob, Jr., learn the family business. "I always wanted to be successful, to show my father that I could be successful. I always had that driving desire to prove to him I was a success, and I think Bobby has that same desire."

By the time he was fourteen, Bob was working at Rich Products during summer months. He loaded trucks and performed other labors. For the most part, it was exhausting work, but he relished it. He also proved to be a down-to-earth communicator, fitting right in with the other workers. "I know Bobby's early work in the plant did him in good stead," his mother says. "He used to come home and tell us how he got to know the men down there, how much their jobs meant to them and how nice it was to be a part of it. Bob has a natural gift of enthusiasm, which I think is a fine thing. We knew he had quite a future ahead of him with his father. Just as my husband's father had set an example, Bobby's father set an example for him. In our family, that is a normal development."

As a youth, Bob "was always outside playing some game," his mother recalls. "In the summer, you could always find Bobby on some corner lot, playing baseball." His favorite player was Ruben Amaro, a slick-fielding shortstop for the Bisons. "I thought it was my destiny to be a shortstop," Bob later said, but he quickly learned that the game was much harder than it looked. He had gone from Public School 22 to a prep school, Nichols, where as a sophomore he was introduced to Uncle Charlie—the curveball. "We're playing against a South Park High School, and their pitcher is a little guy, about five-feet-four," Bob, Jr., remembers.

He literally came up to my belt buckle, and I didn't see how he could throw the ball by me. It turns out he had a great curve. He struck me out four times on twelve pitches. And the last time was with two outs in the ninth inning with the bases loaded, and we're losing by a run. After the game, I went straight to the athletic director's office and put my uniform and equipment in the corner. I told the athletic director that I'd like to go out for the tennis team.

Janet Rich recalls that "in the fall and winter, it was football and hockey. Bobby really liked hockey, but I'd yell at him because he'd play goalie without a mask."

At Nichols School, Bob was a quarterback and—still without a mask—a goalie. As the years passed, he developed a reputation as a bit of a rebel, whose main interests were sports, fast cars, and good times. David Rich saw his brother as "not so much a rebel as he was a person who was trying to find his own way. He was very individually oriented, toward his own life."

When it came to choosing a college, Bob, Jr., and his father had their differences. "I wanted Bobby to go to Ames, Iowa, to Iowa State," Robert Rich says. "That's a cow school; it would be a great place for him to learn the dairy business. Bobby wanted no part of it."

If the son had a consuming passion, it was hockey. He was six feet two inches and 175 pounds and wanted to be a goalie, and Williams College in Williamstown, Massachusetts, offered the best opportunity for that. The social life, too, was more appealing than in cow country. Bob enjoyed racing cars and tooled about in an MG and a Ferrari. He also was big on the party scene. "I had a lot of fun in college," he says. "I knew if I was going to go into business, I was going to need a graduate degree, anyway. So I had a lot of fun. I remember some pretty wild times."

Except during hockey season.

His dedication to hockey was total. Everything else—including social life—was set aside during the season: "From Thanksgiving until the end of March, I never touched a drink, smoked a cigarette, ate junk food, and I always went to bed early. Sports was the thing that always brought me around. From the time I was old enough to drive, meet girls or whatever, sports was the thing that always brought me back. As rebellious as I might have seemed at times, my father and I always shared that background in sports, and he knew I would never stray too far away."

Tom Roe and Bob Rich, Jr., were roommates at Williams. Roe played center on the hockey team, and the two of them shared four years of adventures, both on and off the ice. "Sports was always the priority with Bob," says Roe, now a lawyer in Minneapolis. "He was a goalie and a real showman on the ice. He was a good goalie . . . a tremendous competitor. Bob was one of those jocks who took it very seriously; he was very intense."

Roe and Rich joined the varsity team during their sophomore year in 1961 and soon led Williams to its then-best two hockey seasons ever. In 1961 Williams posted a 16–3–1 record. The next year, the team went 16–4. "Bob was the first goalie at Williams to start as a sophomore," says Roe, who as an All-American led the nation in scoring one year. But the results in the classroom were quite different from those on the ice. "Bob enjoyed college, but he wasn't overly serious about studying," Roe says. "Don't get me wrong, Williams is a tough school, and Bob held his own, but he liked to have a good time. And when hockey season was over, we had some crazy times."

Roe liked the fact that Bob Rich, Jr., despite his wealth, never put on airs. "Bob hated people who did that," Roe says. "When he was in college, Bob was the kind of guy who befriended the janitor in the freshman dorm, or the people who worked in the snack bar." Rich also talked a lot about Buffalo. "I've never seen a guy, or a family, so loyal to their community," Roe says. "Bob always said good things about Buffalo and what growing up there meant to him. I think he knew he was going to be in the family business. Maybe that's why he wasn't too serious about studying at Williams; he knew he would have to get a graduate degree. But I think, down deep, even then, Bob looked forward to working with his father."

Bob Rich graduated from Williams in 1963 with a B.A. in Spanish. Soon afterward, he went to Hawaii to work as a salesman at a Rich Products subsidiary. "Actually, we put him in Hawaii because he was so gung-ho for surfboarding," his father says. "He asked me if he could work mornings and take afternoons for surfing. He told me I'd only have to pay him half a salary." In evaluating the business experience the son gained from working in Hawaii, the father said, "He became a good surfer."

Toward the end of 1963, Bob Rich was back in Buffalo facing important decisions about his future. He had interviewed for a job with the Central Intelligence Agency. He had considered an offer from the Air Force to attend Officer Candidate School and fly jet fighters, but that would require a five-year commitment. There was a job offer from Texaco, too. And then there was hockey: opportunities to try out for the 1964 Olympic team and to play professional hockey for the Los Angeles team in the Western Hockey League. Rich had been a practice goalie for the Buffalo Bisons of the American Hockey League, and during that stint had scrimmaged against players such as Phil Esposito and Bobby Hull. Rich finally did try out for the 1964 Olympic squad and was one of the final cuts.

Time seemed to be running out for Bob Rich, Jr., to make a career move, and that's when his father stepped in.

"He knew how headstrong I was," the son recalls. "While I had worked in the company, it really wasn't on my agenda to come back to Rich Products. So my father told me, 'Look, I'll make you a deal. We're thinking of building a new plant in Canada. You can take over the operation, work on the design, and I'll give you a million-dollar budget to build the plant. You can operate it, and I won't bother you. I won't interfere. You can do with it what you want.'"

Robert Rich was offering his son the opportunity to be his own man in the family business. "That was very compelling for me," the son says. "My father rightly put his finger on the major issue: I had to be my own person. . . . My dad is the only boss I have ever worked for, and I've made a pledge to myself: He *will* be the only boss I will ever work for."

The son accepted his father's offer. He came back to Buffalo, joined the Army National Guard and served six months of active duty. "The idea was, when I got out, I would go to Canada and work," the son says. "I felt, for the first time, my career path had been somewhat established. I wasn't sure I was going to make a career out of Rich Products, but the idea of having my own plant and company in Canada was very appealing."

The business seemed to bring father and son closer than ever. "Every time I ran into a problem, like any manager, I'd look for help from somebody who knew the business," the son remembers.

> What better person than my father? He was right across the border and more than happy to give advice.
>
> I realized how much more he knew than I thought he knew when I was in college. From that time on, we've become good pals. Oftentimes for me, it's not like father and son; it's more like a friendship. We've gone through different things and stages in our lives. He's always been there for me. He has a tremendous capacity for love. He also has a tremendous capacity for letting people have their own opportunities to succeed.

Robert Rich was pleased with his son's efforts. Business in Canada boomed, and Bob displayed a knack for communication and salesmanship. "I remember one time we got a call from our broker up in Boston," Robert Rich says.

> One of the store chains was mad because one of their rivals had copied their carton, and we were packing for them. We couldn't help that; they give us cartons, and we fill them. They said they were going to discontinue Rich Products, and they were one of our biggest customers in the Boston area. Bobby took the next plane out and went to see the buyer. He told him, "We're at fault. Now, what can we do to remedy it?" Just like that, Bobby patched the whole thing up and came home. By the time he got back, we got a call from that company for more orders. Bobby took a bad situation and turned it around. That, you can't

teach in school; you've got to have it inside, and Bobby's got it. I always knew he'd do great in this business.

In 1967 Bob needed to make time to enroll in the graduate school at the University of Rochester, where a business-development program enabled executives to earn a master's degree in two years. But the schedule was hectic. He worked full time in Fort Erie, Ontario, where his plant was located, and on school days he would commute about seventy miles to Rochester for classes, which often began at seven A.M. and lasted until early evening.

"There was a minimum of twenty-five hours' homework a week," he recalls. "I remember a couple of times, driving home from Rochester and just pulling off the road in Batavia and sleeping in the parking lot of the Treadway Inn. It was so tough, with everything else I had to do, that at times I just felt like crying."

But for two years, he managed to juggle it all. He graduated with honors, second in his class, and his business career began to soar. His efforts resulted in huge profits for Rich Products of Canada, and he became president of Rich Sales Company, the sales and marketing arm of the corporation.

The relationship between father and son was flourishing. "I think the emotions between fathers and sons are one of the least-documented and strongest emotions that bind people in humanity," Bob later said.

A lot of human behavior can be traced to the desire of sons to prove themselves to their fathers, and I'm no exception. I was always under a lot of pressure. People used to say to me, "How do you come into a business in a community like Buffalo, where your father has been so successful? Isn't there a lot of pressure?" For me, there never was, because I never really cared what people thought of me, as far as the job I've done, or whether I'm my own person, or whatever. The only person who has really concerned me is my father and his perception of how I'm doing. So the pressure was there, but not from other people. It was really from my desire to prove myself.

THERE IS A WISTFULNESS to Bob Rich, Jr., when he talks of his days as a youngster in North Buffalo, often returning home from street games with an assortment of bumps and bruises. "Whenever I think of growing up, I relate to the physical feeling of being with the kids, playing on the sandlots," he says. "I mean, we'd be out there at the start of baseball season, freezing to death, using some dirt-encased, taped-up ball. It felt more like a shot put than a baseball, but what fun!"

Perhaps the most magical memories of all, though, surround an annual rite of spring. Even though Robert Rich was deeply involved in building his business, and the demands of his time often seemed overwhelming, there was a special time reserved for his son: Opening Day. Janet Rich would write a note to the principal so her son could leave school early. Bob would sit on the curb, baseball glove in hand, impatiently watching for his father's car. At about eleven-thirty in the morning, it would appear.

"Finally," Bob remembers fondly,

he would pull up in his Packard. It seemed like this big, giant car, and I would slide into the front seat and be right next to him. For that day, it was just the two of us, and I was the most important part of my father's life. He would put his work aside, . . . and we would drive over to Offermann Stadium for Opening Day. What a wonderful baseball tradition—a boy and his dad doing something together. . . . It was a mutual enjoyment of the game, and I've always thought that's what the essence of sports should be.

SNAPSHOT—JOE D. AND MARSE JOE

Buffalo is where Joe DiMaggio's first big-league manager, Marse Joe McCarthy, spent most of his life.

DiMaggio was a twenty-one-year-old rookie in 1936 when he came to Yankee Stadium to play for McCarthy. For most of the next decade, these two men—both destined for the Hall of Fame—led the Yankees to unmatched success.

DiMaggio is thinking about that on a June night as he stands in the middle of a banquet room in the Hyatt Regency Hotel in Buffalo. He is attending a banquet with other baseball greats who are in town for an old-timers' game. As usual, he is surrounded by autograph-seekers and other admirers who just want to get close; DiMaggio is like a quarterback in a huddle. These people wear suits and evening gowns, and somehow juggle cocktails along with pens and sheets of paper that are continually thrust toward DiMaggio. In his mid-seventies, he has lost none of his magnetism and savoir-faire. But he is always uncomfortable with so many people around him, and this is no exception.

"Are you a reporter?" DiMaggio asks as I follow him across the room.

"Yes," I say, and he starts to walk away.

"I really don't want to talk," he says, continuing to move gracefully away. The throng of admirers is thinning out, and I'm walking with him, a foot or so away, trying to keep up.

"Mr. DiMaggio," I gingerly persist, "I wonder if I could ask you a couple of questions about Joe McCarthy." He takes a few more steps, then suddenly stops. It's as if a lamp has been turned on in a dark room.

"Wait a minute," DiMaggio says, "are you from Buffalo?" I

nod yes. By this time we're face to face, about six inches apart, and he looks me straight in the eye. "Joe was from Buffalo." DiMaggio stops walking and, once more, about ten people gather around him. He doesn't seem to notice them, though. "Go ahead," he tells me, "ask your questions."

So I do.

"What kind of a manager was Joe McCarthy?"

"Joe was a great manager. He was, I would say, a disciplinarian. . . ."

"What did Joe McCarthy do for you?"

"He didn't do anything; he just managed. Joe wasn't too close to his players. I would say he was all business when it came to baseball. The only time he would really talk to the players would be out in the hotel lobby. He would be sitting there with that big black cigar in his mouth, and he'd talk to anybody."

"But what made McCarthy a great manager?"

Silence from the Yankee Clipper. Then a chuckle. Then a hand held to the mouth, trying to hide a sly grin, as if to suggest that any manager, even Joe McCarthy, is only as good as his players. Then a laugh.

"You have to remember, we had some great players on those teams. And I mean *great* players."

DiMaggio's expression turns serious.

"Joe McCarthy knew how to keep a team together, and he knew how to make it jell. If you played for Joe McCarthy, all he demanded was that you give your best. It didn't matter if you were the number-one man on the team or the twenty-fifth man. It was all the same to him."

DiMaggio then tells a story about how McCarthy might have cost him a chance to hit .400 in 1939. He was hitting .412 in September, when he developed a sinus infection around his left eye. He received a shot of Novocain above the eye, which swelled and started to close. DiMaggio, a right-handed hitter, faced the pitcher with his left eye. So with the swelling, he had trouble seeing the pitcher and even the ball.

"Here, I'll show you what I mean," Joe DiMaggio tells me. Resplendent in an impeccably tailored navy blue suit, sky-blue shirt, and red tie, he proceeds to spread his feet apart and demonstrate his legendary batting stance, right there in the middle of a hotel banquet room in downtown Buffalo. The dozen people or so who are witnessing this can't quite believe it.

"See, I was like this," he says, holding his hand up high as if waving a bat. He points to his right eye. "See, I couldn't see the pitcher."

Nevertheless, McCarthy wanted him to stay in the lineup. DiMaggio's batting average tumbled, ending up at .381, which was still good enough to win the batting championship by 21 points. At age twenty-four, he was named American League Most Valuable Player for the first time.

All this had happened a half-century earlier, but for Joe DiMaggio, it is as if it were a memory from a summer or two ago. Why did McCarthy keep him in the lineup? Because, the manager told him later, he didn't want the great DiMaggio to win the batting title as a "cheese champion."

DiMaggio shakes his head.

"Can you believe it? But that's the way Joe was; he wanted you to play. But I don't have to tell you all this; you're from Buffalo; you already know about Joe McCarthy."

IN BUFFALO, JOE McCARTHY led a far different life than he did in his baseball uniform. He had managed Babe Ruth, Lou Gehrig, DiMaggio, and later with the Boston Red Sox, Ted Williams. Away from the glitter of the game, Marse Joe was a quiet, contented man, who savored life in Buffalo with his wife, Babe. The couple eventually settled on a farm in the suburb of Amherst, where they spent their final years together.

Joe McCarthy was born in Philadelphia in 1887. He was seventeen when he earned a baseball scholarship to Niagara University, and he spent nearly twenty years as a player and manager in the minor leagues. He came to Buffalo in 1914 as a second baseman with the Bisons. (In one International League game, he went hitless in four at-bats against a Baltimore pitcher named Babe Ruth.) That year McCarthy, who never played a game in the majors, appeared in 146 games for the Bisons, hit four home runs and batted .266. In 1915, he appeared in 135 games for Buffalo and again batted .266.

While playing for the Bisons, he met a young woman from Buffalo, Elizabeth McCave, whom he affectionately called Babe. They were married in 1921 and settled in her hometown. In 1926, McCarthy made his major-league debut as a manager with the Chicago Cubs. He came to the Yankees in 1931 and stayed until 1946. He finished his career in 1950 after three seasons of managing the Red Sox.

Every year after the season ended, McCarthy escaped the pressure of baseball and returned to Western New York. Ralph Hubbell, a sportscaster in Buffalo, became McCarthy's closest friend. They had first met in 1939, when Hubbell, just starting as the regular play-by-play man for the Bisons, visited McCarthy in New York.

"I figured Mr. McCarthy was a Buffalonian, and I was a Buffalonian, so I called him at his hotel to see if I could come in and have a chat," says Hubbell, who's eighty now and recently retired after a broadcasting career of fifty-five years. "He told me to stop in around noon. I'm just a young announcer, and I walked in that room shaking like a leaf. He shook hands with me and said, 'We Buffalonians should stick together.'"

Hubbell remained close to McCarthy from that day on. One day, while he was walking to McCarthy's apartment on Gates Circle, he saw a sign that had been put on a nearby tree by a prankster. It read, NO BALL PLAYING ALLOWED. The story made national news, and McCarthy was furious. Hubbell says, "That's the only time I ever saw Joe get really mad."

McCarthy cherished his off-seasons at home. "He liked the people in Buffalo; they left him alone and weren't hounding him all the time," Hubbell says. "When the local reporters went to see him, it was a friendly visit. Babe would get a beer out of the refrigerator, and Joe and the reporters would sit around and talk informally. His door was always open, and being around someone of his stature was a tremendous experience for all of us."

There was a bit of mystery surrounding his nickname, Marse Joe. Hubbell says McCarthy told him that he picked it up when he managed down south. In that part of the country, *marse* meant master, "and I guess that's what he really was," Hubbell says. Others have said the nickname was given to McCarthy by a Chicago sportswriter named Harry Bailey. Regardless, says Hubbell, when McCarthy was in Buffalo, "he was just Joe to everyone."

As a manager, McCarthy could be cold and tough, but there was another side to his personality away from the dugout. "He was completely human," Hubbell says. "Most people in this country knew him only as a baseball manager, but his friends in Buffalo got to know the real Joe McCarthy.

"He was a passionate man, totally committed to Buffalo and the pleasant life he had here. He commanded so much respect, it was remarkable."

Ted Williams, who played under McCarthy for three seasons in Boston, once told Cy Kritzer of the *Buffalo Evening News* that Marse Joe "is the greatest manager baseball ever knew."

Phil Rizzuto, the Yankees' sparkplug at shortstop in the forties and early fifties, described McCarthy as "the greatest manager I ever knew and a wonderful person."

Of all the players McCarthy managed, Lou Gehrig was his personal favorite. He kept a portrait of Gehrig in his home and once told Kritzer that "under championship pressure, Lou was the greatest."

Babe McCarthy was the ideal complement to her husband. "In a lot of ways, she was just the opposite of Joe—talkative, vivacious, and full of life," Hubbell says. "She used to make jokes and kid him all the time."

The McCarthys had no children, and in 1950 when he quit baseball, they moved from the city to the farm. There, in a wooded area near the gently rippling waters of Ellicott Creek, Babe and Joe McCarthy entertained friends, did some gardening, watched baseball on television, and shared the pleasure of each other's company. The estate was called Yankee Farm. "My world is here," McCarthy told Kritzer.

But the years on the farm were far from idyllic. Babe suffered a stroke and was bedridden for years. In 1971, at age eighty-four, she died. "Much of his life went out when she died," Hubbell says. "He was never the same."

McCarthy continued to live on the farm, with the assistance of Fred and Maria Richards, who lived there and cared for him and the grounds.

In April 1977 McCarthy celebrated his ninetieth birthday. He had been in and out of the hospital with a broken hip and other ailments. He grew weaker and more frail with each passing day. "He didn't seem to be in a lot of pain," Hubbell recalls, "but then Joe was the kind of guy who would never let you know if he was in pain."

That winter, McCarthy's condition worsened, and he was taken to Millard Fillmore Hospital in Buffalo, just a few buildings away from his former apartment on Gates Circle. Hubbell went to the hospital every day to visit his friend. On Friday evening, January 13, 1978, Hubbell walked in, and a nurse ran up to him. "Mr. Hubbell," she said, "we've been trying to get in touch with you all day because Mr. McCarthy seems to be slipping away."

Hubbell took the elevator to the fourth floor. He walked into McCarthy's room and saw his old friend lying on his right side, facing the window. Outside, a soft winter snow was falling. Hubbell looked out the window and smiled, seeing McCarthy's old home, outside of which the NO BALL PLAYING ALLOWED sign had once been placed.

Hubbell looked at his watch. It was about seven-thirty P.M. He walked around the bed and sat close to his dear friend. He held his hand and whispered, "Hi, Joe, it's me, Ralph, and I'm back again."

There was no response. McCarthy's eyes were closed. Then, unexpectedly, Hubbell felt a slight, gentle squeeze on his right hand. "Then he went on his way," Hubbell remembers, "and Babe had been waiting for him a long time. I said, 'So long, Joe.' I hope you understand what I mean when I say that it was a very pleasant good-bye."

FOR THE RECORD, Joe McCarthy led the Yankees to eight American League pennants and seven World Series championships. He is the all-time leader in victories among major-league managers with 2,126. His winning percentage of .614 also tops the all-time list.

Joe DiMaggio, reminiscing on this June evening, remembers that McCarthy "would always talk about his life in Buffalo." After the 1950 season, McCarthy's last as a manager, the two all-time greats pretty much lost contact with each other. "He didn't come up to New York much, and I didn't have much chance to come to Buffalo," DiMaggio says. "He used to write me once in a while, and we stayed in touch."

Having played under Marse Joe for eight seasons and against him for three, Joe D. keeps many memories of the man, but perhaps one above all: "Joe loved Buffalo."

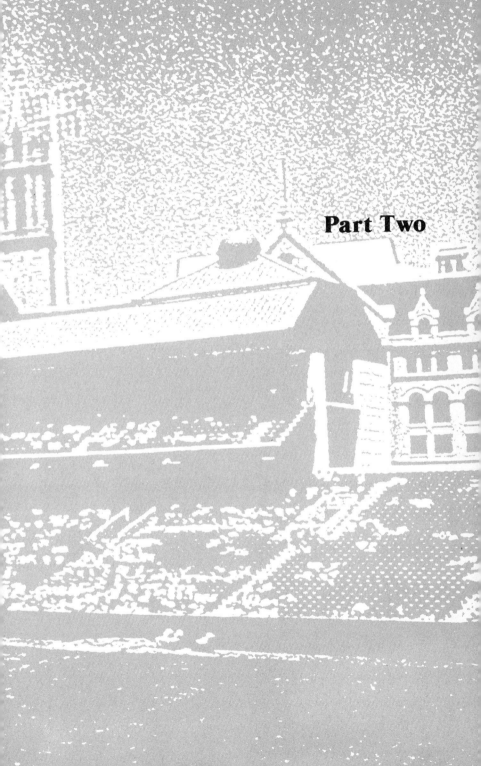

Part Two

5

STARTING OVER

Outside, snowflakes filled the air, and the wind howled; the temperature was about 20 degrees, but it seemed much colder. It was January 1983, and Mike Billoni found himself with Bob Rich in an office at weather-beaten War Memorial Stadium. This was the first strategy session between the Bisons' new owner and the first person he hired for the team's front office. There was no heating system, and the only protection from the cold was a couple of portable heaters near the frosty concrete walls. Billoni looked around the room and noticed paint peeling from the ceiling. As they talked, the two men could see their breath. There were spider webs on the walls, and Billoni was startled to see a rat scurrying across the floor; he began to wonder what he had gotten himself into. Rich, though, was optimistic. He looked at Billoni and said, "Mike, we've got three goals: Number one, I want to get from Double-A to Triple-A as soon as possible. Number two, the mayor's talking about building a new stadium downtown, and we're going to do everything we can to get that stadium. Number three, when we get that stadium, we're going to get to the big leagues."

Billoni, as a reporter, was used to being skeptical. Yet here he was, freezing at the Old Rockpile, watching spiders and rats, and Bob Rich was talking about the major leagues: "I'm thinking to myself, 'This guy is *serious*.' . . . Those were ambitious goals, to say the least."

After their meeting, Billoni and Rich walked down one of the dank passageways toward the field. It was covered with snow. The old end-zone scoreboard still showed Buffalo Bills versus Detroit Lions from 1972, O. J. Simpson's fourth season with the team; it was the last National Football League game ever played there. The Old Rockpile was in a state of suspended animation—a scene straight out of *The Twilight Zone,* Billoni thought, and he knew that he would need to try everything possible to drum up interest in the downtrodden Bisons. Billoni decided to follow the advice of the late Bill Veeck, the man who proved to be his patron saint.

Veeck, baseball's maverick hustler and promoter extraordinaire, was notorious for his gimmicks. As an owner, Veeck made few friends inside baseball's establishment, whose members he referred to as "stuffed shirts." But the fans loved him. When Veeck owned the St. Louis Browns, he once sent a midget, Eddie Gaedel, to the plate as a pinch hitter. In Cleveland, Veeck set a franchise record in 1948 by drawing 2,620,627 fans. In Chicago, with the White Sox, Veeck installed an exploding scoreboard. With Veeck, the game was not a religious experience, and anything that created interest or sold tickets was not only permissible, but preferred. In his *Hustler's Handbook,* Veeck wrote, "You don't have to be a hustler to be a promoter—which is fair enough, since you don't have to be a promoter to be a hustler, either. But it helps."

That would become Mike Billoni's creed.

IN THAT JANUARY of 1983 when Bob Rich saved baseball in Buffalo, Mike Billoni had almost taken a far different job out of town. After the *Courier-Express* folded in September of 1982, there was an opportunity for him to work in the family dry-cleaning business in nearby Kenmore, but he wasn't interested; he still wanted to be a newspaperman. There was nothing for him at the only remaining paper in town, the *Buffalo News,* but the prospects in Rochester seemed better. As as stringer, he had broken the story of Rich's purchase of the Bisons in the Rochester *Democrat & Chronicle,* and the next Monday, he was going to be interviewed for a job there. He was confident that he would be hired as a full-time reporter. "I was sure this was my last weekend in Buffalo," Billoni would recall. "I was calling people up to say good-bye; at the same time, I was asking other people if I should ask Bob Rich for a job. People sounded positive about my working in baseball. They told me, 'What do you have to lose?'"

Rich was in Florida visiting his father, though, and Billoni didn't have his number.

Billoni figured that he might as well go to Rochester, and he was shaving at eight o'clock on Monday morning when the phone rang. On the other end of the line was Bob Rich.

"Mike, how would you like to come down here and talk about a baseball job?"

"Bob, I can't; I've got to be in Rochester this morning for an interview with the paper."

"Mike, we have to talk. Be here at eight-thirty."

Billoni rushed down to Rich Products, and his conversation with the Bisons' new owner lasted all of five minutes. Rich offered him a job and said, "You've got one minute to think it over." Billoni laughed and said yes. Now, all he needed was a title. "We've got to come up with something unique," Rich said. So Billoni was dubbed "director of promotions, publicity, and marketing." Billoni remembers that "it sounded good, but I still don't think that title was ever explained to anybody."

Regardless, he canceled the Rochester interview.

Billoni knew that he had a mess on his hands. In 1982, the Double-A Eastern League team had had a paltry attendance of 77,000. It was a laughingstock in the news media, receiving little coverage and drowning in red ink. Billoni decided that it was time for a change—time to have fun. From then on, the Bisons wouldn't be selling baseball itself so much as the *ballpark experience*.

As jack-of-all-trades for the Bisons, Billoni was on a headlong mission to create community interest. He wanted fans, and he wanted publicity. He believed that the best way to reach those two goals was through hustle and promotion. It wasn't easy to create interest in a minor-league baseball team in a town with big-league football and big-league hockey, but Billoni saw it as a personal challenge. He was like a general in the Bisons' front office, with an army of public-relations workers and college interns at his beck and call. If celebrities came to town—from actress Pia Zadora to a touring Soviet baseball team—Billoni made sure that he knew about them and had them stop off for a picture at the ballpark.

Billoni deluged media outlets with news releases and personal phone calls. He called them night and day, supplying the latest news on the team and setting up media luncheons and dinners. He talked before every civic and church club he could find. Anywhere there was a TV camera or radio microphone, Billoni turned up boosting the Bisons. He would soon be known as P. T. Billoni, Buffalo's answer to Barnum.

During games, Billoni prowled the aisles of War Memorial Stadium, sporting a walkie-talkie, barking out orders, listening to reports, and chatting with fans. His walkie-talkie identification was "Bison One." Billoni carried a clipboard with yellow paper, constantly jotting down ideas and suggestions. At six feet three inches, and more than two hundred pounds, he was an imposing presence; Billoni was everywhere, seemingly carrying on a dozen conversations at once. A workaholic, he became totally absorbed in his role in the Bisons' dual interests: baseball and the bottom line.

Keeping the fun atmosphere in mind, Bob Rich next hired a beer vendor: Earl Howze, who came to be known as "The Earl of Bud." Howze had worked at the stadium, and Rich had seen him in action at the ballpark. There was a flair about him that appealed to the Bisons' new boss.

Rich himself called Howze soon after he bought the team.

"This is Bob Rich; is Earl Howze there?"

"Say what?"

"This is Bob Rich, and I want to speak with Earl."

"Who wants to speak with Earl?"

"Bob Rich wants to speak with Earl," Rich repeated, his voice growing louder.

Then there was a pause.

"Get out of here—this ain't Bob Rich."

"Earl, this is Bob Rich, and I'm buying this team, and I'll keep it if you will consider staying involved with the Bisons."

Another pause.

"You're putting me on."

"No, Earl, I'm serious."

"If this is really Bob Rich, you got a deal."

Howze became famous at the ballpark for performing his Pee-Wee Herman type of dance on top of the dugout to the old rock song "Tequila." The Earl of Bud became the most popular vendor in Buffalo baseball history, and his picture was even printed on tickets. Howze, whose full-time job was in a Buffalo Fire Department rescue unit, became a permanent part of the Bisons' family. "I love being at the park with the people," Howze would say. "I get a kick out of entertaining the fans and making the game a little more special."

Billoni encouraged that kind of spirit. Fun was the name of the game. Not only was there the Earl of Bud, but other zany characters, including madcap vendors such as Conehead, Zorro, and the Lone Ranger, who dressed as if every night were Halloween. Donald "The Butcher" Palmer, a 350-pound bat boy, reached folk-hero status for his antics behind home plate and along the baselines. One of The Butcher's favorite maneuvers was belly-flopping across the infield tarp on rainy days. He also would fling tiny frisbees to the fans and catch foul balls backhanded after they rolled down the backstop net—all to loud cheers. But when a ball would get stuck in the netting, leaving The Butcher with no play, the disappointed fans would boo.

The fans delighted in the interaction, among them Frank "Fremo" Vallone, a huge baseball nut who sat by the third-base dugout with his bullhorn. Fremo owned a bar called Merlin's, which became a favorite watering hole for the Bisons, their opponents, and umpires. Eventually, Fremo joined the Bisons' organization as the team's official host.

Then there was "Meathead," an elderly fan named John Davis who sat behind the plate at the Old Rockpile and earned his nickname by yelling "Way to go, meathead!" every time there was an error.

The interaction of fans and the Bisons' supporting cast made it seem like a day at the circus. "We saw these people around the park, and we knew we had to try something different," Billoni said. "We felt we had to make the park a positive place where fans would have a good time. When we came in, the Earl of Bud was the only thing going. We needed more."

There also was a new team mascot, Buster Bison, who got himself thrown out of a game and suspended for arguing with an umpire. Billoni turned that incident into a publicity bonanza and even had Bob Rich issue a statement that the suspension was "cruel and unusual punishment for Buster."

Managers and players even added to the carnival atmosphere. Profane, hard-living Al Gallagher was manager of the 1983 Bisons, a Cleveland Indians farm club, and Billoni promoted him as "Dirty Al," a carryover from his diving-in-the-dirt days as a player. Gallagher arrived in Buffalo in late February and demanded to see the stadium with the lights on. The only problem was that the light switch was frozen. Billoni persuaded a maintenance employee to climb the pole and turn the switch. Dirty Al was pleased, but then the maintenance man couldn't turn the lights off. "That was our introduction to Dirty Al," Billoni said, "and I'll never forget it." After the first home game of the 1983 season, Gallagher lectured his players to be gentlemen, because they were representing not only the ball team, but Buffalo as well. Later that night, Dirty Al was reported seen dancing on top of a local bar with his shirt off. Said one player, "I guess Al didn't listen to his own lecture."

For that 1983 home opener, Billoni arranged a pregame gimmick of celebrities' playing catch on the infield, featuring such diverse personalities as punk-funk rock star Rick James and the mayor himself, Jimmy Griffin.

Billoni believed that fans in Buffalo would not attend Bisons games just to see who won or lost, so he gave them countless other reasons. He was after the non–baseball fan, so every game became an event. He presented fireworks, picnics, rock concerts, Friday night bashes, Picnic Day, Bat Day, Back to School Day, Polish Night, Italian Night, African-American Night, Irish Night, German Night, and Fan Appreciation Night. He brought ice skaters who performed on a special plastic surface atop the dugout. There were Easter-egg hunts for kids and Dash for Cash races for adults. There were freebies at the gate, such as caps, pennants, and team pictures. Billoni also began publishing a monthly, tabloid-size newspaper called *Bisongram*. Once, when a forecast of rain threatened a big concert promotion involving the Beach Boys, Billoni called the Perpetual Rosary convent in Buffalo and asked that the Dominican nuns there pray for clear weather. That night, despite threatening skies, there was no rain, and the Bisons sent a donation to the convent. That kind of move was typical Billoni, making sure that all the angles were covered.

The wildly eccentric Joe Charboneau was one of the memorably zany Bisons, as was Steve "Psycho" Lyons, who later with the White Sox would drop his pants at first base, to the disbelief of the Chicago fans. But in Buffalo, the flakiest of all was Charboneau, one-time American League Rookie of the Year with the Cleveland Indians. Charboneau's repertoire included chewing on glass. He was fired by the Bisons after making obscene gestures during a televised game at War Memorial Stadium, but except for that, even Joe Charboneau seemed to fit into the Billoni entertainment package.

Before long, people were talking about having fun at War Memorial Stadium instead of worrying about being safe in the surrounding neighborhood, where security was now ample. The atmosphere had an unmistakable flavor: family.

During that first season of 1983, attendance jumped from 77,000 to just over 200,000, although the organization was criticized for announcing tickets sold rather than turnstile count for its attendance. The Bisons answered by saying it was Eastern League (and later American Association) policy to announce tickets sold as total attendance, just as in the American League.

Regardless of any criticism from the news media or ruffled feathers among traditionalists, it was apparent that Billoni had energized a franchise that had been moribund. "Look at it this way," Billoni said,

the year before we came, they drew 77,000. Obviously, people didn't care about anything. We had to bring them back to the park, and we knew the way to do that was to have fun. The game is not bigger than life. We just wanted people to come out and have a good time for three or four hours. The whole thing just started to steamroll. We knew we had to come in wearing the top hat and bells. We had to shake people up and make them see that things were different. Some of it was crazy; some of it wasn't. At the Single- and Double-A levels of minor-league baseball, your main job is to get people in the stands and to make your bottom line as a business. At the same time, we wanted to educate people into being baseball fans. Remember, baseball had been away from Buffalo for most of the 1970s.

EARLY ON, BOB RICH, JR., realized that if his baseball venture was to succeed, he would have to make a point of getting out into the community and making himself available for newspaper, radio, and television interviews. At the ballpark, he mingled with the fans and talked baseball with everyone. "You have two commodities to spend in your life: money and time; I guess your time becomes more valuable as you get older," he reflected. "When I bought the baseball team, it wasn't a major investment in money, but I never thought about the investment of my own time this project would bring. I figured, well, we'll staff it up, and if it works, we'll run the team, and that's it. I never realized just how much time and personal involvement I would be compelled to give to baseball."

Beginning in that first season, Rich would attend games with William Gisel, Jr., a lawyer who served as vice president of the Rich Products International Division and as vice president–secretary and legal counsel for the Bisons. "Bob knows the frozen-food business as well as anybody in the world; he's been with Rich Products for over a quarter of a century," Gisel says. "But in the food business, his profile is not as important as it is in baseball. He knew, especially in the early days with the Bisons, he had to have a high profile and be a visible leader."

At the Old Rockpile, Rich made Gisel stay no matter what the outcome of the game or the weather. "I remember this one game in War Memorial in April 1983," Gisel says.

It was raining, and we were sitting there in bone-chilling cold. We're sitting on the concrete, and I'm freezing. The game is going into the eleventh inning, and there's probably a dozen people left in the stands. It's eleven-thirty at night, and I keep asking Bob to go, but he won't leave. I wanted to go, but I can't leave this guy in War Memorial Stadium sitting by himself. He just wouldn't budge. The twelfth inning starts, and Bob finally realizes there are only a handful of people in the park. He turns and looks at me and says, "Why don't we just invite everybody to my house after the game is over?" Reality finally set in. For the first time, he saw there were about twenty people in a 40,000-seat stadium.

Bob Rich, though, was not easily discouraged. Five years earlier, not long after taking command of the nation's largest family-owned frozen-foods business, he had charted his course in a speech that would mark his emergence as a community leader and a fighter for Buffalo. The company had received lucrative offers to relocate in the Sun Belt, and in the speech, Rich decided to answer those who questioned his commitment to Buffalo. Its message, delivered at the groundbreaking for a new Rich Products headquarters building in October 1978, left no one in doubt:

> Let the meek search for their sunny shores, but don't use our city as an excuse. We choose to roll up our sleeves and work harder in Buffalo—for Buffalo. Companies who have left and those who may still leave, we wish them well but caution them that a little bit of them will die when they leave their home. . . .
> A city is as strong as its people. Buffalo is strong in the quality of people who live here—hardworking, industrious people with spirit that cannot be chilled by the winds of Lake Erie. Spirit like this will never die, and neither will Buffalo.

Still, it was clear to Rich that he, Billoni, and their hardy band of true believers couldn't turn around Buffalo baseball by themselves.

What they needed was a massive dose of credibility. What they didn't know was that it would soon come from the unlikeliest of places: Hollywood.

6

ROBERT REDFORD COMES TO TOWN

He never outgrew his childhood affection for baseball. The game was his constant companion on those long lonely days in the 1940s when his father was away from home working two jobs, as a milkman and a part-time accountant. Young Charles Robert Redford, Jr., found a way to fill that vacuum: He formed an emotional allegiance to a baseball star of mythical proportions—Ted Williams. The boy lived in Santa Monica, California, about 3,000 miles from Boston, where Williams played for the Red Sox. The boy's devotion to Williams, who had grown up in San Diego, transcended space and time; it was downright hero worship. The boy dreamed of the day when he could step on a major-league field, hit home runs and wear number 9, just like Williams. The boy, who was left-handed, played first base on his high school team. The second baseman was a big, burly kid named Don Drysdale. Both of them fantasized about playing in the big leagues. Drysdale eventually made it—as Williams did—to the Hall of Fame. As for the first baseman, he earned a baseball scholarship to the University of Colorado but turned his attention to acting and went on to make it big in Hollywood as Robert Redford. Nevertheless, he remained passionate about baseball.

Baseball had also touched the life of a youngster growing up in Baltimore during the late 1940s and early 1950s. His parents, Irv and Vi Levinson, were the children of immigrants from Eastern Europe. He lived with them in his grandparents' house on Appleton Street in southwest Baltimore. In 1954 Barry Levinson was eleven when the St. Louis Browns became the Baltimore Orioles. The team was terrible. Although it finished that first season in Baltimore with a 54–100 record, the boy's loyalty to the new hometown team was undiminished. He spent many summer days and nights at Memorial Stadium and, when not at the ballpark, listened to the games on radio. In 1955, a young, skinny third baseman named Brooks Robinson made his first appearance with the Orioles, and Levinson had a new hero. He remained a fan throughout his years at Forest Park High School and later when he worked in television and films. During the 1980s, Barry Levinson became one of the hottest directors in the movie industry, yet his bond to Baltimore and baseball remained strong.

In January 1983, Levinson and Redford came together for a business meeting to discuss a possible film collaboration, but the conversation kept drifting to baseball. Levinson was fresh from the success of his directing debut in the 1982 movie *Diner*. Redford had been relatively inactive; his last acting role was in the film *Brubaker* in 1980. That year, he also made his debut as a director with the film *Ordinary People,* which won the Academy Award as best picture and earned an Oscar for Redford as best director. Levinson and Redford both wanted to talk about new movie projects, but the previous baseball season was on their minds. Levinson bemoaned the Orioles' fate in 1982, when the team, led by a young power hitter named Eddie Murray, finished second, one game behind Milwaukee in the American League East. Redford talked about aging Boston star Carl Yastrzemski, the man who twenty-one years earlier had been Williams's successor in left field, and how the Red Sox finished third, just six games behind Milwaukee. "We were just talking baseball," Levinson recalls, "what happened last year and our hopes for the coming season."

Redford then asked Levinson whether he had read *The Natural.* "I read it a long time ago," Levinson replied.

"No, Barry, not the book. Have you seen the script for *The Natural?*" Redford asked. He had wanted to make the movie since the mid-1970s but couldn't obtain the rights. Now, in 1983, the rights were available, and Redford wanted to make Bernard Malamud's novel into a movie, with Levinson as director. To Redford, this movie would be more than just a baseball tale; it would be a mythological view of the game and America—a story of unfulfilled promise, and of failure and redemption. The plot was loosely based on the June 1949 shooting of Eddie Waitkus, a hard-hitting first baseman who had been traded from the Chicago Cubs to the Philadelphia Phillies that season.

Waitkus was in a Chicago hotel when he received a note asking him to visit a woman in a nearby room. The bachelor ball player, who was in an upbeat mood after leading the Phillies to a 9–2 victory over his old team, the Cubs, did not recognize the woman's name but still decided to accept the invitation. As he opened the door, she stood there staring at him.

"What's it all about, honey?" Waitkus asked.

The woman answered, "I have a surprise for you." She then went to a closet, pulled out a .22-caliber rifle, raised it, and fired. The bullet penetrated Waitkus's right lung.

It turned out that Ruth Ann Steinhagen, who had a history of mental problems, had secretly worshiped Waitkus for years. After she shot him, she told police, "If I couldn't have him, I decided nobody could."

Waitkus survived, but he was never the same as a ball player. He eventually became a part-time player with Baltimore near the end of his career. That was in 1954, the same year Barry Levinson began following the Orioles.

Levinson was intrigued with the folklore, stories, and legends of baseball, and fascinated by the prospect of turning *The Natural* into a movie, especially with Redford in the lead role of Roy Hobbs. "Part of the beauty of watching a baseball game is that you are watching the present but at the same time seeing something that happened before," Levinson says. "There's a great mythology and history connected to baseball, like Eddie Waitkus getting shot and Ted Williams hitting home runs. I was interested in the flamboyance and grandeur of a movie that could treat that mythology and history."

Redford, at forty-five, was faced with a daunting challenge as a performer: playing Roy Hobbs from age twenty-one—when Hobbs, like Waitkus, was shot in a woman's hotel room—until he was a 35-year-old outfielder becoming a big-leaguer for the first time with the New York Knights. "This was a difficult role," says Levinson, "but Bob has an effortless way of making the hardest roles look easy." Redford did make one demand of the director—that his uniform be number 9: Ted Williams's number.

Levinson was forty-one and excited about the prospect of tackling his first big-budget movie with a star of Redford's stature. "I took the script home, I read it, and I thought it was great," Levinson says. Redford was delighted. He wanted to shoot the film in Boston's Fenway Park and hoped to have Ted Williams appear in a cameo role.

But Levinson had other, more practical concerns. The director knew that baseball movies were considered death at the box office. The most recent baseball film, *The Bingo Long Traveling All-Star and Motor Kings,* had been made in 1976, and the only other recent baseball movie before that was 1973's *Bang the Drum Slowly.* Neither of the films was boffo at the box office. "We had to convince the studio we could make money on a baseball movie," Levinson says.

Without Redford, that was probably impossible, but with him Levinson knew he could find a producer. Tri-Star Pictures, then a new subsidiary formed by Columbia Pictures, HBO, and CBS, agreed to back the film. That obstacle was out of the way, but there was another problem: The film would have to be shot during the summer months, right in the middle of the 1983 baseball season. This meant that Fenway Park and every other major-league stadium would not be available. Still, Levinson pressed on and assembled an all-star cast, including Glenn Close, Robert Duvall, Kim Basinger, Wilford Brimley, Barbara Hershey, Richard Farnsworth, Darren McGavin, Robert Prosky, Joe Don Baker, and NBC's Bob Costas, to supply an authentic voice of a radio sportscaster. Everything else was falling into place, but the stadium search was fruitless.

The Natural was a period piece, primarily covering the years 1924 to 1939, and the stadium had to look like a park from that era. As the quest for a ballpark dragged on, Levinson became discouraged. "We couldn't use any of the existing big-league parks, and the minor-league parks weren't big enough," he recalls. "We didn't know what to do." It was early May, and shooting was to start in a few months. *The Natural* faced the problem of having a big-name cast with no place to perform. Mel Bourne, a production designer for the film, was also feeling the pressure. He had scoured the country in vain, trying to find just the right old stadium.

Bourne, who had worked on several Woody Allen movies, was bald with a fluffy white beard and spoke in loud tones with an unmistakable New York City accent. Knowing that the film's success depended on finding the right ballpark, a frustrated Bourne found himself in Louisville, Kentucky, checking out Cardinal Stadium. "The stadium was big enough," he said, "but it had that stupid AstroTurf."

While he was there, he took pictures of the locker room for future use. He was getting ready to leave when Frank Evans, who had worked in the Louisville clubhouse for as long as anyone could remember, walked up to the downcast Bourne, tapped him on the shoulder and asked, "What's the matter?" Bourne told him of his unsuccessful search for a stadium and of his disappointment that Louisville did not fill the bill.

Evans had an idea for Bourne.

"There used to be a big old stadium in Buffalo. Have you looked at it?"

"There's no baseball stadium in Buffalo."

"Yes, there is. We played there in 1961."

It was worth a try.

Bourne found a telephone number for the Buffalo Bisons. It was noon Friday, and Marta Hiczewski was at work in the Bisons' office. She had joined the team only a few weeks earlier, working as a secretary from a temporary-help agency.

The phone rang.

The call was from Louisville.

"My name is Mel Bourne. I'm a production designer with Tri-Star Pictures, and we're doing a movie. We want to come to Buffalo to look at your stadium, because we need a location to film at."

Hiczewski laughed. It was her lunch hour, she was new on the job, and she thought that this was a gag. Ever since Bob Rich had bought the team, all kinds of people had been calling with crazy schemes and suggestions. But Bourne sounded serious. He asked how many people could be seated in the park.

"Forty-five thousand."

"Do they have wooden seats?"

"Yes."

"Does the stadium look real old?"

"It sure does."

Bourne was elated. He told Hiczewski that he was going to catch a plane to Buffalo as soon as possible. She asked him to wait until after lunch, so she could talk first with her new boss, Mike Billoni.

Billoni returned from lunch, spoke to Bourne, and then quickly phoned Bob Rich.

"Bob, you're not going to believe this, but there's a guy named Mel Bourne on the line, and he says he wants to come to War Memorial Stadium to make a movie."

Rich laughed out loud. "Sure, Mike, and tell Mel Bourne when his brother Sid Knee calls, we'll all go to Australia for vacation. He's probably some guy with an X-rated movie company. Ask him who the actors are; they're probably a bunch of no-names."

Billoni got back on the line with Bourne.

"Who's in the movie?"

"Well, the star is Robert Redford."

Billoni practically fell out of his chair.

"Bob, they've got an actor to star in the film."

"Who is it, Mike?"

"Ro . . . Rober . . . Robert Redford," Billoni stammered, barely able to get the words out of his mouth.

Rich was so shocked that he dropped the phone. He picked it up and told Billoni, "Get them here as soon as possible."

Bourne said he would be there Monday.

Billoni, with his flair for promotion, decided to go all-out to impress Bourne. He arranged for a stretch limousine with a police escort to pick up the movie man at the airport. Billoni and Bourne jumped in the limo and headed for War Memorial Stadium. "I need an old stadium with a run-down look," Bourne said. Billoni, trying to hold back laughter, said, "That sounds a little bit like War Memorial."

The stadium was forty-six years old, and evidence of decay was everywhere—rusted steel, peeling paint, and eroding concrete. It had been spruced up a bit when Double-A baseball returned in 1979, but it was little more than a patchwork job. This didn't seem to bother Mel Bourne. As the limo pulled down Best Street toward the stadium entrance, Bourne startled Billoni by yelling at the driver, "Stop this car!" Bourne unexpectedly jumped out and stood in the middle of the street, briefcase in hand, gazing at the old stadium. He got back in the car, and the limo went around the block to Dodge Street, on the opposite side of the stadium. Once again, Bourne got out of the car, stood in the middle of the street and stared at the stadium as though transfixed.

Finally, the limo pulled into the tunnel entrance near the infield of the Stonehenge-like stadium. On the field, a couple of city workers were sweeping. Bob Rich and his legal counsel, Bill Gisel, were standing on the side of the field, waiting for Bourne. They decided to play it cool and not appear too enthusiastic. Dale Senn, boss of the grounds crew, was walking near the infield and had no idea what was going on. Bourne got out of the car and starting walking around the infield. "This is it!" Bourne shouted. "This is perfect! This is what I've been looking for!"

Bob Rich had never heard such words spoken about the Old Rockpile; he found himself "wondering what this guy is seeing that nobody else ever saw."

Bourne started barking orders to no one in particular as Billoni, Rich, Gisel, and the stadium workers watched in puzzled amusement. "This has to go," Bourne said, pointing down the right-field line to a concession stand that had just been built there. Then he gestured toward the stands, saying, "These seats have to be painted," unaware that city workers had just finished doing so. Next, Bourne gazed at the outfield. "Those signs have to come down," he said as Rich and Gisel bit their lips over the possible loss of substantial advertising revenue.

Dale Senn could not believe what was happening. "Who is this guy? Who's he talking to? And what's he doing here?" Senn wondered.

Billoni, meanwhile, was trying to humor Bourne. "Sure, Mel, the signs will come down. Right, Mel, the seats will be painted. Move the concession stand? You got it, Mel."

Eventually all those things would be done, because the Old Rockpile was soon to become Hollywood East.

When Bourne was finished, he went into a stadium office to set up a conference call with Barry Levinson, Mark Johnson, the producer of *The Natural,* and Robert Redford. "This guy is calling Robert Redford?" Senn asked in stunned disbelief. "Don't worry, Dale," Rich replied. "Everything will be all right."

On the phone Bourne said, "You guys are going to love this place; it's perfect for the movie." He then told the Bisons' people that Levinson and Johnson would be in Buffalo in a couple of days to see the Old Rockpile for themselves.

Johnson, who had worked with Levinson since the 1970s, came to Buffalo and immediately sensed that the hunt for a stadium was over. "We spent *so* much time looking for stadiums," he said, noting that the film company had checked about seventy facilities across the country.

> When we got to Buffalo, the first time I walked in that place, I said, "What a great stadium! This is perfect." It was a combination of things. I loved the size of the stadium; it was clearly big enough to be a major-league park. I loved the place; it had an old-fashioned feel that was just right for the film. There was the gigantic covering over the grandstand, and the whole place was so enormous. My only concern was how we could get enough people to fill the stands for the game scenes.

In addition to the park, Johnson was impressed with Buffalo. "I had heard it was a slightly impoverished city with high unemployment, a real sort of colorless, working-class town," he says now. "That wasn't true. We loved the architecture, and we shot a number of scenes in Buffalo, outside the stadium. There were wonderful old houses, and they looked beautiful sitting next to the water. I liked Buffalo right off the bat."

So did Levinson, who quickly approved of the site. "It obviously played a major role in *The Natural,*" the director says. "It was the only park we could find that was big enough to resemble a major-league stadium from the 1930s. There was nothing like it anywhere else."

Levinson had a comfortable feeling about Buffalo. "Like Baltimore, I sensed Buffalo was a working-class town," he says. "Both cities had a lot of character, and both cities had gone through a major transition. To me, Buffalo looked like it had more wealthy areas than Baltimore. Buffalo had homes and architecture that were really phenomenal."

Johnson and Levinson were pleased with the stadium, but Redford had to approve the decision also. Rich and Billoni were eager to have the movie shot in War Memorial. Not only would it generate mountains of publicity, but it would add to baseball's credibility in Buffalo and burnish the image of the Old Rockpile. After all, if War Memorial Stadium was good enough for Robert Redford, it was good enough for anybody, right?

The actor was expected in town the following week, but on a Sunday afternoon, Billoni received a call from Mark Johnson. "Keep this a secret, Mike," he said, "but Redford will be at the park in an hour. He wants to take some batting practice."

Billoni rushed to the stadium. A tarp was covering the field when Redford arrived, dressed in sweat shirt, blue jeans and sneakers. He slowly walked around the diamond, looked at the stands and smiled. "I like it," he told Billoni. "Can I take some batting practice?"

Before answering, Billoni had to pinch himself.

"Sure," he said as he nervously ran off the field and into the clubhouse to dig up some bats and balls. By this time, the grounds crew had come by and surrounded Redford. Billoni came back on the field, lugging baseball equipment. One of the members of the grounds crew volunteered to pitch, and Billoni ran out to right field to shag balls. The rest of the people in the park were startled by the sight of Redford's hitting style. Soon, he began smacking line drives at Billoni, who was huffing and puffing trying to catch up with the fusillade of baseballs. "I'm the only one out there, and I'm dying," Billoni recalls. "He's hitting them out there left and right, but then he got tired, dropped his bat, and left." Billoni, out of breath and sweating profusely, raced back toward the infield.

With Billoni in close pursuit, Redford made his way down the long, dark tunnel that led to the ballpark and said, "This is a great stadium."

War Memorial Stadium wasn't the only Buffalo edifice to play a role in *The Natural*. Ellicott Square, an ornate office building that at the turn of the century was called the world's largest, filled the bill for a hotel lobby. Parkside Candy Company, a landmark sweet shop, retained a frozen-in-time atmosphere that proved ideal for Roy and his sweetheart Iris to become reacquainted over lemonade. The venerable Buffalo Psychiatric Center was the setting for the hospital scenes, and the shots at the Hobbs farm and the carnival train stop were well-suited to the rural communities of Stafford and South Dayton. The need for a Wrigley Field look-alike in one of the "Chicago" scenes was satisfied by fifty-five-year-old All-High Stadium, behind North Buffalo's Bennett High School, where Robert Rich, Sr., had long ago gained glory not only as a football player but as a coach.

And in a trademark Billoni brainstorm, the old *Courier-Express* building, an Art Deco classic where Joe Alli and he had worked before the paper died eleven months before, was transformed into the home of the *New York Daily Mirror* and its sports columnist, Max Mercy.

Filming in the stadium began in July, and it lasted until September. The Old Rockpile was treated to a face lift so it could meet Hollywood standards, and the community as a whole was given an economic boost estimated at five million dollars. Buffalonians were captivated at being in the center of Robert Redford's baseball film, and thousands of them turned out as extras and sat in the stands. "We had no trouble getting extras; the people in Buffalo were great," Mark Johnson said. "Obviously, they wanted to see Robert Redford." The reclusive actor was uncomfortable with the crowds and the constant attention; the Bisons' chief of security, Joe Petronella, served as his bodyguard. During preparation for scenes, he would retreat to study in his trailer parked near the stadium. While most of the cast and crew stayed downtown, Redford kept to himself at a house on the lakeshore, about an hour away. At times, he appeared aloof and uncommunicative; he was serious about his work and would not tolerate distractions from fans or anyone else.

For Levinson, directing *The Natural* proved to be trying. "The most difficult thing was doing a baseball movie in period. This was a

movie in a specific time, and every extra had to be in the right
costume and right place for every shot. No one had anticipated how
difficult the movie would be. To me, it was exhausting. But my
experience in Buffalo, away from the set, was pleasant."

It didn't take long for Levinson to discover that the stereotyped
image of Buffalo was vastly overdrawn. "I never knew much about
Buffalo, except for watching the Colts play the Bills in the cold
weather on the frozen tundra." Levinson laughs. "But I'll tell you,
that summer we spent in Buffalo was beautiful. Buffalo is the type
of city you could hang around in, in an easy way. Buffalo is laid-
back, comfortable, and not pretentious. That's what stood out to
me: It was an easy city to be in."

He, Redford, and the others connected with *The Natural* also
enjoyed the city's restaurants, with their remarkable ethnic diver-
sity. A special favorite for gourmet dinners was a Buffalo standby,
Oliver's, which had gone out of business a year earlier but was res-
urrected in March of 1983 by a young restaurateur named Henry
Gorino. Redford and Levinson went there frequently, and Kim
Basinger absolutely fell in love with the place, eating there about
five nights a week.

"Buffalo is a great food town," Levinson says. "Whatever nationality you are, you'll find something good to eat. I went to the
Anchor Bar and ate chicken wings; I never had chicken wings that
tasted that good. There were great Italian restaurants in Buffalo.
We were always eating."

The filming of *The Natural* also was memorable for the local
baseball players, umpires, and other residents who were given
minor roles in the film. One was Kevin Lester, who played the part
of catcher for Redford's team, the New York Knights. He custom-
made some thirty-four-inch bats for Redford and improved the
pocket in the star's glove. The two men developed a strong rapport.
"He was a kind of a shy, quiet guy who didn't like to be bothered,
but once you got to know him, he opened up," Lester says. "I had a
couple of personal talks with him. He was a good hitter, a line-drive
hitter. He often said you had to have a lot of little boy in you to
play this game. He was one of those guys who you could tell just
loved baseball. A lot of people tried to cozy up to him, and you got
the sense he didn't know who to trust."

Duke McGuire, a former number-one draft pick of the Detroit Tigers, also played for the Knights in the movie and grew to like Redford. "I kind of felt sorry for him, in a way," says McGuire, now public-address announcer for the Bisons. "He couldn't walk twenty feet without getting mobbed. But when we were on the field or in the dugout, he was a regular guy. He liked to hang out and talk with the rest of the guys. And he was a good athlete; he could hit and throw. For me, it was great just to be in the movie with him. It's something I'll remember the rest of my life."

Paul Sullivan, Jr., then thirteen, played Roy Hobbs as a youngster. "It didn't mean a lot to me back then, but now it means a lot more," says Sullivan, today a student at Canisius College. "Redford was great to me; we'd play catch and I'd go to his trailer on the set and talk about the scenes." Sullivan had auditioned with hundreds of other young, blond, blue-eyed, Buffalo youngsters, and the significance of the role didn't hit home until he saw the movie. "I'll never forget looking at the screen and realizing it was me up there. I still can't get over it."

George Wilkosz, who played Bobby Savoy, the bat boy for the Knights who let Hobbs use his bat for the game-winning swing, was discovered by a member of Levinson's staff amid the bazaarlike bustle of the Broadway Market, where his family still runs a food stand. He has now entered his twenties and still feels a strong bond to the film. "I have the video at home and I play it all the time. I've changed a lot over the years, but people still come up to me and talk about the movie."

Other local baseball personalities were given roles as players and umpires. Knights players included Joe Charboneau, who had recently left the Bisons, Phil Mankowski, Larry Couzens, Rick Oliveri, Steve Poliachik, and Ken Kamholz. Phil Rosenberg played the Pittsburgh Pirates' starting pitcher in the climactic game, and Chris Rehbaum portrayed the reliever who served up the magical home run to Hobbs. Tom Kennedy was a Phillies pitcher, Bill Truman a Pirates catcher and Ron Nero a Cubs pitcher. Sibby Sisti, former infielder with the Boston Braves, was cast as the Pirates' manager. Among the local umps were Joe Strnad, who was behind the plate for the finale, Nicholas Koleff, James Quamo, and a jolly giant named Jerry Stockman, who years later would boast that he was still getting royalty checks for his one line of dialogue ("That *is* the ball, Augie."), even though moviegoers never got to see his face. Perhaps the most poignant presence on the set was umpire Pete Calieri, without whom Buffalo's baseball prestige might never have been restored.

Music for the party scenes was provided by the Buffalo Swing Band, and individual Buffalonians popped up in *The Natural* from all walks of life. The fellow operating the soda fountain, for instance, was an advertising executive, Jim Mohr, and young Iris was played by Rachel Hall, a local schoolgirl. A diminutive fifty-four-year-old accountant and corporate executive, Peter Poth, had one of the more unusual casting calls. He had brought his son, Paul, for an audition as a bat boy but ended up landing a role himself—as Dr. Knobb, the "two-bit carny hypnotist" who droned that "losing is a disease."

There was a Robert Rich in the movie, too, but this was neither the chairman of Rich Products nor the owner of the Bisons. This was Robert E. Rich III, who was sixteen and appeared in the last scene in the ballpark as Ted, the son whom Roy Hobbs had never known. He and Redford played an idyllic father-and-son game of catch in a wheat field to close the film, which had begun with a shot of Paul Sullivan, Jr., as young Roy with his dad, in a similar setting.

No movie had ever conveyed more of Buffalo's flavor.

The people, as well as the city itself, made a favorable impression on Redford. On September first, with the shooting nearly done, the Bisons held a Robert Redford Appreciation Night at the old stadium. "Bob really didn't want the attention, but he agreed because everybody with the Bisons had been so nice to us," producer Mark Johnson says. "He doesn't like that kind of thing, but I think he did it for Buffalo."

A crowd of 12,084 showed up, and Billoni introduced Redford to a standing ovation. He wore jeans and a baseball jacket with the insignia of the New York Knights. "I stood out here last week in front of 5,000 people for quite a while trying to hit a home run, and I thought *that* was tough," Redford said, referring to the climactic scene that had required more than thirty takes. "It's a lot easier and more gratifying to stand here tonight in front of you people and say thank you."

There was another loud ovation.

"The fact is, since we've been here, the people of Buffalo have been very kind and very friendly, and I'm especially appreciative of the friendly atmosphere and warm hospitality we've received. I want to again say thank you . . . and let's play ball."

A few days later, just before he left Buffalo, Redford amplified those feelings in an interview with Scott Brown, a television reporter with WGRZ-TV, Buffalo's NBC affiliate. "I think Buffalo's gotten a bum rap; I really do," Redford said. "You hear all these exaggerated stories about a place, but they're not true. I think it had a lot to do with the snow; I don't mind snow. I imagine the people who were here for the blizzard of '77 feel differently about snow. I think that's where a lot of the exaggeration came from. . . . I would defend Buffalo; in fact, I already have. Some people said to me, 'You've been in *Buffalo;* are you all right?' I told them I enjoyed it. . . . This has been just wonderful."

Asked what he enjoyed about the city, Redford said,

> For me, personally, I like the sense of tradition that's still left in Buffalo. There's a feeling that you feel from the people about pride in their city—that means a lot to me. I was driving over the Skyway bridge the other day. It was a very clear day, and I looked out because the wind had blown all the storm clouds across the water, and I saw all these steeples that just dotted the horizon. It was just beautiful, and I thought Buffalo was really something. . . . The people here were great. I liked their friendliness and their openness. They really got behind us and were supportive and enthusiastic. That means a lot to me, and the people here who helped us are very much a part of this film.

As for the oft-mentioned subject of his being mobbed by the public and reacting with aloofness, Redford said,

> It's very hard, harder than many people realize. It's easy to see why you might develop a shyness, because as much as everybody wants the attention or likes being the

target of affection, finally you begin to feel you can't get any place by yourself to breathe. There was a really difficult situation here. We were working with thousands of extras . . . and because we were shooting in fragments, we had to shoot and jump from different parts of the script; you had to keep your mind on track with what your character was doing in terms of sequence.

It took a lot of concentration, and it was very hard to concentrate because a lot of people came up and wanted you to sign something, or pose for a picture, or say hello. You wanted to accommodate them, but if you did, it would start something you could never finish. Also, you would lose all your ability to concentrate, which is what you are required to do. So you had to sometimes walk through a crowd of people and try not to be distracted. . . . That could be interpreted as rudeness by some who don't understand . . . but that is one of the negative parts of being in that situation.

Brown asked Redford whether there was any comparison between himself and the character he played, Roy Hobbs. "No, I don't think it's now or never for me. I haven't done a film in some time, but I haven't been out of the picture for fifteen years like he was. There is a little bit of a connection, certain places in this film that feel close. . . . When I was a little kid, I wanted to be a baseball player."

The story of *The Natural* was not easy to present on the screen, Redford said:

I wouldn't classify it as a baseball movie. It's an allegorical piece by Bernard Malamud; you could hardly just simplify Bernard Malamud. It's so unique and so untypical that it's very hard to define and describe. I'm not at all comfortable describing what this film is about. I know it has something to do with reclaiming a lost dream. I know it has something to do with a second chance. I know the allegory of baseball and life has something to do with everyone wanting a chance at bat.

What about turning forty-six and playing a character at the ages of twenty-one and thirty-five?

The film is very stylistic; if we were just doing a dead-on accurate thing here, we'd be in a lot of trouble. It has more to do with attitude; that part of the film where he is a young man is almost dreamlike in a way. . . . But if you asked me point-blank: 'How does it feel playing a twenty-one-year-old?' I'd say (laughing) 'Sure.' My kids asked me about that; they're older than twenty-one, and they say, 'Well, Dad, how are you going to pull that off?' I say, 'Well, I don't know, I'll just go see.' . . . Roy Hobbs was a hard character to play, much harder than I think a lot of people realized.

His most lasting memories of Buffalo, Redford said, will include "the ease with which the people and the place made this experience. I'll also think of the contrast about what I heard about Buffalo and what I was supposed to feel about it, and what I actually felt. I really like this city."

The Natural was released in 1984, and gala premieres were held in New York City and Buffalo. It became a financial success, with gross receipts of almost $60 million in its first release. The film started a trend, leading to baseball movies such as *Bull Durham, Eight Men Out,* and *Field of Dreams.* Reviews of *The Natural* were mixed, though, with some critics complaining because Malamud's dark ending was changed. The objection was to the upbeat movie climax in which Roy Hobbs hits a game-winning home run onto the stadium roof, setting off a shower of fireworks.

"I felt good about the movie," Levinson said.

The thing you have to remember is that it wasn't just a baseball movie; some critics didn't like it because they saw it as a baseball movie. Redford was outstanding. He played a sort of mythical character, but he gave Roy Hobbs honesty and simplicity . . . kind of the child and the man and the disillusionment of the man, and that made for a great performance by Redford. I remember that one scene where Redford is in the hospital room with Glenn Close, and he tells her how much he loves baseball and why he has to keep playing. That was great.

For Buffalonians such as Kevin Lester, who for a few shining moments had been a member of Roy Hobbs's New York Knights, *The Natural* was to leave an abiding impression. Lester, thirty-four at the time and the father of three sons, was teaching physical education at an elementary school and keeping himself in the game as a catcher in the municipal league. After the filming ended, he returned to teaching and also worked as a youth clinic coordinator with the Bisons. He, like Redford, had been captivated as a child by dreams of playing in the major leagues. *The Natural* was as close to fulfilling those dreams as either man would ever come. To Kevin Lester, though, this was as if the dream had come true: "I can't tell you what this movie meant in my life. Next to my wife, Janet, and my children, this is the most unique thing that ever happened to me. For me, this was the big leagues."

For Bob Rich, however, this wasn't the big leagues, by any means. But it was a start.

7

TILTING AT WINDMILLS

Bob Rich's office, with a view of the churning Niagara River, is on the fourth floor of Rich Products Corporation headquarters on Buffalo's West Side. Behind his desk is a bronze statue of Don Quixote, in full knightly armor, lance in hand, ready to battle another windmill. "This guy is my patron saint," Rich says. "I studied all the Spanish philosophers in college, and they formed my personal philosophy of life. To me, striving for the goal is the goal itself."

Major-league baseball in Buffalo.

The impossible dream.

Cervantes had written that "every man is the architect of his own destiny," and Bob Rich, Jr., was taking those words to heart.

By the 1984 season, Rich's second as owner of the Bisons, he was already tiring of Double-A baseball. Jack Aker succeeded Dirty Al Gallagher as manager and led Buffalo to a 72–67 record and a fifth-place finish in the Eastern League. Attendance at War Memorial Stadium barely increased to 223,443. This time, there was no Robert Redford to provide excitement and, despite the increase in attendance of nearly 23,000, Rich could sense that interest was waning. "We felt Buffalo would support Double-A baseball for only so long," he says. "This is a major-league city, and we knew that compared to the Bills and Sabres, it was tough for fans to get excited about the Lynn Pirates or teams from smaller cities in the Eastern League. We had to do something."

He knew that it was time to go out and get a Triple-A franchise, and he wanted the best possible man at his side: his father.

Buffalo's Dan Carnevale, who has spent more than fifty years in baseball, including one season as manager of the Bisons, said later that "when you put Bob Rich together with his father, look out, because nothing is going to stop those two."

In September 1984 Bob Rich, Jr., and his father took the first step toward acquiring a Triple-A franchise for Buffalo, when they went to Pawtucket, Rhode Island, in a Rich Products jet.

Ben Mondor, owner of the Pawtucket franchise in the International League, was fascinated with the jet. Senior and Junior kept trying to make a pitch for the club, but Mondor wanted to talk airplanes. Finally, as the Riches were getting ready to leave and Mondor was finished inspecting the jet, he said, "I'm surprised you came to see me when the Wichita team is available. I think you could probably get that club for less money than some of the other teams."

Bob Rich had heard that Wichita had turned down an offer of $750,000 for the team, then considered high for a minor-league club. His father told Mondor, "No, no, we're here with you. You're our guy." But then he thought about Pawtucket's proximity to Boston, and he thought that the Red Sox would be upset if they were to lose their nearby farm club.

The Riches said good-bye to Mondor and told him that they would get back to him. On the trip back to Buffalo, the jet rose above the clouds. Suddenly, "I looked at my father, and he looked back at me at the same instant," Bob Rich recalls. "Sometimes, we both think so much alike it's frightening. He said, 'Do you want to make the call, or should I make it?'"

Bob Rich used the portable phone to call A. Ray Smith, who was running the Louisville Redbirds of the American Association, which also included Wichita. "I said, 'A. Ray, this is Bob Rich. We'd like to get a Triple-A team in the association; would you support us?' He said, 'Absolutely.'" The price, Rich soon learned, might be $1 million. Rich then called Wichita to set up an appointment.

Father and son flew straight to Wichita and met the owner, Milton Glickman. He had earned a fortune in the scrap-metal business and had been one of a group of community owners who took over the struggling franchise. Glickman, a gregarious, outgoing man, took the Riches out to dinner and kept telling them corny jokes throughout the evening. "God, the jokes were terrible," Robert Rich, Sr., remembers, "but he kept laughing, and so did we."

Finally, the Riches told Glickman that they wanted to buy the team. Bob Rich, Jr., said Glickman told them, "I've been here all these years. These are my neighbors. My wife and I are getting near retirement. This team is like a child to us. I just don't see myself ever getting out of this." Glickman then left to go to the men's room.

Robert Rich looked at his son and said, "What are we doing here? This is ridiculous."

But when Glickman came back, the negotiations turned serious. When the figure came close to a million dollars—$950,000 to be exact—Glickman agreed. At that time, it was a record price for a Triple-A team. Robert Rich acknowledges that "it was a lot of money, but we thought it was a good business deal, because we believed we could make it work."

Bob Rich had been chasing a Triple-A team for more than a year but wasn't able to bask in his moment of glory. When the news conference to announce the deal was being held in Buffalo, he was flying a few hundred miles to Williams College to be with his daughter. Kimberly Rich was in the first week of her freshman year and was having a hard time adjusting to college life at her father's alma mater.

"A lot of the orientation was geared to social life, the kids' getting to know each other at parties and things like that," Bob Rich recalls.

> My daughter is very bright, but she was shy at that time and had never been away from home before. She called me up that first week and was upset. "I'm out of here, I want to come home," she said.
>
> I told Kimberly I had some work to do there; we sell a lot of products in Massachusetts. I rented a hotel room for a week, and I said she could stay with me. I set up an office in the hotel, and I'd see her every day. Each day, I saw her less, and by the time Friday rolled around, she had

made many friends. She was just loving it. I missed the announcement in Buffalo on buying the Triple-A franchise, but so what? My family is my priority.

Kimberly MacKenzie Rich eventually graduated with honors and hopes to pursue a master's degree in child psychology. Now in her mid-twenties, she works for an executive and business travel agency in St. Louis.

Bob Rich also has three sons. Robert E. Rich III, now in his early twenties, graduated from St. Lawrence University. He works as youth coordinator for Western New York United Against Alcohol and Drug Abuse. "He's very cause-oriented and very interested in youth affairs and the environment," Bob Rich says. Theodore Watson Rich, also into his twenties now, is into the second half of his undergraduate studies at the University of Vermont. He works summers as a sales trainee for Rich Products. Barnaby "Barney" Webb Rich, just finishing his preteen years, is the youngest child. He grew up in baseball and has been serving as a bat boy for the visiting teams at Bisons games.

Barney, in particular, inherited his father's quick wit. "Hey, Barney," Rick Wrona, a catcher then with the Iowa Cubs teasingly yelled in front of everyone in the visitors' dugout in Buffalo as Barney was putting away some bats and balls. "I heard your father's worth 80 million bucks."

Without skipping a beat, Barney, who was ten at the time, shot back, "He's worth a lot more than that to me."

"It broke up the other players," Bob Rich recalls, "and that's the last time that guy tried to go one-up on Barney."

LITTLE BY LITTLE, the people of Buffalo began to believe in the baseball dream that Jimmy Griffin and Bob Rich, Jr., were doggedly pursuing. As if inspired by the high hopes, the community began to turn the corner. Better times were on the horizon and, if anything, overdue.

Despite all the hard times, the people of Buffalo never stopped believing in themselves—they never lost their spirit. "On a grassroots level, there was a tremendous sense of community activism," says author and educator Mark Goldman. "It's easy to say that Buffalo was defensive or Buffalo had low self-esteem and was declining. But on a smaller level, in the neighborhoods where people lived, there was a tremendous effort to fight back."

Buffalo might have procrastinated in coming to grips with some of its problems, but it made up for lost time. Goldman points to the successful and peaceful integration of Buffalo public schools that began in the mid-1970s. There also was wise use of tens of millions of dollars in federal urban-development grants to revitalize neighborhoods. Thousands of needy residents benefited from subsidized housing, and there was an infusion of more than $90 million in business loans for start-ups and expansions. There was much to praise in what Goldman describes at the "tremendous cooperative efforts between the public and private sectors" to invest in the community and, in many respects, to rebuild it. Organizations such as the Erie County Industrial Development Agency and the Western New York Economic Development Corporation played critical roles in rebuilding Buffalo, transforming public and private energies into a single positive force for the common good.

Buffalo had bottomed out and was beginning to bounce back with vigor. Says Goldman, "There was no question that by the mid- and late 1980s, people in Buffalo were feeling much prouder of their community."

"The work ethic is alive and well in Buffalo," says George Smyntek, economist for the New York State Department of Labor. "People here know what a job means, and they will work hard to keep it. Due to the adversity and economic uncertainty, the attitude of people in Buffalo towards each other is much more friendly and open than in most places. We've all been through a lot together, and we seem to care more about each other."

In a metropolitan area of about 1.2 million people, the city's population stabilized at about 324,000. Unemployment dropped to about 5 percent. A theater district, a light-rail rapid-transit line, and a pedestrian mall, Buffalo Place, helped reinvigorate Main Street downtown, and nearby streets formed a corridor for high-tech industry. Hotels, restaurants, office towers, and small businesses sprouted from the cityscape, and the long-neglected waterfront was being developed in earnest—a marina complex, office buildings, restaurants, even expensive condominiums—to the tune of more than $200 million.

Jimmy Griffin, who came into office complaining that there had been no private development downtown for a decade, had tackled the problem and was getting results. Griffin, ever the political maverick, shrewdly distanced himself enough from his Democratic roots to support Ronald Reagan and later George Bush for president, thereby staying in the good graces of the White House. Griffin's individualism lost none of its ruggedness, but he managed to mend fences with his former adversaries in banking and business, turning them into allies. The man who came in as an outsider was now being welcomed in executive offices and boardrooms. In 1985, Griffin faced a tough election against Common Council President George Arthur, one of the city's most skilled politicians, and won an unprecedented third consecutive term, 53 percent to 43 percent.

As Buffalo shifted from an industrial foundation to a service-based economy, the keystone was jobs. In 1970, there had been only 328,000 nonmanufacturing jobs in the Buffalo area; by 1980, that figure had increased to 367,000, and by 1988, it was 426,000. With more than $2.5 billion in new development either in place or in progress toward the end of the eighties, there were more than 547,000 jobs in the metropolitan area, an all-time high. More than 55,000 of those jobs had been created in the mid-1980s.

Smyntek notes that "the economic devastation of the late seventies and early eighties taught Buffalo a painful lesson: Unless we can compete, we're dead." With the city having learned that lesson, he says, the comeback could be complete. "By the year 2000, like the year 1900, Buffalo can be a great city again."

In 1993, Buffalo will be the first U.S. city to serve as host to the World University Games, attracting athletes from 120 countries. In a new spirit of city-county cooperation, Buffalo's bid for the games succeeded largely through the efforts of Dennis T. Gorski, who took office as Erie County executive in 1988.

Down the road, the biggest economic boost of all is expected from the U.S.–Canada free-trade agreement, which will phase out tariffs over ten years and allow a border town such as Buffalo to benefit with millions of dollars in new business. Attractive prices have drawn Canadian shoppers to the Buffalo area in droves. The relatively cheap labor and real estate markets have provided additional incentives for Canadian businesses, which already have opened dozens of offices in the city and its environs.

USA Today wrote of Buffalo, "This city of cold winters and hot chicken wings, long a victim of hard times, seems to be on the threshold of a resounding economic boom." Dominic Bellissimo, who runs the family-owned Anchor Bar and Restaurant—the birthplace of Buffalo-style chicken wings, thanks to his mother, Teressa—is among those who will take advantage of free trade. As he told *USA Today,* "I'm going to truck my heat-and-serve wings into Canada."

The *New York Times* took note of Buffalo's turnaround:

> There are not many bright spots in the New York economy these days, and one of the few can be found in the unlikeliest of places: Buffalo. . . . Job growth in the Buffalo region, which is defined as Erie and Niagara Counties, has outpaced the state average in each of the last four years. At 2.8 percent, it was almost triple the state rate last year. . . . Buffalo is brimming with the self-confident boosterism of a boom town.

The *Washington Post* praised Buffalo for combining "big-city amenities with small-town intimacy." William Hoyt, a state assemblyman from Buffalo, told the *Post* that "this battered old town that was the epitome of the Rust Belt is on the verge of greatness."

Even the much-maligned Buffalo weather was being viewed from a positive perspective. Steve McLaughlin, a meteorologist from Buffalo, compiled thirty-year average figures showing that the city was a summer haven, featuring dry, sunny weather. McLaughlin's study showed that summers in Buffalo had more sunshine and less rainfall than those in Boston, New York, Baltimore, Washington, Philadelphia, Albany, and Pittsburgh.

By the end of the eighties, the *Wall Street Journal* had given Buffalo the ironic label of "hot new city."

Rain or shine, Buffalo's enduring love affair with its big-time sports teams has rarely been anything but hot—even in the hardest of economic times. Since 1973, the Bills have played in one of the National Football League's largest stadiums, and their fans have regularly filled it. In 1988 Buffalo football fans set an NFL single-season attendance record of 622,793 for eight games, all sellouts; they then came close to matching it in both 1989 and 1990, making it three years in a row as NFL attendance leaders. Just as the Bills had not yet won a Super Bowl trophy as 1990 ended, the Sabres had not yet won a Stanley Cup, yet their announced average attendance of nearly 15,900 for the 1989–1990 National Hockey League season put them at nearly 97 percent of capacity, about where they have been for most of the last two decades.

Still, Buffalo's longest professional sports tradition has been baseball, minor-league though it might be. Austin Fox, an architectural historian and member of the Buffalo Preservation Board, was an all-star baseball player when he graduated from Buffalo's Lafayette High School in 1930, after years of rooting for his beloved Bisons. In the twenties, he took his mitt to the Bisons' games: "Just in case one of the players got hurt and they needed someone to take his place, I was ready."

More than sixty years later, Fox says, "Baseball is still a very important part of this community. It's part of the pride people have in Buffalo, and they show it by the way they support the sports teams."

Buffalo's appetite for the big leagues—to be part of "the show"—was thought to have been long lost, but that, too, was restored in the eighties as Bob Rich, Jr., embarked on his quest.

"I think Bob Rich and baseball have been a highly positive force for Buffalo," says one of the city's adopted sons, Jack Kemp, who became the Bills' quarterback in a hundred-dollar waiver deal and then went on to become a nine-term congressman and U.S. Secretary of Housing and Urban Development. Kemp has known Rich since the mid-1960s and is familiar with Buffalo's comeback story: "This city went through some hard times, but it has changed. Buffalo even looks different; it is different, and you can't help but notice. There's a much greater sense of pride in the faces of the people. I see it everywhere in Buffalo, and I think baseball is part of the reason."

IT'S SAFE TO SAY that no one has wanted major-league baseball for Buffalo more than Bob Rich. His near-evangelistic zeal has become contagious, so much so that even his once-skeptical father joined the ranks of the converted. "I have to admit that when this baseball thing first started, I wasn't as enthusiastic as Bobby," says Robert Rich, Sr. "But I've changed, and now I'm hoping that it goes all the way."

"When you get down to it, Bobby is a hardworking jock. Nobody will outwork him or outhustle him. He's not a natural, but he will do anything he has to do to win," says George Ostendorf, his friend and classmate since boyhood and later his partner in winning two city squash doubles championships.

> For me, squash was easy; it wasn't easy for Bobby. But he wanted to do it, so he became a champion. That's how he does everything: He throws himself into a project and is unrelenting. When he makes his mind up that he's going to do something, he does it to the hilt. There's no halfway with Bobby. It can be squash, polo, football, baseball, business, whatever. When Bobby wants something bad, he'll kill himself to get it and then move on to the next challenge. It's always like that; I call him 'Mr. Toad.' He keeps hopping from one challenge to another. . . . Sports has always been important to him, but I think relationships are more important to him. He comes across as very competitive, but he's a very sensitive person. I don't think he's as competitive as he appears, and he's much more sensitive than he appears.

Seymour H. Knox III, like Bob Rich, is a member of a prominent Buffalo family and has long been active in business and sports. In the mid-1960s, Knox and his brother, Northrup, made a bid for a National Hockey League franchise. The first try came in 1965, and Robert Rich, Sr., was a part of their group of Buffalo investors.

That attempt was unsuccessful, but in 1969, Knox and other Buffalo investors, including Bob Rich, Jr., agreed to purchase the Oakland Seals franchise, which had been struggling. Because of internal politics, the NHL asked Buffalo to sell controlling interest in the team, although Knox and his partners held on to 20 percent of it. This gave Knox and the Buffalo group an inside role in NHL business, enabling them to lobby for expansion, and Buffalo was granted a franchise in 1970, along with Vancouver. Seymour Knox, chairman of the Sabres, wasn't at all surprised that young Rich was interested in the hockey business:

> I knew Bob played hockey in college and had tried out for the Olympic team, but we had been friends long before that.
> The thing about Bob and his family is that they have always loved sports. The first time we put the syndicate together to get an NHL team, we failed, but Bob wanted to be part of the group. I think he learned the ins and outs of what it takes to get a team and what it means to run a major-league sports franchise.

The tedious, time-consuming effort to gain an NHL franchise was an indelible learning experience for Bob Rich, who was in his late twenties when he became a member of the Sabres' board of directors, a position that he holds today. "So much of what I've learned in sports management has come from the Sabres and the Knoxes," Rich says. "I watched the way they set up their ownership group and the infrastructure of the organization. I watched the way they politicked the owners and the time they spent getting out in the front lines, where the votes were. The way they handled the presentation for a major-league team was very insightful to me."

Such insider information plus his formidable bloodlines and increasing maturity made Bob Rich an ever more dynamic presence in the realms of both sports and business. "I think Bob inherited his father's managerial instincts and desire for excellence," says Bill Gisel, chief legal counsel for Rich Products and confidant of both father and son for nearly a decade. "He's determined to do the absolute best he can; Bob puts tremendous demands on himself. . . . He's extremely facile-minded, and knows how to judge situations and people. Above all else, he's a leader."

Robert Rich, Sr., would tell his son that "there are many similarities between baseball and the food business. It's the same thing: promotion, promotion, promotion. In the food business, the most important thing besides promotion is the quality of your product. You've got to have the product, and you've got to have the promotion. In baseball, you don't have to win every game, but every game should be special."

Bob Rich took the advice to heart. "He never lost sight of the fact that the success of the franchise depended 100 percent on the fans," Gisel says. "They are the customers."

Jack Kemp has remained an ardent admirer: "Bob Rich has carried on the family tradition, in terms of expanding the business and continuing the business and social responsibility in the community."

Steadily, the image of Bob Rich, wealthy young individualist, has evolved into that of Bob Rich, pillar of the community—and, at the same time, regular guy. There are even certain iconoclastic touches to this Man Who Would Be a National League Owner. "These things have evolved as I've aged," he says with a laugh. "When I was younger, I always had a hot car. I just got to the point where I was tired of having cars that broke down all the time. So now I just grab the first thing out of the mail-room car pool. Everybody kidded me because I used to drive this Celebrity station wagon that had over 100,000 miles on it. I didn't even think about it; cars just aren't important to me anymore."

Then, too, there's his appreciation of music, ranging from the show tunes of Andrew Lloyd Webber's productions on Broadway to contemporary country songs that emanate from the Grand Old Opry. The trademark of his wardrobe is cowboy boots. From leather to lizard skin, from brown or black to naturally patterned, from custom-made to off-the-rack, Bob Rich lives with his boots on. He swears that this footgear isn't just a fashion quirk, but purely practical:

I, like a lot of Buffalonians, go to many public events during the winter. There's a great tradition in Buffalo. You go to the cloakroom, and you take your galoshes off; then, when you leave, you have to find the right ones. You try to get out ahead of the crowd, so you can make sure you have your own boots. It never works. No matter how hard you try, you always end up with somebody else's galoshes. And if you're honest, you end up with the worst ones in the city. One year, I got a pair of Western boots, and I found out how nice it was not to have to search for your galoshes in the winter. It was so nice, I've got about fifty pairs of Western boots; I don't wear shoes anymore. I guess I'm the Imelda Marcos of the cowboy-boot set. One time, a banker looked at my boots and said, "What are you trying to do?" I just told him, "Hey, this is me, I'm a boot guy."

Bob Rich, Jr., the hard-charging man in his mid-forties, was many things, but he wasn't a machine, even though to most people he seemed like one. He was a civic leader and the embodiment of Buffalo's baseball dreams. He was the president of a major corporation. His baseball ownership responsibilities were now at the Triple-A level and much more demanding than before. He had had two unsuccessful marriages, and he was the father of four. His time was already being stretched near the breaking point. There didn't seem to be room for further complexity in his life. But, in fact, there was. Her name was Melinda Roth.

SNAPSHOT—SPAHN

The winningest left-handed pitcher in major-league history is entering his seventies now, and his famed hook nose is no longer surrounded by the cold, fearsome expression that for twenty-one seasons made batters shudder. He is balding and gray, and his athlete's trim physique has turned paunchy. His smile is warm and sentimental—grandfatherly—as he visits the city of his youth nearly a half-century after he left it for good. Amid a chorus of echoes from old-timers'-night applause, he becomes reacquainted with many ghosts. Haunting memories seem to come alive for him everywhere, a sign that he will always be one of Buffalo's own: Warren Spahn.

Especially vivid for him are those long walks home from Bison Stadium that he used to take with his father. During the summer, Edward Spahn and his son would journey a couple of miles on foot from South Buffalo to the ballpark. The father was a wallpaper salesman and an outstanding amateur third baseman who shared his passion for the game with his son. The son's hero was legendary Bisons home-run slugger Ollie Carnegie, who never played in the majors.

"When I was a kid growing up, I idolized the players on the Bisons, especially Carnegie," says Warren Spahn, who developed as a young ball player during the Depression. "My dad would take me to the ball games, and we'd sit in the bleachers watching and talking baseball. After the game, we'd walk home to South Buffalo and rehash what happened on the field. Then I'd wash up, go to bed, close my eyes, and pretend I was playing for the Bisons. That was my fantasy."

Warren Spahn's decision to become a pitcher was made when

he was ten. Coming home one day, he asked his father's opinion of whether he could throw as hard as a kid who lived on the next block. Edward Spahn assured his son that he could, and so that very day, the son pitched his first game, for the Lake City Social Club— and he won.

Pitching became a family affair for the Spahns. Warren had four sisters—Eleanor, Marjorie, June, and Gertrude—and a brother, Ed. Eleanor became his baseball partner. She was a natural athlete and spent hours with Warren, acting as catcher while he threw pitch after pitch. "Eleanor was a heck of an athlete, probably the best in the family; she really helped me," Spahn says. So did his father. As a teenager, Spahn played first base on an amateur team with his dad, who was at third base. "To be on the same field as my father," he recalls, "was a real thrill."

The German-American household of Edward Spahn, his wife, Mabel, and their six children was typical of Buffalo in that era: hard-hit by the Depression, but resolute, close-knit, and proud. "We were a poor family," Warren Spahn recalls, "and I feel you have to be deprived to appreciate; that was an important lesson for me, and lessons like that stick for a lifetime."

During the spring and summer, young Warren practically lived at Cazenovia Park, playing baseball on the diamonds and swimming in the creek. "Buffalo had a great baseball program, and I'd play all day, every day," Spahn says. "I played in the weekend leagues, the Muny leagues, and the twilight leagues." He quickly established a reputation with his fastball that he took with him to South Park High School. Spahn also had a wicked curveball. He later developed an effective change-up and screwball. This variety of pitches, combined with his high-kick windup and left-handed delivery, enabled him to dominate and confuse hitters. Buffalo's Dan Carnevale, now an advance scout with the Cleveland Indians, played against him on the sandlots of Buffalo: "I tell you, he had the greatest overhand curve I've ever seen for a left-hander. You would stand at the plate and watch that ball go by you. Then you'd sit down."

Sibby Sisti, who grew up in Buffalo during the same years as Spahn and was signed by the same scout, Billy Myers, remembers seeing Spahn play American Legion ball: "Even then, you knew he was something special. Warren was like a lot of kids who grew up in the Depression; we didn't have a lot of money, but we always had baseball."

Spahn's coach at South Park High, Joe "Chief" Shoemaker, who had developed several professional players, took Spahn under his wing. Spahn not only pitched but played first base, and many talent scouts took notice. In 1940, Spahn, then nineteen, caught the attention of Myers, a ticket-seller for the New York Central Railroad in Buffalo who moonlighted as a bird-dig scout for the Boston Braves. He offered the young man a contract, and Spahn signed. "It was like all those dreams I had as a kid came true," Spahn recalls. "It was such a wonderful thing to be able to make money by playing baseball."

Spahn was sent to Bradford, Pennsylvania, to pitch in the Pony League. The wiry six-footer posted a 5–4 record there before throwing out his elbow when breaking off a curveball. Myers took him to Erie for treatment by a chiropractor, who manipulated his injured arm and told him to rest it for the balance of the season. "I was scared," Spahn says, "but I always believed I would come back."

And he did.

In 1941, for Evansville of the Three-I League, Spahn finished 19–6 and struck out 193 batters in 212 innings. The next year, he made the big leagues with the Boston Braves. "That's when my dream really came true," he says. But life in the bigs wasn't easy. For one thing, Spahn didn't hit it off with Manager Casey Stengel. Once, after Stengel ordered him to throw at a batter and Spahn hesitated, the manager called him "gutless" and soon farmed him out to Hartford, Connecticut, where he hurled seventeen victories.

After the 1942 season, Spahn joined the Army. "Where I grew up," he says, "you figured you owed something to this country." Spahn was wounded as a combat engineer in the battle to reopen the Remagen Bridge over the Rhine and earned a battlefield commission. When he came back to the Braves in 1946, he recalls, "I was a much more mature, worldly person. I learned a lot of good things in the military; I think I just grew up. The military taught me discipline, and so much of playing baseball is discipline. When I went back up this time, I was ready." In 1946, he posted an 8–5 record with the Braves to go along with a 2.94 earned-run average. The next season, Spahn came into his own, winning twenty-one games and taking the first big step on his long journey to the Hall of Fame. Sibby Sisti, who was a teammate of Spahn's with the Braves, recalls that "when we were in Boston together, Warren would always talk about what was going on back home in Buffalo."

Birdie Tebbetts, who managed Spahn in Milwaukee, remembers him as

a hardworking, great player. Spahn could pitch, field, and he could hit—he won a lot of games with his bat. You'd think with the high kick that runners would be able to steal off him, but it wasn't true. Spahn had a great pick-off move. He never stopped working; he'd come to spring training ready to go nine innings the first day, and he was like that the whole season. Pitching was a business to Spahn; he took it very seriously. Nobody wanted to mess with him, he was very tough and one of the strongest guys I ever saw.

Tebbetts and Spahn did have at least one difference of opinion. It came in the early 1960s, when Tebbetts was a vice president of the Braves and the team commissioned an artist to do a portrait of Spahn to be given to him on a special night in Milwaukee's County Stadium. There was only one problem: Spahn hated it.

"He looked at the picture and said, 'I don't like it; my nose is crooked,'" Tebbetts recalls. "I told him that it did look like him and that he had a strong face. I told him to take it home to his wife and see what she thinks."

Spahn took the picture to his wife, LoRene, and also showed it to his teammate and close friend Lew Burdette. He came back and told Tebbetts, "You know, Birdie, Burdette said it was the best thing he ever saw; my wife didn't like it at first, but she kind of got used to it. You were right, Birdie. I guess I just never realized I had a crooked nose."

There was no such complaint about his Hall of Fame plaque, which was placed in Cooperstown in 1973. Despite not winning his first major-league game until he was twenty-five, Spahn won twenty or more games thirteen times, a National League record. His 363 victories are the most ever by a left-hander and fifth on the all-time list. Before he retired in 1965, he had led the league in victories eight times, a National League record; had pitched the most innings (5,246) in league history, and had recorded the most shutouts (63) by a National League left-hander. Along the way, he picked up a World Series ring, hit thirty-five home runs and, according to Boston sportswriter Harry Kaese's estimate, won forty games with his bat. Today, his durability is mentioned in the same breath with Nolan Ryan's; Spahn pitched his first no-hitter at age thirty-nine and his other one at forty, and seventy-five of his victories came after his fortieth birthday.

For nearly four decades, Spahn has lived on a ranch in Hartshorne, Oklahoma, where his various business interests include real estate. His late wife was from Oklahoma, which is where his son, Greg, was born in 1948. Despite the years away from his hometown, Spahn has never lost his affection for the city of his birth. "For me, it all started in Buffalo," Spahn says. "That's where I learned about caring and sharing. I grew up playing for neighborhood teams. We didn't play for money; we played because we loved the game, and you busted your butt, and you hated losing. I carried those traits on to pro ball, and I carried on what my father and my family taught me."

His father is gone now; Bison Stadium, too. "So many of the places I used to frequent are no longer around, and I'm sorry about that," Spahn says wistfully,

> but that's what happens when you get older. But you know something? I always get a good feeling when I come back. My brother and sisters still live here, and my life in Buffalo was certainly good for Warren Spahn. When you get to be my age, you think more about counting your blessings, and Buffalo is a very important part of my blessings. . . . You have hardy, loving people in Buffalo. . . . The people play as hard as they work, and I think that's what Buffalo represents. I am forever grateful that I grew up here."

As it always has, South Buffalo holds an irresistible attraction for Warren Spahn. "I went to Cazenovia Park, and the kids are still out there playing," he says. "I spent half my life there when I was growing up. You know, back then, the little creek in the park seemed like a big river. Now, it seems so small. Everything seems different when you get older, but when I saw those kids playing ball, it made me feel good."

Part Three

8

MINDY

Pete Rose, Johnny Bench, Joe Morgan, Tony Perez, George Foster—Sparky Anderson's Big Red Machine—they were the toast of Cincinnati in the seventies, and Melinda Roth enjoyed cheering them on with her family in Riverfront Stadium. "I loved Joe Morgan," she recalled years later, after becoming Mrs. Robert E. Rich, Jr. "He was scrappy, always got on base, and he had speed." The same might have been said of young tomboy Mindy Roth, who discovered early in life that "when you're born in Cincinnati, being a baseball fan is part of your birth contract."

Mindy, who had a younger brother and a younger sister, grew up in a neighborhood dominated by boys. There were few girls her age, so she capitalized on her athletic, competitive nature and turned to sports. "I played everything—football, baseball, you name it," she says. "That's all we would do was play sports on the street and in the backyards. I'd come home after school, eat, and then go out and play sports until it was dark. There was a group of about ten of us who always played together, and I was the only girl."

Even as she was turning into a teenager, she was still playing football and baseball with the boys. "I sort of grew up as one of the guys in the neighborhood," she says. "Then, when I first got asked out on a date, the guys in the neighborhood, like my cousin and my brother, couldn't understand why anybody would want to go out on a date with me. After all, I was one of the guys."

But all that began to change one day in the huddle of a neighborhood football game. "One of the guys was the quarterback, and he used to draw plays on your stomach," she recalls.

You know, he puts a finger on your stomach and says, "Go this way, cut that way, and then go deep." Well, he does that with one receiver and then he comes to me and starts drawing the play on my stomach. He says, "Okay, Mindy," points his finger, but then he stops. He looks at me, and I look at him. Suddenly, we both had this realization he couldn't draw the play on my stomach anymore. So he points to his hand and says, "Go this way, cut that way, and run deep."

That was the first time I can remember that there was any realization among the neighborhood guys that I was a girl. I was a good player; I was usually picked before a lot of the guys. I was fast, I had good hands, and I could catch the ball. But I'll never forget that day the quarterback couldn't draw a play on my stomach. It was my first realization, especially in sports, that things are different for a woman.

As a twelve-year-old, Mindy started working as a cashier in her uncle's pizza shop, and although she was too short to reach the register, she solved that problem by standing on a metal crate. "It was great to be working," she says. "I told my parents I didn't want an allowance anymore because I didn't want them to tell me how to spend my money. I figured if I went out and earned my own money, I could be as independent as I wanted to be."

Her parents, Richard and Judy Roth, were not surprised by her attitude. "Mindy was always very hardworking and very independent," her father says. The Roths, like the Riches of Buffalo, were in the food business. The Roth family operated Rubel Baking Company in Cincinnati for nearly a century. Richard Roth later went into the frozen-foods business with a company called Prestige Donuts and also with VIP Products, which specializes in pizza crusts and other dough products. "I come from a family business," Mindy says, "and in that culture, work is an integral part of your life *and* your pleasure."

The Roth family had its own box at Crosley Field and used to sponsor some Reds games on radio. Today, sitting on the deck in the backyard of the Roth home in Cincinnati, are two seats from Crosley, which the Reds left in the seventies in favor of Riverfront.

"I used to take Mindy to Crosley Field when she was just a little kid," her father remembers. "She always loved baseball."

Mindy brought a spunky disposition to both work and play. She was rebellious, "but not in a bad way," her father says. "Mindy had indefatigable energy; she pours herself into everything she does." She placed high demands on herself. As a youngster, she took up skiing, which became a lifetime passion. On the slopes, as in life, Mindy Roth was driven toward perfection. "But I wouldn't call her a perfectionist," her father says. "Mindy has always been steeped in the work ethic. Whatever she does, she's determined to do it to the best of her ability."

That was evident during one unforgettable day in Aspen. On that winter afternoon, the Colorado sky was clear, and a burnt-orange sun peeked over the white mountains. Her skis glided effortlessly over the snow, as if she were riding a cushion of air. It was the quest that every skier strives for: the perfect run.

"It was such a great feeling, that one time when everything went right," Mindy said later. "Right then, at that exact moment, you knew all the work and preparation paid off. It might never happen again, but at least you had that moment when everything was right. That's what you strive for all your life."

She brought that same kind of dedication to every job. At sixteen, she landed a cashier's position at Dino's, a men's clothing store in Cincinnati that was frequented by members of the Reds and visiting National League teams. "All the players came in there," Mindy remembers. "I could tell you George Foster's waist size. He had one of the smallest waists of any baseball player; I think it was a twenty-eight."

After high school, she enrolled at Jacksonville University in Florida. It was the mid-1970s, and Jacksonville, primarily known as a basketball school, developed an outstanding baseball team under coach Jack Lamabe. Mindy Roth happened to date a catcher on the team and became part of a booster group. "There were no concessions on the field, so we started a stand," she says, and she worked behind the counter selling hot dogs, popcorn, and soda. "At first, the fan base was real low; baseball had never been that big at Jacksonville before. But it began to grow as the team kept winning." As for the concessions operation, "it was pretty rinky-dink at first, but by the second year, we were making money. We had uniforms and everything. That was my first real baseball job."

After two years, Mindy grew restless at Jacksonville. She missed skiing, so after her sophomore year, she enrolled at the University of Colorado, near some of the best slopes in the world. The university also offered the opportunity for her to study both psychology and business. She was particularly fascinated by the field of organizational development.

After graduation in 1979, Mindy had the best of both worlds: a job as business manager for a subsidiary of Aspen Ski Company and the opportunity to spend countless recreational hours on the slopes. She became a ski instructor but eventually realized that skiing would not be her life's work. In 1982 she came to Buffalo and worked as a broadcast producer and as an advertising account executive. In January 1985 she became a product manager for a Buffalo pharmaceuticals firm. "I never had any plans or ambitions to get involved in pro sports," she says now. "It just kind of happened."

It started to happen during the 1983 baseball season, when Mindy Roth was attending a Buffalo Bisons game in War Memorial Stadium. Bob Rich, Jr., owner of the Bisons, saw her at the game and introduced himself. He had met her father about five years earlier, through business dealings with Rich Products. Mindy and Bob Rich hit it off immediately; they had much in common. Both were reared in family businesses, both were considered rebels while growing up, both were self-described "sports nuts," and both had the same aggressive, independent attitudes. If that wasn't enough, Rich also liked to ski. "Mindy has an infectious personality when she meets somebody she likes and has a lot in common with," her father says, "and, boy, she had a lot in common with Bob. I think they make a great couple."

In September 1985, soon after the Bisons' season ended, Mindy Roth, twenty-seven, and Bob Rich, Jr., forty-four, were married. They spent a few weeks in Paris for their honeymoon, but it wouldn't be long before Mindy Rich would learn something her husband already knew: The baseball season never ends.

THE HONEYMOON WAS OVER. On his first day back on the job after returning from Paris, Bob Rich proposed to Mindy again—this time about baseball. For the first time, he was ready to make a move to acquire a major-league expansion franchise, and he wanted her help.

The 1985 season had been Buffalo's first in Triple-A since 1970. Despite a team that finished seventh in the American Association with a 66–76 record, Buffalo had enjoyed a banner year at the gate. The Bisons, a Chicago White Sox farm club managed by John Boles, drew 362,762 fans to the Old Rockpile, an increase of nearly 140,000 over the previous season. But Bob Rich was more concerned about the future, and that future was being shaped by decisions at high levels of government and baseball.

The timing was perfect because expansion was suddenly a prime concern of Major League Baseball. "Expansion is a front-burner item, something we have to look at in a positive way," Commissioner Peter Ueberroth said during the winter meetings in December 1984. The National and American Leagues had been out of balance since the American League added Toronto and Seattle in 1977: The American League had fourteen teams, the National League twelve. But Ueberroth had more in mind than two teams for the National League. His ultimate goal was thirty-two teams, divided evenly between the two leagues, with each league having two eight-team divisions.

The prospective expansion cities were lining up, including a veritable Lazarus of a city named Buffalo. With one year of Triple-A behind him and a new stadium on the drawing board, Bob Rich was ready to roll.

Ueberroth, however, was not going to jump headlong into expansion. "I only favor expansion when there's a city that qualifies under three criteria: local ownership with roots in the community, fan support, and support from the city, county, state, and their politicians," Ueberroth said in a 1985 news conference.

In August 1985 the commissioner's office announced that there would be a meeting for all expansion candidates. Representatives from thirteen cities, including Buffalo, would travel to New York in early November to meet with baseball's Long Range Planning Committee. When Bob and Mindy Rich returned from their honeymoon in mid-October, Bob received a letter from the commissioner's office stating that the meeting was four weeks away.

Four weeks. Bob Rich needed someone in the Bisons' front

office to take charge of preparing Buffalo's presentation to Major League Baseball. Pronto.

Well, he thought, who better than his own wife?

"We had just come back from our honeymoon, and I quit my job when we decided to get married," Mindy Rich recalls. "I figured I wouldn't worry what I was going to do until I got back. . . . Well, the day we get back, Bob calls me into his office. He says Buffalo has been invited to make this presentation and how would I like to do it."

It didn't take her long to make up her mind.

Having added a husband to her life but subtracted a job "was an adjustment," she acknowledged.

> I mean, you come back from your honeymoon, everything is wonderful, and you're completely relaxed. Then you wake up the next day, and the hard, cold reality hits you in the face: What are you going to do with your day? I didn't know what to do with myself. I always had a purpose. I always had work. I was panicking.
>
> That's when Bob asked me to work on the presentation. I said, "All right. Sure." I was so glad I had a job, and I had to try and pull it off in four weeks. It was a real challenge. . . .
>
> We knew that when we went to that meeting, we were the dark horse. We were a joke. People thought there was no chance for Buffalo; 1985 was our first year in Triple-A, we needed a new stadium, and we still had a long way to go. But I believed in Buffalo, so I figured: Why not give it a shot?

Mindy Rich worked on the presentation with Charles F. Rosenow, president of the Buffalo Development Companies, the economic-development arm of city government. He had been instrumental in Buffalo's baseball comeback. Among the others involved were Mike Billoni, general manager of the Bisons, and Alden Schutte, president of the advertising agency that had been working with the team.

Mindy Rich's experience in marketing and advertising had paid off in her creation of an extensive brochure detailing Buffalo's strengths as a candidate for major-league expansion. It was a crucial part of the Buffalo group's presentation.

Among those who went to New York with Bob and Mindy Rich were Mayor Jimmy Griffin; Northrup Knox, president of the Buffalo Sabres, and Chuck Rosenow.

This Buffalo contingent met with Ueberroth, National League President Chub Feeney, American League President Bobby Brown, and about nine owners of major-league teams. The meeting was supposed to last one hour, which was the time limit the other twelve cities followed. The Buffalo group's presentation lasted eighty minutes.

Rich and company used cold, hard facts to make Buffalo's case, as outlined in the brochure prepared by Mindy. "We didn't just make hopeful promises; we stuck to the facts about what we can do and what we've accomplished," Bob Rich said.

That would become the cornerstone of Buffalo's philosophy to land an expansion franchise: Use facts to show that Buffalo can meet the criteria set by Major League Baseball. On this first trip to New York, it worked.

"Buffalo went into this as a dark horse, but we left as a real eye-opener," Bob Rich said in a news conference after the flight home. "I think we knocked them dead with our presentation, and nobody could have received a better reception from the owners."

Mindy Rich said that "when we left that meeting, we all felt good. Buffalo had a lot more recognition as a baseball town. . . . I think it was the first time we all began to believe we might pull this off and make the major leagues someday."

After the presentation, Billoni asked Mindy to join the Bisons full time to work on marketing projects. "At that point, I wasn't sure what I was going to do," Mindy Rich recalls. "There were other projects I was thinking of working on for Rich Products. But when Michael came to me, I thought it was a great idea. It fit in with my sports background, and it was great to work in baseball. It just kind of evolved."

With the demands on his time ever greater and with the stakes of his major-league quest rising to the tens of millions of dollars, Bob Rich knew that he not only needed a capable person to run his burgeoning baseball operations on a daily basis, including the Double- and Single-A teams in Wichita and Niagara Falls, but someone in whom he could place his complete trust. Given those criteria, his choice was easy.

"Let's face it, sports ownership clearly does not keep one in silk shirts," he says. "So I try to have the best of both worlds. I spend my days with Rich Products, and when I come home, I can catch up with Mindy on baseball. . . . We've had some points of disagreement in baseball, as any baseball people would have. But we've always been able to work through those disagreements."

Says Mindy, "Bob and I have a special rapport. If I don't agree with him, I tell him. I don't always argue a baseball point; there are times I concede, but I like people to challenge. I've learned a tremendous amount from working with Bob. I think we've been good for each other."

"What I see in Mindy is a motivated person who shares the same interests as Bob," says Tom Roe, Bob Rich's college roommate and longtime friend. "She speaks up to him and holds her own, and I think he likes that."

RIGHT FROM THE START, Mindy Rich made it clear that she was more than the boss's wife.

"What it comes down to is, you have to be your own person and believe in yourself," she says.

> I tried to be conscious of the fact that when I came here, some people were thinking, "Oh, yeah, she got the job because she's his wife." Some people looked at my being his wife and my being with the company as possibly a threat or possibly as a way of getting to him.
>
> You have to be secure enough to deal with the circumstances surrounding your own situation. I happen to be the boss's wife, and I happen to be a woman; those are considered two handicaps in the working world, and especially the baseball world. I deal with that as best as I can. I figured the way to deal with that is to gain the respect of my peers and the people who work with me. If they can respect me for the job I do, then that is how you prove your-

self. I'm not a feminist; I just want to be appreciated for the job I do.

Mindy Rich, after having worked her way from consultant to marketing vice president to executive vice president, directs the day-to-day operations of the Bisons. That rapid rise, she likes to joke, was because "in this family, nepotism works," even to the point of her awakening her husband in the middle of the night to tell him an idea about improving the baseball franchise. "I'm totally dedicated to my work, which, by the way, is the key to this organization," she says. "The people in this organization who don't have a high level of dedication or don't care, those people aren't going to make it, because the other people, who do care and are dedicated, aren't going to put up with it."

That kind of attitude impressed Bob Rich. Mindful of his grandfather and grandmother, and of his father and mother, he was well aware of the value of a husband and wife working closely together in business. "She's not only my wife," he says, "she's my partner."

Mindy Rich quickly established her own identity within the organization as a hands-on executive. When there were complaints about long waits at concession stands, Mindy would go stand in those lines to find out what was causing the delay. If someone got a cold hot dog, she wanted to know why. At the stadium, she developed a commanding presence to which everyone in the organization—from the ushers to the front office—responded.

With each passing month, Mindy Rich became more important within the organization. Slowly but surely, the Bisons operation began to take the shape of her business philosophy: relentless effort to meet customer needs. She became a demanding leader who would place the greatest demands on herself. She would arrive at her office each morning sharply at eight and stay until five, or well into the night if the Bisons were playing at home. A slender five feet, six inches, she prefers business suits and a generally conservative wardrobe, and the image she projects is of a lean, energetic executive. Her dark brown hair is cut short, her words are rapid-fire but soft, and she listens intently—legs crossed, elbow on knee, chin on palm, brown eyes focused like lasers.

Creative, outspoken, sometimes blunt, Mindy Rich emphasizes details, and the Bisons' staff, at every level, follows that lead. There is a spirit of responsiveness: The fans come first.

Suggestion boxes were placed throughout the ballpark, and fans were sent questionnaires. Good ideas were acted on promptly.

When fans bringing infants to games had problems finding a place to change diapers, the Bisons set aside special areas for that purpose. To better serve fans with dietary restrictions, a low-cal food counter was opened.

On game days, Mindy Rich seemed to be everywhere. She would walk through the stands and talk to fans, asking opinions. The goal was to create a family-oriented, fun atmosphere. "When I'm at a game, I'm looking at the whole experience of being in the ballpark," she says. "If I get a stale peanut, I'll go to the concession stand and tell them to get rid of those stale ones. We're selling fun and entertainment and the special flavor of being at the ballpark. I don't care if you are a ticket-taker, an usher, or a salesman; everybody who works for the Bisons is marketing the Bisons."

That's why appearances are important. At games, members of the front-office staff wear blazers with a Bisons insignia—and ties. Ushers wear red vests with white shirts—and ties. Each inning, ushers walk the aisles of the ballpark to help fans and make their presence known. Security personnel, exuding an aura of comfort rather than intimidation, have gained the reputation as low-key guardians of the family atmosphere.

Through both marketing and fate, the names *Rich* and *Bisons* were becoming increasingly evident in Buffalo's everyday life. Bob and Mindy Rich also are chairman and president, respectively, of Rich Communications, which operates both a highly rated FM rock station and an AM sports/talk station that has exclusive rights to Bisons, Bills, and Sabres games. Bob's younger brother, David, who is vice president and treasurer of the Bisons, had held the top two titles at Rich Communications before becoming head of the Rich Foundation.

The Bisons even developed a signature hot dog, and they offered lines of team-insignia merchandise on a par with those found in the any big-league city. Eventually, there was a food court that functioned almost as a town square, with passersby stopping for lunch or a snack and eating right in the stadium seats.

The blur of their hurried pace sometimes makes it easy for their fellow Buffalonians to forget that the Riches are people. "We have no social life," Mindy Rich says with a good-natured shrug. "We try to spend as much time with the family as possible."

Once a year, during the off-season, Bob and Mindy Rich do treat themselves to a ten-day vacation. They spend most of that time fishing and skiing. The rule: no baseball talk. But it's a rule made to be broken. "The first two days, we're so exhausted from baseball, all we do is sleep," Mindy says. "Then we talk about everything we think we can possibly talk about. Then we enjoy where we are. It takes four days to chill out, so we get about five days not thinking about baseball."

Yet even when they seem to have no time, there's always time for the community. For instance, Bob and Mindy Rich are co-chairs of Western New York United Against Drug and Alcohol Abuse. "There is a lot more than baseball that matters to us in Buffalo," Mindy Rich says. "This is our home, and we have a strong desire to do what we can to help this community."

IN THE MINOR LEAGUES, unlike the big time, player contracts and salaries are not a major concern. The parent team pays most of those bills and controls player transactions. The emphasis for a minor-league front office is on promotion, concessions, ticket sales, and off-the-field activities.

On the field, the Bisons of 1986 posted a 71–71 mark, but attendance at War Memorial Stadium jumped to 424,113, a Buffalo record. In 1987, the team dropped to 66–74, yet attendance rose again—to 497,760—setting another record.

"When you have a winning team, you will draw fans," Mindy Rich says. "The real challenge is to sell tickets if you're not winning."

She stressed interaction and motivation. Brainstorming sessions in and around her office were what made things happen. "I want people to be open and honest," she says. "I don't mince words. I put my cards on the table and let people know where I'm coming from. I'm open to ideas and suggestions, and if I don't want to use them, I will say why. One of the reasons we have done so well is because of that open atmosphere."

All the while, the Bisons' front office kept improving on its formula of blending the baseball entertainment experience with first-rate customer service. The rationale was quite simple: Why wait to act big-league?

Mike Billoni, with a new title of vice president and general manager, was still Sancho Panza to Bob Rich's Don Quixote, right down to the cowboy boots. Billoni was, if anything, expanding his already outsized reputation as a latter-day Barnum, earning praise from Bob Rich as "the spirit of the Buffalo Bisons."

That special spirit manifested itself in the atmosphere at the ballpark. Every Friday night, there was a "bash" at the park, with rock music and beverages served at a tent party, and a fireworks display after the game. Buffalo also became one of the first minor-league franchises to schedule rock concerts and baseball games as doubleheaders.

Amid all the state-of-the-art hoopla, the Bisons never lost sight of tradition. One of their eating enclaves was named Luke & Ollie's, in memory of the legendary Luke Easter and Ollie Carnegie, and in 1985 they established a Buffalo Baseball Hall of Fame.

Billoni's counterpart in nonbaseball matters is Jon Dandes, vice president and general manager of stadium services, who is responsible for the ballpark food-service and restaurant operations not only in Buffalo, but in Wichita and in Niagara Falls, where the Single-A Rapids play at Sal Maglie Stadium. Dandes started with Rich Products in 1986, but his first contact with the Rich family was in 1974, under rather strained circumstances, when he was student government president at the State University of New York at Buffalo. Robert Rich, Sr., was chairman of the university council, and Dandes was an outspoken, long-haired, blue-jeaned student leader who had his share of clashes with the council. "That's when I first met Mr. Rich; we fought a lot—you know, that was the heyday of student rights. But he was pretty nice to me when I came to Rich Products." Says Robert Rich, Sr.: "Jon has done a terrific job."

Dandes worked in hotel and restaurant management before coming to Rich's. He joined the baseball operation in 1987. "There's a dynamic tension in this organization, and that's what makes it work," he says. "The point is, when the time comes, everybody pulls together to make it work. It starts with Bob and Mindy and holds true for everybody else."

At times, it appears that everyone in the organization is going at 78 rpm while the rest of the world is at 33.

"There's a degree of spontaneity, creativity, and energy, but also, sometimes, flat-out madness," says Dandes. "There are times you have to get away or you can wind up in a padded room."

"Jon and I have sat back and seen some pretty good baseball arguments," Billoni says. "Bob has his opinion, and Mindy has her opinion, and they don't bend. That's when Jon and I have to be referees. But seriously, I think it's great; they refuel the fires. In this organization, there's an open atmosphere, and everyone can speak their mind."

But there's still time for fun. "We try not to take ourselves too seriously," says Mindy Rich, who one day picked up a rake and jumped on the diamond to help her husband and the grounds crew work on the field after a rainstorm. Another time, during the dog days of summer, when Mindy, Dandes, and Billoni had reached the point of exhaustion, Bob Rich loaded them on a plane and took off for a weekend in Nassau. They sat on the beach and forgot about baseball. "Sometimes, things get crazy, and you have to get away from it all," Billoni says. "Bob and Mindy understand that."

Marta Hiczewski, whose answering of the phone at the Old Rockpile back in 1983 had been the first inkling that Buffalo would forever be identified with *The Natural,* became the Bisons' assistant general manager, Billoni's second in command, in 1986 at age twenty-nine. She points to the "tremendous impact" of Mindy Rich and to 1985 as "a turning point—that's when we really started thinking big-league, and a great deal of that came about because of Mindy Rich."

Mindy Rich sees the Bisons' phenomenon as so complex that it's simple: "There is still something magical about this game to Bob and me. We both love baseball."

"This was an organization that started out with enthusiasm and talent, and Mindy pulled that together very well," Bob Rich says. "She brought order to the plan of moving to the major leagues."

"I think she's firmly established herself as a baseball executive and a good baseball person. She's earned the respect of the people in this organization and the people in baseball's hierarchy."

Jack Kemp adds, "She's a fantastic teammate and partner for

Bob Rich, not only in marriage, but also in business." Syd Thrift, former general manager of the Pittsburgh Pirates and New York Yankees, emphasizes that "too many people in baseball have tunnel vision. Mindy is very open-minded, and baseball needs people with her marketing sense." Paul Beeston, president of the Toronto Blue Jays, says that "Mindy Rich has made her mark in this game. She's one of the major reasons the Buffalo franchise has been so successful." Marge Schott, owner of the Cincinnati Reds, says of Mindy, "She's done a great job."

Bob Rich sees Mindy's role as crucial: "Baseball in Buffalo wouldn't be where it is without her."

SOON AFTER THE 1985 news conference in which Baseball Commissioner Peter Ueberroth established three criteria for any city with a hope of joining the big leagues, he added a fourth: a suitable stadium, preferably for baseball only.

For Bob and Mindy Rich, this posed a problem, because Buffalo didn't have one. Just a Rockpile.

There was a plan for an expandable 20,000-seat ballpark downtown, but this was at a time when both the City of Buffalo and the County of Erie were wrestling with monstrous budget deficits. Help would be needed from New York State: $22 million or more. But in October 1984, the governor had held a news conference in Buffalo where he said, "I would not now want to commit to a stadium only to find there is a more compelling need for Erie County." He stressed that "Erie County has serious problems," implying strongly that there indeed might be more pressing needs than a ballpark.

It would be up to the Democratic governor to ask the state legislature for the money. But he certainly didn't owe Mayor Jimmy Griffin any political favors, and the county executive was a Republican. Such considerations might have come into play if this had been a different governor. This governor, however, was Mario Cuomo, who, as a young man, had hoped to be another Joe DiMaggio.

9

CUOMO: IN DIMAGGIO'S IMAGE

The count is three and two as Matt Cuomo digs in at the plate. It is the summer of 1952 in Brunswick, Georgia, and prejudice seems to be everywhere. That is why Mario Matthew Cuomo, a twenty-year-old Italian-American Catholic from Queens, goes by his Anglo-sounding middle name. His position is center field, Joe DiMaggio's position. His number is 5, DiMaggio's number. But his team is *not* the New York Yankees; it is, instead, the Brunswick Pirates, a Class D outfit in the Georgia-Florida League, on the bottom rung of the professional baseball ladder.

Pitching for the Cordele Athletics is Jack Barbier, another Italian-American, who comes from Schenectady, New York. The temperature is nearly 100 degrees as the second game of an August doubleheader continues. Cuomo has stung Barbier for two hits in two previous at-bats today. Now, the pitcher is determined to teach the batter a lesson. Cuomo, with characteristic on-field combativeness, crowds the plate, daring Barbier to throw inside. The late-afternoon sun is glaring in Cuomo's eyes. Sweat is pouring from his forehead. He is exhausted. He feels dizzy. But, damn it all, he's going to fight off any inside pitch.

Barbier, a right-hander with a side-arm delivery, has a deceptive windup. He unleashes a pitch from the third-base side, and Cuomo, right-handed like the Yankee Clipper, can't pick up the ball. "Curve—the ball's going to curve," Cuomo thinks. Refusing to back off the plate, he braces for the curve. But instead of curving, it's coming straight in, high and tight: a fastball. He wears no batting helmet; such protection, he thinks, is not for a tough kid from the streets of New York City. Suddenly, he sees the ball clearly, its red seams spinning in the blazing sunshine, speeding right at his head. There's no time to think; there aren't even any flashbacks about his parents or his buddies 800 miles away in South Jamaica. Everything's happening too fast. In this broiling heat, with a deadly fastball hurtling toward his face, instinct takes over: a flinch. And he ducks, dropping the bat and turning his head away—all in an instant. But not quick enough. In a split second, there's the sickening sound of a baseball thunking against the back of his skull. As a tense hush snakes through the crowd, Cuomo slumps to the dirt and everything goes black as a blood clot begins forming near his brain.

Mario Matthew Cuomo lies there on the dusty earth of coastal Georgia, unconscious and unaware that his baseball career is over.

NEARLY FORTY YEARS later, Mario Matthew Cuomo, the governor of the State of New York, is in Albany, sitting behind a huge, dark-oak table in one of the Capitol's enormous, ornate, high-ceilinged meeting rooms. It is resplendent with sculpted, pale magenta walls and shiny marble floors; near the entrance are velvet ropes, held three feet above the floor by brass posts, to keep visitors in line. When Cuomo talks, there is a slight echo. On the hour and again on the half-hour, one can hear the sound of a clock tower ringing nearby. Cuomo, no longer a skinny outfielder, has a stocky but powerful build, about six feet and 185 pounds, with wide shoulders and large hands that project strength when he greets you with a handshake. He wears a dark blue suit, white shirt, striped tie, and weary expression. He has been governor for two terms, soon to be elected to a third, and this has been a typically demanding day, full of meetings with legislators and special-interest groups and a seemingly endless flow of official papers requiring his attention. But when late-afternoon conversation turns to baseball, this chief executive appears re-energized, almost as if by a magic wand. The topic is not only baseball, but Buffalo.

Cuomo's first visit to Buffalo had been in 1974, during an unsuccessful campaign for lieutenant governor, and his fondness for the city has grown since. "My first day there," he recalls, "I said this place reminds me of home."

Buffalo, like Queens, was an ethnic mix of blue-collar, working-class families. In 1980, as lieutenant governor, Cuomo helped set up an economic-development task force to help Western New

York, which had been devastated by layoffs, plant closings, and a sinking economy.

"I told Governor Carey we had to do more for Buffalo, because it was having such a tough time," Cuomo says. "I didn't have any power; I was only the lieutenant governor, but I was able to bring people in to talk to the locals and come up with ideas. The people there appreciated what I did; they were grateful that somebody was interested in Buffalo. One night, I'll never forget, they had a dinner with about 250 people, and they presented me with a watch; it was given to me by Jimmy Griffin."

Cuomo pauses.

"This isn't a prop," he says as he takes the watch off his wrist and slides it across the oak table. On the back of the watch, there is an inscription: "To Mario Cuomo From Your Friends in Buffalo, 1980."

"I have never worn another watch in ten years," Cuomo says. "That watch means everything to me. The truth is, the things I receive now, as governor, I receive practically ex officio. You don't give it to a lieutenant governor, which I was when they gave me that watch, and that's why it means so much to me. I never take it off; it annoys Griffin when I whip it off during a speech and he's in the audience and I say, 'Thanks for the watch, Jimmy.'"

New York State's governor and Buffalo's mayor have long had their political differences, and in 1984, they disagreed on Buffalo's proposed stadium project. That was the same year that Cuomo was Walter Mondale's campaign manager in New York State, while Griffin backed President Reagan in the race for the White House. When it came to a stadium, Griffin favored a study that supported a dome and asked Cuomo and the state to contribute $40 million toward a project estimated at $89 million.

Cuomo was hardly thrilled at the large amount requested or the idea of having baseball played under a dome in Buffalo. "I'm not sure people in this part of the world want to see baseball played this way," Cuomo said, noting his own experience as a minor-league ball player. "You should sit out and get rained on from time to time. That's baseball."

Griffin was not amused. He said Cuomo "must have got hit in

the head with a pitched ball if he thinks people enjoy sitting out in the rain. That's why he only made it to Class D baseball."

Leave it to Jimmy Griffin to remind Mario Cuomo of that long-ago moment in Georgia that could have meant the end of his life. But on this hot August afternoon, Cuomo is reflective, even wistful. "You know the movie *Bull Durham*? Well, that's how it was, and the stuff about sex was exactly right, except it was hyperbolic," Cuomo says. "And nobody down there looked like Susan Sarandon."

The Brunswick Pirates were a mediocre collection of farmhands back then; the club had three managers and finished seventh in the eight-team Georgia-Florida League with a 62–78 record. Cuomo was a smart, intense athlete who played with élan. "You learn some things about anybody who plays baseball," he says.

For example, thresholds; people quit at different thresholds. When you play baseball, you learn whether or not a person can handle adversity. I remember Tony Sarmiento, a big right-hander from Cuba, who pitched in the league. He struck me out four times in the same game with the same pitch. Four times! I knew it was coming . . . but I couldn't hit it. I don't know if it was something in my eyes or my mind; the pitch would come, you knew it was going to break, but you just could not hit it. That's a tough thing to take in front of a big crowd, and we had big crowds down there for that time: two, three thousand people.

In baseball, you learn competitiveness, and I think you can tell something about intelligence, too, because you can't really be stupid and be a good baseball player. There are so many judgment calls: You've got to know when to run and when not to run, what base to throw to, when to take a pitch, and so many other decisions that have to be made in an instant.

Mostly, baseball tells you about a person's ability to deal with adversity and ability to deal with success—you can be spoiled by too many championships—and your ability to play with the team and give yourself up for the good of the team. Are you willing to hit behind the runner? Are you willing to take a pitch? Are you willing to sacrifice?

To this politician so at home in the corridors of power, there is an almost spiritual sustenance to be drawn from a game he once described as "a uniquely American tradition that binds generation to generation, unlike any other ritual in society."

"To me, it is better than all other sports," says Cuomo.

> Baseball . . . has less insistence on size than football or basketball. . . . You can be Hank Aaron and be the greatest home-run hitter of all time, or Yogi Berra and do nothing but flick your wrists at bad pitches and make it to the Hall of Fame. You can be as small as Phil Rizzuto [five feet six, 150] and be a great player. You can be Dom Di-Maggio, who wasn't much bigger than Rizzuto, and play center field.
>
> As a game, it's exciting; there's a symmetry to it. There's a niceness to baseball that appeals to me because it is so merit-oriented. . . . There's something about base-ball—the chance that you can win as the most improbable underdog, the chance that with two strikes on you and with two outs in the last inning of the World Series, a catcher [such as Brooklyn's Mickey Owen in 1941] can drop the ball that was the third strike, throw it wild, and then you can score four runs or whatever, and the Yankees beat the Dodgers. Mickey Owen! Man, I mean, you know, Cookie Lavagetto!
>
> Baseball is a wonderful game that teaches lessons: Never quit; the game's not over until the last batter is out. It is a game that instructs, and I like the lessons that come out of baseball—the fact that you can't win it alone; you can't even throw a pitch alone; you need somebody to catch it. The pitcher and catcher can't win it alone. I won-der if in the Don Larsen perfect game, if there were any other heroics by anyone else in that game, besides the pitcher and catcher. Were they all routine outs? He couldn't do it without those players in the field. You have

to depend on everybody doing their job to do a perfect game. That's an important lesson.

The roots of Italian immigrants such as the DiMaggios were in the suburbs of Palermo; those of the Cuomo family were in Salerno, south of Naples. Joe DiMaggio's father, Giuseppe, immigrated to America's West Coast, where he became a fisherman in the San Francisco area. Mario Cuomo's father, Andrea, came to the States in 1926 and settled in the East, taking work as a ditch-digger in Jersey City. In 1927, he was joined by his wife, Immaculata, and their infant son, Frank. The family settled in Queens and started a grocery store in 1931, during the Depression. At first, neither could read or write English, but working around-the-clock, they made the store a success. Mario was born in 1932 in the back room of the store, with the help of a midwife. He was about twelve when a family friend named Tony Boscaino took him to a game at Yankee Stadium. "Mario," Boscaino said when he arrived at the grocery store, "today, you're going to see the great DiMaggio."

No one had to tell the boy about DiMaggio; Mario was always hearing the ball player's name throughout the neighborhood, where the Italian people sang songs about Joltin' Joe in their native tongue. Mario would read the stories about DiMaggio in the newspapers and listen to games on the radio. He would close his eyes with the radio on and imagine the graceful DiMaggio running back to the wall in center field and leaping at the last second to make a sensational catch. Young Mario possessed a vivid imagination; to him, DiMaggio strode with the gods. But more than that, he was an Italian. "He's a world hero, and he's Italian like you, and some people try to make fun of you because of that," Cuomo reminisces, "but then you think and hear about Joe DiMaggio, and you are proud and reinforced."

The melting-pot neighborhood where Cuomo grew up was a forest of tenements. There were no big dreams; all anyone yearned for was a home and a job. It was a place where few people could afford college and many were unable to speak English. "We didn't have any teachers; we didn't have any cops," Cuomo recalls. "We had a lot of laborers."

Mario's brother served two hitches in the service; his sister worked in the family store. "Once, my sister got to be Stanley Gerts's secretary in the S. Gerts Department Store in Jamaica, which meant she could get jobs for all the guys for inventory-taking. Let me tell you, in my neighborhood, that meant my sister was a queen. All the guys would say, 'Mary—be nice to Mary.'"

Jobs were at a premium, and when Tony Boscaino landed a civil-service position with the Sanitation Department, there was a block party in his honor. A civil-service job was something to be treasured, a sign of security and status.

Money and jobs might have been scarce in the neighborhood, but there was plenty of baseball. The quiet, somewhat introverted Mario shared his baseball heroes with his close friends, Boscaino, Willie Golowski, and Artie Foster. When Hank Greenberg came to town with the Detroit Tigers, Foster, who was Jewish, would tell his friends to call him Hank. When Whitey Kurowski of the Cardinals came, Golowski, who was of Polish descent, told his pals to call him Whitey. Mario, of course, wanted people to call him Joe. "There was a strong identification," Cuomo remembers fondly. "You were so proud of those players."

When Boscaino took him to Yankee Stadium, the only seats they could afford were up in the bleachers. Mario watched DiMaggio's every move, although as seen from the bleachers, the Yankee Clipper was merely a white-uniformed speck on the green expanse of the outfield. Cuomo didn't care. On that day, he finally was sharing the stadium with his idol. To him, DiMaggio represented dignity and excellence; he was an uplifting role model who led by example and espoused the values that shaped Cuomo's moral philosophy. Joe DiMaggio was everything Mario Cuomo wanted to be.

"The game was easy to become attached to, and yes, of course, it was particularly meaningful to me because Joe DiMaggio played center field," Cuomo says. "Baseball was a wonderful game of imagination because it was on the radio all the time. You had to imagine everything: the ball hitting the wall, what DiMaggio looked like and—what is a Pee Wee Reese?" By the time he was twelve, he knew the statistics of every Yankees player by heart.

In 1947, when he was fifteen, there was something new in the neighborhood—television. On one October afternoon, Cuomo rushed off the subway in Queens and ran up to the Jamaica Refrigeration and Television store, across the street from his parents' grocery. There, he stood among a crowd staring at a small black-and-white screen inside the store window. They were watching a telecast of the World Series, and Bill Bevens of the Yankees was working on a no-hitter against the Dodgers in Brooklyn. With two out and two on in the bottom of the ninth inning, Cookie Lavagetto came to bat. Cuomo raised himself on his tiptoes, trying to get as close as possible to the window. He could barely hear the sound—there was no outside speaker—but the door to the store was open. Cuomo was delighted that Bevens was on the verge of becoming the first player to pitch a no-hitter in a World Series. Then came the shock. Lavagetto lined a double, scoring two runs, and the Dodgers won, 3–2. The Brooklyn fans were delirious. Cuomo just hung his head and slowly walked home.

As a player, Cuomo would create his own baseball heroics. He was an outstanding player on a talent-laden high school team at St. John's Prep. Five of his teammates signed professional contracts and played in the minor leagues. Cuomo was an excellent student, and his college options after graduation in 1949 included an athletic scholarship to Hofstra University and an academic scholarship to St. John's. He was determined to play center field in college, and his first choice was Hofstra. "I was there one day," he recalls, "and they told me, 'You have to go out for the track team.' I asked them why. They told me, 'Because we want you on the track team; you have an athletic scholarship, and you're very fast.' I told them, 'Yes, I am fast, but I'm not going to run. I play baseball. When I'm not playing baseball, I have other things to do, like going to school and working.' They said, 'No, you have to go out for track.' I told them, 'Forget about it.' And I went to St. John's."

In September 1949 he enrolled at St. John's. He won the center-field job for the school's freshman baseball team, coached by Lou Carnesecca, who went on to become one of the nation's most successful college basketball coaches. Cuomo finished with an average of .286, and Carnesecca was impressed. "He was young, but he was a heck of a player," Carnesecca recalls. "He was an excellent fielder, had a gun for an arm, could run, and had some power. The guy was a tremendous competitor, and he was a natural leader. The other players looked up to him."

Off the field, Cuomo also made his mark. "He was a good student and very serious about school," Carnesecca says.

> But Mario was a regular guy; he mixed in with the other guys, he liked to play basketball, and he was a lot of fun. I got to know him as a person, and he was always concerned about other people and helping them. He was interested in what you might call the little people, and he hasn't changed in that regard.
>
> He likes to be with people, regular people. I can't remember if we had a captain for the freshman team, but Mario was the leader. He had talent, he was competitive, and everyone respected him. He was a ball player who was fun to coach.

During the spring season of 1950, Cuomo raised his average to .360, but there was a problem: What position would he play? Cuomo was determined to play center field, but an injury to the team's catcher changed those plans. The varsity coach was Frank McGuire, who, like Carnesecca, would go on to earn national fame as a basketball coach. McGuire wanted to convert Cuomo to catcher. One day, after practice, McGuire came up to Cuomo.

"You're going to be my catcher," Cuomo remembers the coach telling him.

"No, I'm not going to be your catcher," replied Cuomo, stubborn and independent as ever.

"Why not?"

"I don't catch. I play a little first, I pitch once in a while, but mostly I play center field."

"But why don't you catch?"

"Because I don't want to get hurt catching. I'm no dummy."

Cuomo says McGuire then decided to demonstrate his own brand of hardball. Joe Repice, a close friend of Cuomo's, was also a member of the team. "Listen, Repice is a good friend of yours," Cuomo recalls McGuire telling him. "If you catch, I keep Repice. If you don't catch, Repice is off the club."

Cuomo was furious. "I went to Repice, told him the story and said, 'Joe, what does it mean to you?' He cursed for about five minutes and said, 'He can't do anything to me because my scholarship is good whether I play or not.'"

As for himself, Cuomo wasn't worried because he had an academic scholarship. "I didn't have to play baseball," he says. "So the next day, I go up to McGuire, hand him the catcher's mitt and say, 'Coach, you know what you can do with that glove.'"

Cuomo left the St. John's team but didn't give up baseball. He spent most of the 1951 season playing semipro ball under such assumed names as Matt Dente, Glendy LaDuke, Connie Cutts, and Lava Labretti. "I can't use my real name," he explains, "because I'm illegal; I'm getting money to play baseball."

While playing semipro ball, Cuomo competed against such future big-league stars as Whitey Ford and Billy Loes. During one game in which Cuomo faced Ford, Pittsburgh Pirates scout Ed McCarrick was impressed by Cuomo's speed and intensity, and wrote in one report: "He is aggressive and plays hard. . . . Will run over you if you get in his way."

In August 1951 McCarrick offered Cuomo a $2,000 bonus to sign with the Pirates. Cuomo, who was about to start his junior year at St. John's, would be due to report to the minor leagues in the spring of 1952. He would be sent to Class D, where most untried prospects reported. Cuomo wasn't sure about signing, and there was another problem: He was underage and would need his father's permission. One day, McCarrick showed up at the Cuomo grocery store to talk it over with the father and son. There, with salami and provolone hanging behind the counter, a heart-to-heart talk began between an immigrant father and his American-born son.

Andrea Cuomo told his son to forget baseball and concentrate on school.

"Pa, do you realize they want to give me $2,000?" young Mario told his dad.

"I don't care. You have to go to school; you're still in school."

"Pa, I'll go to school. Don't worry."

"No, no, no. I checked with Tony Boscaino, and he says they start playing very early in the spring, and you're supposed to be in school, and you won't go to school. You can't sign no contract."

"But, Pa, it's $2,000. Do you know how hard you have to work and how long it takes to make $2,000?"

"I don't care about money. You're staying in school. Forget baseball."

Then, Mario Cuomo had an idea. He asked McCarrick to find out whether Branch Rickey, the legendary baseball executive who was running the Pirates, would intervene. Rickey, who had left the Dodgers to become general manager at Pittsburgh, was building a farm system based on speed, and Cuomo was his type of player. McCarrick persuaded Rickey to write a letter to Cuomo's father.

"He went on and on," Mario Cuomo recalls. "Rickey told my father what a wonderful thing it was that he wanted me to stay in school and what a smart man he was to want his son to have an education. He said he agreed with my father and said his letter was a guarantee that his son would never have to play baseball while he's in school; he can come to spring training during Easter vacation and join the team when the school year ends. He said I would not miss one day of school."

Rickey's word was good enough for the father, who proceeded to sign his son's contract.

In 1952, Cuomo was ready to leave for spring training in Florida but was filled with self-doubt: He wasn't sure he even wanted to be a baseball player. He loved school and had met a young woman named Matilda Raffa, a student at St. John's. She didn't care for baseball, especially if it meant that Mario had to leave home and play in Georgia for the entire summer. "I'm not marrying any baseball player," she told him. Cuomo had his own doubts. "I just didn't think I was good enough," he remembers. "I never saw the scouting report; I never knew that they thought I was that good."

Mario Cuomo was confronting a moral dilemma. He had already accepted the $2,000 bonus; in fact, he used part of it to buy Matilda an engagement ring. Now, he didn't want to play, so he decided to talk the situation over with the Rev. Edward Caulfield, an English professor at St. John's.

"First, I asked Eddie McCarrick, the scout who signed me, what would happen to this contract if I decided not to play," Cuomo recalls. "He told me that nobody could force me to play and that I could keep the money. He said if I decided to play someday, I would have to play for Pittsburgh and nobody else; that's all it meant."

Still, he needed to talk with Father Caulfield. "Father," he said, "I don't think I should go down there. I'm not good enough to play with those guys."

"Why not?"

"I'm just not. I'm a sandlot player, and this is professional ball. I can't see myself making a living playing baseball. That's not the way I want to spend my life. I'm not in shape, I've been in school, I've been working, I'm playing ball once a week on Sunday, but these guys down there have been playing every day. I can't go down to Georgia and play every day."

"Look, literally, technically, you're not doing anything wrong if you don't go. But the truth is, it will disappoint McCarrick's expectations—he will look very bad, and it's unfair to him."

"Well, Father, if I go, I'm not going to last, anyway. I'm not good enough."

The priest looked Cuomo in the eye. His voice was stern yet soft: "I think you should go and make an effort."

"Okay."

There was a pat on the back from the priest. And a good-luck handshake. Then, in what seemed like a blur, Mario Cuomo went home to Queens. Inside his room behind the grocery store, he packed a little bag, trying to hide his nervousness. He kissed his parents good-bye and boarded a bus heading due south—for a long, hot summer in a place where you just didn't find people named Mario.

At first, everything was surprisingly easy in Brunswick. Cuomo even seemed to play somewhat like DiMaggio. He had ample strength, and his swing was smooth. In the outfield, he had more than enough speed, enabling him to catch everything that came his way. In his first game, he went 1 for 3, and after about six weeks, he was hitting .353. But then the problems began. He was chasing a fly ball that had been hit over his head when he ran at full speed into an outfield wall. His wrist was badly sprained, and he wanted to rest. "They told me, 'Don't worry; keep playing,'" he recalls. "I said, 'I can't throw.' They said, 'That's okay; we want you to get game experience.'"

The pain affected his batting stroke, resulting in an 0 for 32 slump. "Playing with that injury ruined me," he says, not to mention the heat. The Pirates played seven days a week, including doubleheaders on Sundays; the temperature was known to reach 115 degrees. "Georgia was the worst state in the universe for heat; it was suffocating and oppressive," Cuomo recalls. "I wouldn't take salt tablets; nobody ever told me to take them. I played in the civilized Northeast; you didn't take salt tablets. If it was hot, it was hot for one day, and you didn't worry about running out of liquids in your body. It was different in Georgia. Down there, you would sweat so much you dried up like a Ry-Krisp." One day, Cuomo passed out from dehydration, but he was back in the lineup the next day. "I had to," he says. "I was a tough kid from Queens trying to make it."

How tough? You might ask the opposing catcher who once made an ethnic slur while Cuomo was at bat. He got punched in the facemask by Cuomo, who at six feet and 170 pounds was about two inches shorter and about twenty pounds lighter than his idol, Di-Maggio. Years later, Cuomo would dismiss the incident as nothing more than self-defense. "Mario was one real tough son of a gun," says Fred Green, who was a twenty-game winner with Brunswick that year and later pitched a handful of big-league seasons, including 1960 in Pittsburgh, when the Pirates won the World Series. "He wasn't a bully, and he wasn't a loudmouth, but when he got on the field, he wasn't going to back down from anybody. In the clubhouse, Mario was a lot of fun, and a nice fellow. I'll tell you, he was a darn good outfielder who could run, and he went all-out on every play. You won't find a tougher competitor; I thought he had pretty good potential to be a major-leaguer."

So did Branch Rickey, who five years earlier had brought Jackie Robinson into the big leagues. In one of his scouting reports, he wrote that Cuomo was "potentially the best prospect on the club."

During the 1952 season, Mario "Matt" Cuomo had these statistics in 81 games: offensively, 254 at-bats, 31 runs, 62 hits, a .244 batting average, 79 total bases, 10 doubles, 2 triples, 1 home run, 26 runs batted in, 6 sacrifices, 7 stolen bases, 54 walks and 55 strikeouts; defensively, in center field, 170 putouts, 10 assists, 6 errors, 2 double plays, and a .968 fielding percentage.

He also was hit by three pitched balls, but the only one that anybody seems to remember is the third. "That was one of the scariest things I've ever seen happen on a baseball field," says Fred Green, who now watches his son Gary play in the majors. "We were all scared because Mario got hit right in the back of the head and was knocked out. We knew it was bad. We were all young kids down there, and when we saw our teammate put on a stretcher and taken to the hospital, it shook everybody up."

In that game of Thursday, August 28, 1952, on a sunny day in Georgia, Mario Cuomo's professional baseball career ended. "I never knew how seriously he was hurt," Jack Barbier, who threw the fateful pitch, said in an interview with Ken Goldfarb of the *Schenectady Gazette* in 1988, when Cuomo recalled with amusement that he and Barbier were "probably the only Italian guys in the league and were beating up on each other." After Cuomo was hit, Barbier remembered, someone ran out with a cup of water—and the umpire drank it.

But none of it seemed funny at the time. Cuomo was diagnosed as having a blood clot near the brain and was hospitalized for nearly two weeks. After he was released, he went straight home to Queens. With no regrets. "When I got hit, it was the end of my baseball career, but it was probably the best thing that could have happened to me," Cuomo says now. "I wanted to go back to school; I wanted to be a teacher. I just didn't want to give my life to baseball. To succeed in that game, you have to want it bad, and I didn't want it bad enough."

What he did want badly enough was to graduate from St. John's *summa cum laude* in 1953, marry Matilda Raffa in 1954, and get a degree from St. John's Law School in 1956, tying for first in his class. The fact that Judge Adrian Burke of New York State's highest court, the Court of Appeals, had been a college shortstop at Holy Cross helped Cuomo land a job as Burke's confidential legal assistant that same year.

Eventually Cuomo entered private practice and taught law at St. John's. He turned to politics and in 1974 lost in his first bid for the statewide office of lieutenant governor. Governor Hugh Carey named him secretary of state in 1975, but Cuomo once again lost an election in 1977, when he ran for mayor of New York City. Finally, in 1978, Cuomo won an election as lieutenant governor. From there, for this father of five, it was on to the governorship in 1982 and a meteoric rise to the upper reaches of American politics. A long way from center field on a Class D ball club.

Mickey Mantle, who was DiMaggio's successor in center field

for the New York Yankees, has teased Cuomo about their early baseball careers. "Cuomo couldn't hit a curve with a barn," Mantle said during a visit to Buffalo. Cuomo, though, is quick to remind the Hall of Famer that his signing bonus was $2,000—$900 more than Mantle's. "I played one season, and Mantle goes on to become one of the greatest of all time," he notes with a laugh. "That's how good the scout was who signed me."

For Mario Cuomo, such irreverent repartee evokes animated memories of all the bench-jockeying that enlivened those dusty, sun-baked diamonds of the Deep South in that summer of 1952. He's reminded that even though his batting average was a modest .244, his on-base percentage—which takes into consideration the fifty-four times he walked and the three times he was hit by pitched balls—was actually .383. Before leaving the Capitol meeting room with the high ceiling and the huge dark-oak table, the governor of New York State stops and flashes a contented smile. "Three-eighty-three," he says with a surge of self-satisfaction. "When they ask you how Cuomo did, you tell them, 'Three-eighty-three.'"

Jauntily, he leaves the room, going back to the business of trying to keep 18 million people happy. Quite often, that business takes him back home to New York City, the place where he fell in love with baseball. It is there, in his office high in the World Trade Center in Manhattan, that he keeps two of his most prized possessions: a baseball and a picture, both autographed by Joe DiMaggio.

IN THE END, Jimmy Griffin and Mario Cuomo knew that baseball—so identified with the public interest—was bigger than both of them. Its impact on a community went far deeper than the game itself. "There's the pride factor and morale factor," Cuomo says.

> That's very important and badly needed. Baseball is important to a place like New York City or Buffalo. New York City is now having its days of sadness. God forbid you took away the Yankees or the Mets. They need it. They represent the community's identity; you know, "We are a city—Buffalo—and we can compete with New York. We can compete with Toronto and Cleveland; we're going

to eat Cleveland alive." They do it in football, but it's more important that you do it in baseball, because that's the American measurement more than football. So baseball is important to a community's morale; it's a cause. And a major-league team is important to the economy.

Buffalo's deteriorating downtown commercial district was sorely in need of a symbol of hope, and to Griffin and Cuomo, the question answered itself: What better than a ballpark?

When Cuomo first went to Buffalo, "it was really down, and he's a big guy when it comes to pulling for the underdog," says New York public relations man Marty Steadman, who had been in the New York Yankees' front office for seven years before serving as Cuomo's press secretary for a few years beginning in 1984. "He likes to target assistance where it's needed most, and back then, Buffalo needed it bad."

Pure and simple, Buffalo needed $22.5 million from the state for a stadium project that would cost $56.4 million. After holding a public meeting in Buffalo in the autumn of 1984, and then talking to local business and government representatives, Cuomo had the answers he needed. "We tried to do as much for Buffalo as we could," Cuomo says. "I was confident they would draw fans in that park. I thought it was a good investment, good for the spirit of the community, but I have to say Jimmy Griffin was the principal force and deserves the credit. He made a good case for Buffalo."

It was a case made by one former street kid—one former sandlot player—to another.

In February 1985 Cuomo submitted a bill to appropriate $22.5 million for the Buffalo stadium. Cuomo told the state legislature that "the Buffalo sports stadium will be an especially important component of the overall economic revitalization program for that area so much in need of economic expansion," and the lawmakers agreed.

Jimmy Griffin and Bob Rich were ecstatic. Griffin gave the governor an effusive public thank-you. Rich spoke for Griffin and the rest of the baseball fans in the community by putting the news in a major-league context: "With the stadium, Buffalo has become a legitimate expansion candidate."

But first things first. "Building a baseball field," W. P. Kinsella wrote in his novel *Shoeless Joe,* "is more work than you might imagine." Buffalo and Erie County had scars to prove it. This time, things had to be different.

10

CUTTING A DIAMOND

In 1985, with the big hit for $22.5 million by Mario Cuomo and the state legislature, the financial bases were loaded for Buffalo's proposed baseball stadium. This time, the path to home plate didn't seem to be a mine field, but Chuck Rosenow knew better. "The implication in the media was, "Okay, we got the money, we got the stadium,'" Rosenow recalls. "But it wasn't going to be that easy."

Two years earlier, Buffalo Mayor Jimmy Griffin had named Rosenow to head the Buffalo Development Companies, the city's economic-development agency. Rosenow had been community-development coordinator under Griffin's predecessor, Stanley Makowski, and worked on the mayoral transition team before Griffin took office. Rosenow left city government in 1977 and spent five years with the Erie County Industrial Development Agency before returning to City Hall as full-time coordinator of the stadium project. He had been following the downtown stadium proposal since day one, in the late seventies, because it was classified as an economic-development project. He also was a student of local history: "There was a horrendous inferiority complex in this community—that no civic project could be done right."

He was well aware that the city and county governments had the reputation of shooting themselves in the foot when faced with big projects. Beginning in the late sixties, there was the seemingly endless saga of the domed stadium that was never built in the suburb of Lancaster. Before it was over, a couple of former Erie County legislators went to jail for conspiracy to take bribes, several architects were indicted, and the county spent fifteen years—and untold legal fees—in court before being ordered to pay the developer more than $10 million as a settlement. The proposal to follow Kansas City's example and build twin stadiums—one for football, the other for baseball—never got off the ground. Two possibilities for revitalizing downtown—an 80,000-seat football stadium and a mammoth campus for the State University of New York at Buffalo—ended up being built deep in the suburbs at sites that weren't easy for city residents to reach by public transit. Once such proposals entered the Byzantine labyrinths of City Hall or County Hall, the outcome was anyone's guess. In the midst of it all, the vital core of the city had been shriveling away.

Now that the downtown stadium proposal had taken wing, Griffin was confident that Rosenow would keep it from crash landing. "Chuck," said Griffin, "is the best technician in New York State who works for government." Rosenow himself was ready to go as many extra innings as necessary, quipping that "I always used to get an A in perseverance at School 38."

Another factor working in Chuck Rosenow's favor was passion: He loved baseball.

Rosenow, who grew up on Buffalo's West Side, graduated from Canisius College and earned a master's degree in urban planning from New York University, treasured his memories of Buffalo baseball. As a youngster during the fifties, he and his brother, Al, who was three years older, would walk about thirty minutes to Offermann Stadium to attend weekend games. They would buy fifty-cent tickets and sit in the bleachers. "Luke Easter was my favorite player," Rosenow recalls fondly. "When you were a kid in Buffalo back in the fifties, baseball was a big thing in your life. I remember they would let us out of school early on Opening Day so we could go to the game." Rosenow spent many a summer evening in his bedroom listening to Bill Mazer announce Bisons games on radio. Mazer, who later gained fame as a TV sportscaster in New York City, spent nearly fifteen years in Buffalo, starting in 1948. "Bill Mazer was my hero," Rosenow says. "He knew everything about baseball and made the game come to life on the radio. I remember one time I even went so far as to try to sneak into Mazer's radio booth at Offermann Stadium."

But like most fans, Rosenow began to lose interest in the Bisons after 1960, when the team moved from homey Offermann Stadium to uninviting War Memorial Stadium. Nevertheless, Buffalo's loss of professional baseball ten years later hurt him as much as anyone. Now, in charge of the downtown stadium project, he saw this ballpark-to-be not only as an insurance policy for keeping pro baseball in the city, but as a down payment on a dream he shared with many other fans: bringing big-league baseball to Buffalo.

In the summer of 1982, Rosenow and the dozen members of the Downtown Baseball Stadium Committee, recently appointed by Griffin, visited Chicago's Wrigley Field and Kansas City's Royals Stadium to observe their operation and design. While in Kansas City, committee members visited the service operation in an area under the ballpark. Griffin noticed hundreds of employees getting ready for a game—ticket-takers, ushers, vendors, parking lot attendants, and dozens of other workers. "There's an awful lot of jobs connected to a baseball team," Griffin said. "We could use those jobs in Buffalo." He also knew that there would be hundreds of construction jobs involved in building the stadium—a shot in the arm for the city's struggling economy.

During the visit to Kansas City, Rosenow arranged a meeting with Ron Labinski, an architect originally from Buffalo, who, like Rosenow, grew up during the fifties with baseball and Luke Easter. Labinski proved invaluable in the early stages of the stadium planning.

Labinski worked for Howard Needles Tammen & Bergendoff design consultants in Kansas City, and he had personally worked on the design of Royals Stadium. When he and Rosenow got on the subject of Buffalo, Labinski asked, "Do they still sell charcoal-broiled hot dogs at Ted's?"

"They sure do," Rosenow replied, "and when you come back, we'll get some." Rosenow sensed immediately that Labinski retained a strong feeling for his native city. Labinski, who had grown up on Buffalo's East Side, talked about going to baseball games at Offermann Stadium and cheering for Luke Easter. After discussion with other committee members, the architect agreed to participate in the stadium project as supervising architect. Warned by Rosenow that there was little money, Labinski still agreed to do much of the preliminary work and said that even if the group ran out of money, he would keep working until more funding could be obtained.

Labinski, Rosenow, and the stadium committee believed that

Royals Stadium was the perfect model for Buffalo's ballpark. "We wanted to keep the stadium small, about 40,000 seats, and we wanted to keep it filled," Rosenow says. "It would be a regional franchise and reach out to small towns and to people who would bring their families to the games. The psychology was that you could have a good time at the ballpark and that you would keep coming back." Labinski understood Buffalo and its goals for a baseball stadium. Although his role in the project would eventually diminish, he was able to articulate those goals forcefully during public meetings in the project's early stages.

By the end of the summer, the stadium committee was ready to have plans put on the drawing board. A group known as the Buffalo Architects Collaborative had been reviewing four prospective sites, and the architects and stadium committee selected the one at Washington and Swan Streets, catercorner from Ellicott Square, where some scenes for *The Natural* had been filmed, and near the heart of the Joseph Ellicott Historic District. Although the stadium plan was gaining considerable publicity, most people in Buffalo weren't taking it seriously; they had been burned before. Soon the project was dubbed "Griffin's folly."

Chuck Rosenow not only had to contend with public cynicism, but also with the New York State bureaucracy, politicians, taxpayers, contractors, architects, labor unions, citizen groups, environmentalists, the news media, preservationists, funding shortages, and a pervasive mood of impatience.

Of Rosenow's myriad headaches, perhaps the most persistent was money: There never seemed to be any. The stadium committee had already spent its entire $25,000 budget, yet Rosenow needed seven times more to pay for a stadium study. After five months, appeals to the private sector, including the Greater Buffalo Chamber of Commerce and labor unions, had raised a grand total of $8,800. So Rosenow, with the help of William Donohue—director of the Erie County Industrial Development Agency and a crucial figure early in the stadium project—went scrounging for public funds and managed to scrape up the $175,000 through grants. Also instrumental in obtaining funds for the stadium was Richard Swist, who succeeded Donohue as director of the county agency in 1983. Early in 1983, the city created Buffalo Development Companies to combine public, nonprofit agencies and to provide a way to get things done outside the normal mechanics of city government.

The stadium study was completed in November 1983, and its primary recommendation was for an $89 million, 40,000-seat, multipurpose domed stadium. An alternative proposal in the study was to build an open-air, 20,000-seat, baseball-only ballpark. Nobody paid much attention to the alternative, especially after a plastic model of the dome was unveiled by Rich at the 1983 baseball winter meetings in Nashville. (The stadium committee used the $8,800 raised in private funds to pay for the model. "We had to do something with that money," Rosenow said. "The people who donated were calling up demanding we give it back to them.")

Rosenow advised Griffin that the stadium project should follow a dual strategy. "We thought the community could afford a 15,000-seat, Triple-A stadium," Rosenow says. "If we can get something more, we'll try to get it. But if we ended up with a 15,000-seat, Triple-A stadium, that was certainly a lot better than playing Double-A ball in War Memorial Stadium."

Griffin still wanted a dome and asked Cuomo and the state to contribute $40 million for the $89 million dome project. But in 1984, Cuomo was skeptical.

Buffalo was not the only state city seeking aid for a sports facility. The state had formed an authority known as Sportsplex to decide on funding for sports projects, and Buffalo was competing for funds with New York City, Albany, and Binghamton. Griffin and Rosenow believed that there was a decidedly anti-Buffalo bias in Sportsplex, which sent a consultant to Buffalo in an effort to determine how many people the city would draw in a new, 20,000-seat stadium. The Sportsplex consultant calculated that about 237,000 people would turn out for Triple-A baseball.

Frank McGuire, a businessman who was the lone Buffalo representative on Sportsplex, spent most of his time fighting for his city and making its case. "McGuire prevented the state consultants from killing the whole project," Rosenow says. According to Griffin, "the state had it in for Buffalo, and without Frank McGuire, we would never have had a chance." Griffin and Rosenow continued to plead with the state for funding, and McGuire told them that Buffalo's best chance would be to build a smaller, expandable stadium. Griffin, abandoning his hope for a dome, agreed.

Rosenow and the stadium committee weren't waiting for the state. In March 1984 they hired architects from Hellmuth, Obata & Kassabaum Sports Facilities Group in Kansas City to continue design work, and ordered an environmental-impact study. In June, Sportsplex recommended that the governor approve a $22.5 million grant to Buffalo for an expandable, 20,000-seat stadium. Three months later, Bob Rich bought the Triple-A baseball franchise that had been in Wichita. All things considered, the stadium project seemed to be picking up the momentum it needed.

Politics in Buffalo, though, resembled rugby more than baseball. The first political scuffle involving the stadium project came in the Buffalo Common Council, whose members had been warring with Griffin for years. For six years, the council had little or no input into the stadium project. Now, in 1985, it was the council's turn at bat, and there was certain to be opposition. After heated discussions, the council did approve the stadium site at Washington and Swan Streets but would not approve a bond issue, which included money for land acquisition. Despite the state money, it appeared that the stadium project might not get off the ground.

Griffin was incensed and called the dissenting council members "goofs" for their lack of leadership. Rosenow, suddenly without a means to buy the land for the stadium, devised an alternative plan in which the stadium committee and the Erie County Industrial Development Agency obtained a loan commitment from local construction unions' pension funds. The only problem was that the interest rate would be about 14 percent, compared with 7 percent if the council had approved the bond issue. Rosenow worked out a compromise with Council President George Arthur—who would run against Griffin for mayor in November—and Councilman David Collins to gain their support. Finally in July 1985 the council saved the city millions of dollars in interest costs when it approved, 11 to 2, the issuance of $5.6 million in city bonds. "Things like this kept happening throughout the project," says Bill Gisel, Bob Rich's coordinator for the stadium project. "Just when we were about to give up hope, Rosenow would figure something out. Every time there was an obstacle, he came in to save the bacon."

The next test came in September, when Councilman Alfred Coppola, one of the dissenters on the bond vote and a staunch foe of Griffin, spearheaded a petition drive to force the stadium-funding issue to a public referendum. The drive needed 18,519 signatures to put the issue on the ballot, and 26,964 signatures were secured, but the whole issue became moot when the Erie County Board of Elections ruled them all invalid because the signatures had not been "properly acknowledged" by the people soliciting them.

The state Department of Transportation expressed concern that the stadium as originally designed would encroach two feet onto Thruway property. The department told Rosenow that it would take up to eleven years to complete an environmental-impact statement for the Federal Highway Administration. Rosenow was incredulous: "Eleven years, can you believe it?" The design was changed, and the stadium site was moved about thirty feet back to ensure that it was not on the highway. The result of this thirty-foot switch was that seats were moved closer to the field, giving the park a cozier atmosphere.

Supporters of the stadium finally received some good news when U.S. Senator Daniel Patrick Moynihan of New York engineered a change in the tax code language, allowing the project to be financed with tax-exempt bonds. That saved "millions of dollars," Rosenow said, cutting the cost of building the stadium to about $42 million and the total price of the stadium project, which included two parking ramps, to $56.4 million. Another boost came when Pilot Air Freight Corporation bought naming rights to the stadium for $1.02 million. Ironically, it was the Rich family who in 1972 had purchased naming rights to the county football stadium, although the Riches had no ties to the Bills' ownership, which was based in Detroit.

There seemed to be no end to the hurdles confronting Rosenow, whose diplomacy prevented any of them from becoming insurmountable. The name of the game was "compromise."

"Preservationists were upset about the visual impact of the stadium and parking lots in the Joseph Ellicott Historic District. They threatened to file suit to halt the project, until there was some compromise on its design. Griffin appointed a nineteen-member design committee to help solve the problem. Even though the resulting change added about $4 million to the cost, Rosenow said, "It was well worth the money."

But there was always another brushfire to put out. Common Council demanded money to demolish War Memorial Stadium and redevelop it as a neighborhood athletic facility. The council required guarantees that at least 15 percent of the construction workers and 30 percent of the operational personnel on the stadium project be minorities. In addition, a no-strike clause was negotiated with construction unions.

At long last, everything appeared to be in place for a ground-breaking in July 1986. But another problem surfaced when it was determined that there would be a $1.7 million cost overrun. The council would not approve the bids and was threatening to delay the entire project.

Griffin and Rosenow were determined that the ground-breaking would not be delayed. The mayor called the governor and told him that the ground-breaking would be held Thursday, July 11. Rosenow quickly arranged public funding to make up the $1.7 million overrun but needed council approval. The council scheduled a meeting Tuesday night and approved last-minute funding, after agreement was reached that the contractor, not the city, would pay for cost overruns. Councilman David Rutecki, chairman of the stadium task force, was instrumental in the compromise, and it came none too soon. "If they hadn't," said Rosenow, "we might have had a ground-breaking with no money for the project."

Cuomo, Griffin, Rosenow, Robert Rich, Bob Rich, Council President George Arthur, and council members attended the ceremony, which attracted nearly 300 spectators. Cuomo described the stadium project as a "celebration of Buffalo's spirit."

For the time being at least, it was full speed ahead. Jimmy Griffin and Bob Rich, both jubilant, echoed each other's words: Without Chuck Rosenow, there would be no downtown stadium.

The same could be said for an inspiring little white-haired gentleman who was in the crowd on this sunny summer afternoon that symbolized so much to his city. It was the same white-haired gentleman who seven years earlier had spoken out about a stadium during the meeting that got the ball rolling in the right direction.

VINCE MCNAMARA LOOKED around the room and sensed that this would be a momentous meeting. It was July 1979, and the Citizens Committee of the Erie County Sports Board was ready to make the first symbolic gesture toward the building of a downtown stadium in Buffalo: giving the go-ahead for a study. McNamara was determined that it be done right, because he knew that baseball's future in Buffalo depended on it. Although a new stadium was only in the talking stage, McNamara believed that he had to make a point: "Fellas, this has to be an open-air stadium with natural grass. That's the way baseball was meant to be played."

The talk back then was that northern cities needed domed stadiums, but Vince McNamara wouldn't hear of it—not for baseball: "There's no reason to put a roof on a stadium and play baseball on a pool table." And that was that.

At age seventy-one, the fiery McNamara still had vivid memories of his childhood, of the streets and coal yards of South Buffalo's First Ward. There was a place called Gaelic Field, where all the neighborhood kids gathered for pickup baseball games on warm summer afternoons. There weren't any bases; the kids used bricks instead. And when there was a close play, young Vince would slide into the brick, get up and slowly pick the stones and splinters out of his behind. To Vince McNamara, that was what baseball was all about: a summer game to be reveled in with childlike joy, under warm sunshine and on the green grass he never knew at Gaelic Field.

The Erie County Sports Board and its Citizens Committee were formed in 1979 with a joint $25,000 grant from Erie County and the City of Buffalo. The Citizens Committee had sixteen members, including such dedicated baseball people as Frank Offermann, Jr., son of the former Bisons owner, and sportscaster Ralph Hubbell. The mayor knew that such a group wouldn't be complete without Vince McNamara, so he appointed his old friend from the First Ward. "Vince McNamara was unlike most people in sports or politics or public life," Griffin says. "If he saw something he thought was wrong and should be corrected, he didn't talk about it or ask others to take care of it, he did it himself. That's Vince, a real doer."

In 1981, consultants hired by the Erie County Industrial Development Agency completed a study showing that Buffalo could support a major-league team.

This was no news to Vince McNamara. He had known it all along. But with more Opening Days behind him than ahead, he wanted—more than anything else—to make sure that it happened in his lifetime.

That lifetime had been devoted to the community and to the game.

Although only five feet, seven inches, and 138 pounds, McNamara the youth was a ferocious competitor in football, basketball, and baseball. A devout Catholic, he recalls that as an altar boy he had to fight his way across the railroad tracks in the tough First Ward to serve Mass.

McNamara had made his mark in basketball as a member of the 1929 Buffalo YMCA national championship team. His football career came to a sudden halt, though, when he suffered a broken collarbone while diving for a loose ball in his first day of practice at Canisius College.

He was nineteen when he realized a boyhood dream by playing in an International League game for his hometown team. On September 27, 1927, he played in the second game of a Buffalo-Syracuse doubleheader at Bison Stadium, replacing regular shortstop Andy Cohen. He was hitless in two at-bats but handled three fielding chances flawlessly. For McNamara, who was to spend most of the rest of his life in baseball, that was to be his only game as a full-fledged professional, although he was to perform in hundreds of amateur and semipro contests. While regularly employed by the Buffalo Parks and Recreation Department, McNamara found time to become a highly regarded official in baseball, basketball, and football. He umpired for a while in the Pony League, now called the New York–Pennsylvania League, on which he left an indelible imprint.

Bob Stedler, sports editor of the *Buffalo Evening News,* was president of the league, which began play in 1939 and is the oldest continually operating Class A league in professional baseball. When he retired from that part-time position in 1948, Vince McNamara succeeded him. For the next thirty-seven years, McNamara guided the rookie league through a rocky struggle to survival, coping with perpetual money shortages, a lack of working agreements, and inadequate ballparks. Many times, he dipped into his own pocket to pay urgent bills.

In the early 1950s, McNamara designed one of the first working agreements in rookie-league history between the Boston Red Sox and the Corning franchise. By 1962 he had lined up player-development contracts for every club in his league. Cy Williams, a longtime major-league talent scout from South Buffalo, says flatly that "Vince was the guy who made that league work."

There was an irascible, even pugnacious, manner to McNamara. He enjoyed deflating the egos of pompous baseball owners and executives. He stuck up for umpires and would not tolerate players' abusing the officials or fans, or using profanity. Thanks to McNamara's efforts, the New York–Penn League not only survived, but became an incubator for such future stars as Sal Maglie, Don Zimmer, Nellie Fox, Pete Rose, Tony Perez, Phil Niekro, Dwight Gooden, Wade Boggs, and Don Mattingly.

As the years went by, just about everybody in baseball knew Vince McNamara, who went by the nickname "Mr. Mac." He was named to baseball's Rules Committee, and one of his most memorable days was when he went to New York for his first meeting with that group.

"I was awed when I walked in and saw I was in the company of Hall of Famers like Bill Terry, Hank Greenberg, and Joe Cronin," McNamara says with emotion. "I just realized how far a kid from the First Ward could go in this country."

In 1972 McNamara was honored by organized baseball at its winter meetings as the year's "King of Baseball." When he retired as New York–Penn League president after the 1984 season, baseball again honored McNamara with the George M. Trautman Excellence Award for his years of service to the game.

When Mayor Jimmy Griffin appointed a new group, the Buffalo Stadium Committee, in 1982, Vince McNamara was again called to serve. It was hardly the best of times for Buffalo baseball. The Double-A Eastern League team playing in War Memorial Stadium was in debt and suffering at the gate. There was no interest from big-money people in Buffalo to support the club, which again was in danger of being moved. McNamara was among those working feverishly not only to keep things afloat but to make some progress.

In 1982 he helped coordinate a December meeting in New York with Baseball Commissioner Bowie Kuhn and his staff; McNamara had worked with Kuhn as a member of baseball's Rules Committee. McNamara, whose baseball reputation and sheer force of personality were helpful in any forum where Buffalo's big-league dreams were discussed, made the trip along with Jimmy Griffin, Chuck Rosenow, and Erie County Executive Edward Rutkowski, a former Buffalo Bills player who was a personal and political ally of then-Congressman Jack Kemp. "We just wanted to talk baseball and ask about possible expansion and Buffalo's future," McNamara recalls. "At this point, baseball wasn't even considering expansion, and some people thought we were nuts."

Nuts, yes, to think that Buffalo had much hope of landing a big-league franchise without a new stadium in place. And the lack of an influential prospective owner—or *any* prospective owner, for that matter—didn't help Buffalo's cause, either.

Bob Rich's purchase of the Bisons a month later brightened the ownership picture for the first time; suddenly, there was big money behind baseball in Buffalo. "Once Bob Rich came along, everything took hold," Vince McNamara says. "He was ready to climb every rung of the ladder and do what had to be done, one step at a time. And he did it beautifully."

BOB RICH'S COORDINATOR for the stadium project, Bill Gisel, then the Rich Products corporate counsel as well as vice president and secretary of the Bisons, was in his early thirties and, like Rosenow, had grown up with baseball in Buffalo, with memories of Offermann Stadium. Gisel often had attended games with his father.

"In 1961, when I was eleven, my dad arranged for us to see the World Series between the Yankees and the Reds," Gisel recalls. "He was in Washington on business, and I had to fly alone and meet him in New York. My mom put me on a plane in Buffalo, and I really thought I was cool flying to the World Series by myself. I was so nervous on the plane, I spilled a container of milk on my lap."

The boy and his father made connections at the airport and headed for Yankee Stadium, only to find that their seats were in deep left field and behind a pillar. "I didn't care," the son says. "I saw Roger Maris, Mickey Mantle, and Hector Lopez in the outfield. It was the greatest day of my life."

There would be other memorable baseball days ahead for Gisel, connected with the building of the new stadium in downtown Buffalo. "It was," Gisel says, "the possibility of the new stadium that got Bob involved with baseball in the first place. Once we were in the baseball business, there was never a day that we doubted there would be a new baseball facility."

Like Bob Rich, Gisel graduated from Nichols School—where he played soccer, hockey, and tennis—and Williams College and earned an MBA from the University of Rochester. Gisel, whose law degree is from Emory University, worked with Rich on the deal to buy the Bisons. He says that "from the start, we thought we could make a difference and make baseball work. . . . When Bob took over this team, he certainly wasn't in it for the money. His motivation was to do something for the community and to save baseball."

The stadium project was a textbook example of how business and government can work together for the common good. Rosenow and Gisel made an intriguing team: young, each over six feet tall, slender, intense, athletic, and aggressive. The mustached Rosenow, who was forty-one when ground was finally broken on the project, worked in a cramped, spartan City Hall office, chain-smoking and drinking endless cups of coffee. Gisel, who also was fueled by coffee, pored over papers and blueprints in his spacious office at Rich Products headquarters. Rosenow tends to roll up his sleeves, loosen his tie; Gisel always maintains a buttoned-down look and wears his suitcoat just about everywhere, including at construction sites. Whereas Rosenow tended to be quiet and studious, Gisel employed a quick, darting wit, especially in exchanges with Rich. "You pronounce his name Geezil, as rhyming with weasel," Rich would tease his friend and colleague. Gisel laughingly would reply that Bob Rich is never satisfied and that he won't be happy just owning a major-league baseball team. "Not him," says Gisel, "because once he gets the team, he has to win the World Series."

Gisel, like Rich, was itching to get the stadium project moving.

"We knew we couldn't sit back and wait," he recalls. "We wanted to take bold action and let people know we were fully behind the stadium project. Our rallying cry was that we wanted to bring Triple-A baseball to Buffalo, and then we were going after the major leagues."

Gisel was generous in his praise for Rosenow: "He is far and away the single person most responsible for the success of this project. He was the cog in the wheel that kept everything moving, and all parties moving forward." Rosenow says, "We are a team, and this project showed what can happen when the private sector and the public sector work together. Bill and I understood our responsibilities, and we knew what a new downtown stadium would mean to this community."

The man from municipal government and his sidekick from private enterprise were managing to work their way forward, but when the course seemed steady, a problem would come out of left field— in some cases literally. In the fall of 1986, for instance, Rosenow was contacted by the state Historic Preservation Office concerning archaeological digs. Rosenow said three archaeological studies had already been done on the stadium site over eighteen months, but the state agency wanted another. It believed that the site might be a cemetery from Buffalo's early days. Rosenow said studies had shown that there had been a cemetery there but that it was moved in 1803. "I had to prove to the state that Buffalo wasn't settled by white settlers until 1797," Rosenow recalls. "In the year 1800, our research showed, there were only twelve white settlers in Buffalo. How many people could have been buried in the cemetery by 1803?"

There was another problem: Construction had already started. "I told them on the phone we already had $10 million worth of steel in the ground." The state agency relented, and the long-awaited stadium was one step closer to reality.

There was something to be learned every day. As it turned out, the ballpark's third-base line at one time had been the site of Randall's Boarding House, where Mark Twain lived briefly before getting married in February 1870. Twain lived in Buffalo for a year and a half while he was editor and part-owner of the *Buffalo Express,* which later was part of the merger that created the *Courier-Express,* whose journalistic roster would one day include the likes of Joe Alli and Mike Billoni.

For Chuck Rosenow, Bill Gisel, Vince McNamara, and everyone else connected with the stadium project, the vision—Pilot Field—was no longer a mirage. Mercifully, the winter before it opened was one of the mildest in Buffalo history. January, a month notorious for such natural furies as the blizzards of 1977 and 1985, actually had little snow, low winds, and thirty-one days of sunshine.

The stadium was completed on schedule and $400,000 under budget by Cowper Management Incorporated, the principal stadium contractor. Rod Conrad, stadium project manager for the Erie County Industrial Development Agency, played a crucial role in ironing out construction problems.

The new ballpark turned out to be a bargain for city government, which according to Rosenow paid only $7.7 million of its own funds toward the $42 million stadium. Along with the $22.5 million from the state, he said, there was also $4.2 from Erie County Industrial Development Agency bonds, $4 million from the Buffalo Development Companies, about $3 million from the Riches, and $700,000 from Erie County itself.

Financially, functionally, aesthetically, and symbolically, it was a grand slam.

"Pilot Field symbolized that the city had turned a corner; it was a symbol of the renaissance of Buffalo," Rosenow says. "I think Bob Rich had a lot to do with it. His work with baseball captured the spirit of the community and its people. Griffin was the same way; he believed in baseball and respected what Rich had done. He knew Rich wasn't in this just for the money."

IT WAS BEAUTIFUL.

And if there was an opinion to the contrary, nobody was saying so.

The nightmare had vanished along with the false hopes—all burned away by the radiance of Pilot Field.

Even though the afternoon of Thursday, April 14, 1988, was cold and rainy, nothing so mundane as weather was going to detract from the magic of the moment. This particular Opening Day—Pilot

Field's first—signified not only the rejuvenation of a sport, but the revival of a city.

Buffalo was back.

And the nation was taking notice.

ABCs *Good Morning America,* for instance, did a live remote from Pilot Field, and the reason was obvious: It was quite a sight.

The story behind this phenomenon was even more special: Not only was this a ballpark, it was a symbolic connection of Buffalo's past to its future. "It's a baseball place in the heart of Buffalo," Bob Rich says. "It's like what they talk about in baseball as a mystical kind of experience: a patch of green in the middle of a city where you can withdraw and your cares go away."

The amenities were something to behold.

The playing surface was classic—72,000 square feet of Kentucky bluegrass that shimmered with emerald luster. The 19,500 seats were bright red. It was a pitcher's park, to be sure, with dimensions of 325 feet to left and right fields, 384 to the power alleys, and 410 to dead-center. "I had seen too many high-scoring, crazy games in War Memorial Stadium," Bob Rich would say of the old park, with its right-field porch of about 280 down the line. "I wanted the new park to have honest dimensions."

That it did, yet on this extraordinary afternoon, the game was won by a home run. It was, by every measure, a day for beating the odds.

The exterior of Pilot Field harked back to a majestic baseball era. It was an almost ghostly reincarnation from a long-gone time of intimate ballparks such as Connie Mack Stadium and Ebbets Field. The outer walls featured marble tiles set in precast concrete panels. Punctuating the skyline, classic cupolas rested atop each end of its roof, which is a bright green shade that the architects call weathered copper. Windowpanes above the gates adorned the main entrance. Old-fashioned, gas-lantern-style street lights surrounded the outside of the ballpark. It was an eerie yet comforting step into baseball's yesterday, and it blended in just right with the Joseph Ellicott Historic District, which bordered Buffalo's resurgent downtown business section. "We wanted the features of Pilot Field to be real friendly with its surroundings," said architect Joe Spear, who did most of the design work. "There was an attempt to relate the stadium to the area around it."

Pilot Field's exquisite attention to the details of its neoclassical architecture befitted a cityscape whose visual appeal included such landmarks as five houses designed by Frank Lloyd Wright. Within the walls, the ambiance was decidedly big-league. Not only was there a computer-operated color scoreboard, a food court, and a variety of individual food stands with a wide array of ethnic specialties, there was a classy 300-seat restaurant called Pettibones Grille that would be open year-round. A first-class aura distinguished places that most people don't see: a state-of-the-art press box for sixty reporters; locker and weight rooms for the team; dressing rooms for bat boys and umpires; and a lounge for players' wives.

Down on the field, as game time approached, two political antagonists could be seen—playing catch. There they were, about forty feet apart, Mario Cuomo wearing a Bisons uniform shirt with number 5 on it—the same number worn by Cuomo's idol, Joe Di-Maggio—and Jimmy Griffin wearing the symbolic number 1. The trappings of power forgotten for the time being, the governor and the mayor resembled a couple of kids tossing the ball back and forth, but this was in front of nearly 20,000 fans. The crowd chanted, "Mario! Mario! Mario!" and also cheered Griffin at every opportunity. Griffin delighted in his panoramic view of the jam-packed stadium during this, the crowning moment of his decade as mayor. "This is the jewel of downtown Buffalo," he said. Cuomo added, "This is what it's all about. Buffalo is coming back; Buffalo is on the rise."

Bill Gisel sat in the stands and felt like a kid again. "This is not the least bit anticlimactic," he said. "For me, it's tremendously exciting, and I'm enjoying every minute of it. Forget baseball; Pilot Field is the most significant municipal project for Western New York in the last ten years. Nothing comes close to this for the impact on Buffalo's psyche. We needed this."

"I think I'm in as much awe as anybody," Chuck Rosenow said. "I feel a little bit of relief. . . . I was concerned that something would go wrong. So much has happened, I never stop worrying. But Opening Day makes up for everything."

There had been a parade to mark the opening of the stadium, featuring speeches by Cuomo, Griffin, Erie County Executive Dennis Gorski, and Bob Rich. On the field amid all the pomp and circumstance stood Vince McNamara, now eighty years old and invigorated by the realization that this dream—this stadium—had come true after so many years of uncertainty. McNamara was given the honor of raising the flag for this historic Opening Day, and as he slowly pulled the rope, tears welled in his eyes. When the flag reached the top, a marching band played the national anthem, and—unbelievably—it was time to play ball. In a brand-new stadium. Downtown.

McNamara smiled. Bob Rich gave a thumbs-up sign, and the crowd gave a thunderous standing ovation that lasted about a minute. Buffalo went on to win the game, 1–0, over the Denver Zephyrs as Bob Patterson pitched the shutout and catcher Tom Prince hit the decisive home run.

This was Buffalo, and it was perfect.

When the game ended, the crowd—with an unusual number of backward glances—slowly began to leave Pilot Field. The drizzle continued, the wind had picked up, the sky was darkening, and the late-afternoon traffic was getting heavier. Before long, the stands were nearly empty, but Vince McNamara remained in his seat. He wasn't yet ready for this afternoon to end. It reminded him too much of those long-lost summer days of his boyhood back in the First Ward. "Baseball is baseball," he said softly, "whether it's in the coal yards of the Ward or Pilot Field." Slowly, deliberately, he finally rose from his seat, took one last look at the field and then savored his view of the stadium. "Baseball is baseball," Vince McNamara repeated as he slowly headed out to the streets of this city he had loved for so long.

On this emotional day in the rain, Bob Rich articulated what so many people were feeling but couldn't quite express: "I think Pilot Field symbolizes the future of Buffalo. It's a place where you can dream what it can be like around here."

SNAPSHOT—NEW KIDS: TONY PENA, KELLY GRUBER, STEVE FARR, DOUG JONES, AND JAY BELL

Visit any minor-league clubhouse and you'll find them: the cocky young slugger who still strikes out too much; the raw, flame-throwing pitcher who can't yet find the plate; the hungry Latino who must adjust not only to pro ball but to American culture, and the aging veteran who hangs on against all odds for one last shot at the big time. Down in the boonies, every player has a story. They come; they go. Each spring, there are new faces, new idiosyncrasies.

Buffalo, in its baseball reincarnation, has been a stop on the circuit since 1979, and the new-era Bisons are much like the old: coming to town for short stays and then leaving with soothed psyches or broken hearts. Reality is unforgiving in the minor leagues; the harsh message can be delivered physically, by a nasty curveball, or clinically, by a stopwatch or a radar gun. For many of the ballplayers who pass through, it signals the end of the line—an anything-but-subtle hint that perhaps it's time to forget the game and find a new life back home. It's a Darwinian struggle in which only the strongest and the most talented survive and go on to the majors.

In the minors, you find out how good you are. Dreams die. Or they are reaffirmed. And the next year, there is always someone new. For every Bench, Boudreau, Bunning, May, or Wine whose rite of passage includes Buffalo, there are always new kids—a Pena, a Gruber, a Farr, a Jones, or a Bell.

TONY PENA

When he arrived in Buffalo in April 1979, twenty-one-year-old Tony Pena saw something shocking: snow.

"In my country, it was warm all the time," says the catcher from the Dominican Republic.

I never saw snow until I got to Buffalo. When I played early in the season, I wore two pair of long johns, plus my baseball pants. I was freezing early in the year. I remember when we got to Buffalo, Luis Salazar and some of the Latin guys, we all lived in a boardinghouse a couple blocks from the stadium. We used to walk to the park at night, and I remember walking home after the games. It was a tough neighborhood, and sometimes people worried about us, but nobody ever bothered us. We had six, seven guys all living in the same building. It helped; we could do things together and talk together.

Before coming to Buffalo, Pena had kicked around the Pittsburgh Pirates' farm system for three seasons. His highest batting average had been .276, and his highest output of home runs had been 10. In 1979, with the Bisons, Pena batted .313 and hit 34 homers, including three in the final game of the season as Buffalo knocked Reading out of an Eastern League playoff spot. He went up to Pittsburgh in 1980 and stayed there until 1987, when he was traded to the St. Louis Cardinals. Although the Cards lost the 1987 World Series to Minnesota, Pena hit .409 in the seven games. He made the National League all-star team five times.

After the 1989 season, Pena became a free agent. He signed a multimillion-dollar contract with the Red Sox and played a crucial role in Boston's 1990 pennant drive. "He's helped this club not just in the field, but in the clubhouse," says Red Sox Manager Joe Morgan. "Tony is an inspirational player. He'll go out to the mound and tell pitchers to concentrate on the game; he stays on them. In the dugout, he talks and keeps everybody's spirits up. Tony's not only a good player, he's a good human being, and he's made a big impact on this team." Pena, whom Buffalo fans voted to the Bisons' team of the decade 1979–1989, is considered one of the premier defensive catchers in the game. In 1990, he hit .263, with 7 home runs and 56 runs batted in.

"I loved Buffalo; I think the year I played there was the year I opened up my career," Pena says in a Spanish-English dialect his teammates call Spanglish.

It was the best year I ever had in the minor leagues. It built my confidence as a hitter and as a catcher. I just came to Buffalo at the right time. I'll never forget that last day of the season, hitting those three home runs against Reading. They were going for the playoffs, and we beat them— that was something.

A lot of people didn't like War Memorial Stadium, but I think it made me a better hitter. I used to be a pull hitter until I got to Buffalo. Then, with that short fence in right, I tried to find a new stroke and learned to hit the ball the opposite way. The fans in Buffalo were great to me. That year was the first year they had baseball in a long time, and they gave us good support. They liked me, and I think the reason was my attitude and the way I play the game. I play hard every single day—that's the only way I know how to play. I'm still the same.

I can never forget Buffalo. Steve Demeter was the manager, and I played for him three years. He knew me better than anybody, and he believed in me. He helped me so much, and I think in Buffalo, I finally became the player he wanted me to be.

Things are so different when you get to the major leagues. Baseball can be a hard business. I signed with the Pirates when I was just a baby, seventeen years old. I grew up in that organization. That was the organization where I learned to be a man. It was really hard to leave Pittsburgh behind when I got traded. I had so many memories.

I had a good time in St. Louis, and I like Boston. Fenway is a great park to play in. I make a lot of money now, but one thing I ask God is, "Good Lord, don't ever make me change, no matter how much money I make, no matter where I play." . . . I consider myself, still, as a poor person. I think money is one thing, and the way you think and the way you act is another thing. . . . You should care about people; that's the way you have to live your life. And when it comes to that, I didn't change at all.

It makes me feel good to know the people in Buffalo still remember me. Those people in Buffalo are my people; I will never forget them.

KELLY GRUBER

In the summer of 1983, Kelly Gruber was a homesick, confused twenty-one-year-old with an injured shoulder. Buffalo was a long way from his hometown of Bellaire, Texas. He had been the Cleveland Indians' number-one draft pick in 1980 but had failed to distinguish himself as a shortstop during his first three seasons in pro ball. Cleveland was growing impatient, and Gruber would have to prove himself in Buffalo.

"I had a good year up in Buffalo," Gruber says.

They switched me from short to third, and I didn't know how it would turn out. But I did all right, and I met a lot of people I won't forget, especially the Rich family and the Earl of Bud.

I enjoyed playing at the Old Rockpile. It had a lot of tradition, and the fans were fun. That was the year they filmed *The Natural,* and I got to meet Robert Redford.

I played for Dirty Al Gallagher, and he was a character. Joe Charboneau was my teammate and roommate, and he was always doing something crazy.

It was a lot of fun, but there were some tough times. I collided with [pitcher] Robin Fuson and collapsed my shoulder. I didn't have anywhere to stay, and [general manager] Don Colpoys took me in his house and put me up. It was incredible. He took me in, and I was like a member of his family. Here I am, a young kid, I'm hurt, and I'm way up north, a long way from home. I'm a Texas boy, and I want to be home with my mom to comfort me. I wasn't married then; I didn't have anybody to care for me or love me. That's exactly what the Colpoys family did for me, and I'll never forget it.

That season in Buffalo, Gruber batted .263 with 15 homers and 54 runs batted in, but it wasn't good enough for the Indians, and they didn't protect him on their forty-man roster. In December 1983 Toronto drafted him, and after a couple of seasons in Triple-A at Syracuse, he went up to the Blue Jays. At third base, Gruber has been one of their best players, developing into an effective hitter and a solid home-run threat. He has twice been named to the American League all-star team. "Kelly has worked hard on his hitting," says Jays Manager Cito Gatson. "I think he can hit twenty to twenty-five homers every year. He's a strong kid and a tough competitor. He means a lot to this ball club."

The 1990 season was one of Gruber's most productive at the plate, with 31 homers and 118 runs batted in, both career highs.

"Some people were surprised about the home runs," he says,

but I never put limitations on myself. . . . I've changed since Buffalo. I'm more mature as a ball player, and I feel more comfortable. It's a combination of things: You get older, you get good coaching and instruction in the majors, and after you have some success, you build confidence.

When I played in Buffalo, the city was going through some tough times; there wasn't a whole lot of excitement, and I think that's why I cherished playing there. I felt like, hey, maybe I can bring a little excitement to this city. Buffalo has come a long way since then. I wish them all the best, I hope they get a big-league team. Bob Rich is a great owner, and if the fans support the team, I think they'll get a major-league franchise. It's great to see what baseball is doing there now, and how the city is flourishing.

Buffalo's fans developed an affection for Gruber and voted him to the Bisons' team of the decade.

"For me, Buffalo wasn't just a place where I played baseball; the people there made me feel like it was home. And when you're a ball player in the minor leagues, you never forget that feeling."

STEVE FARR

They called him "The Beast," and appropriately so. In Buffalo, or anywhere else, pitcher Steve Farr didn't take any guff, on or off the mound. Signed by Pittsburgh as a free agent in 1976, Farr was twenty-five when he joined Buffalo's Eastern League team in 1980. In three seasons, he was 11–6, 8–3, and 5–8.

"I had a lot of fun and a lot of hangovers in Buffalo," Farr recalls.

It was a good party town, I was young, and the bars were open until four in the morning. I got into a few fights in those bars, but, really, the people were great to me.

I remember pitching in the old park. I think it helped. After a while, you realize that you have to stay with your same game and throw strikes. You can't worry about the wall in right field. If somebody hits one out, they hit it out; it's not a big deal. I enjoyed Buffalo, except for the fact I was fed up with the Pirates.

In 1983, when the Pirates tried to send him to their new Double-A affiliate in Lynn, Massachusetts, Farr resisted and went home to Maryland to pitch in a beer league. He was through with Pittsburgh.

"It was a combination of things," Farr says.

I wasn't a high draft pick; I just walked on and signed. There was really no interest by anybody in Pittsburgh to get me up to the major leagues. Every time there was a meeting to pick somebody to go up, it was probably between me and another guy. Well, the other guy always went up, and I got sick of it. It happens in a lot of organizations, you get a few people making decisions, and they are stale on you.

Finally, I got so frustrated I went up to Pittsburgh and sort of snapped. I told them what I thought of them and their organization, and I just went home.

Within weeks, the Bisons, now working with Cleveland, engineered a trade, and Farr was back in Buffalo. "Any time you change organizations, you feel you've got a new life," Farr says. "I think it sticks a little needle in you, and that's how it was for me."

Farr responded with a league-leading 13–1 record and 1.61 earned-run average: "I don't know why, but during that 13–1 year in Buffalo, everything went right. It was like my time had come."

Farr's outstanding 1983 season in Buffalo earned him a promotion to Cleveland in 1984, but he was released by the Indians the next year. He then signed with Kansas City and has been one of the Royals' most effective pitchers ever since, both in the bullpen and as a spot starter. In 1985, Farr pitched in the American League Championship Series against Toronto, and the Royals went on to win the World Series over St. Louis in seven games. In 1988, he saved 20 games; the next year, 18. In 1990, Farr enjoyed one of his best seasons, with 13 victories, a career high, and an earned-run average of 1.98. Then, as a free agent, he signed a three-year contract with the Yankees for $6 million.

"It's funny, all this has happened after I went back to Buffalo in 1983," Farr says. "At that point of my career, I didn't know what was going to happen and had kind of said, 'To hell with it,' as far as baseball was concerned. But Buffalo gave me a second chance. I think it was the turning point of my career."

DOUG JONES

The 1987 season was the last year for baseball in War Memorial Stadium—and in some ways, the last chance for Doug Jones. He was twenty-nine, had been stuck in the minors for nearly a decade and, after spending the first three weeks of the season in Cleveland, found himself back in Triple-A. "That was his time for survival," says Buffalo native Dan Carnevale, an advance scout for the Indians. "I'm not kidding when I say he came within one game of being released."

One person who believed in Jones was Buffalo baseball historian Joe Overfield, who watched him pitch in the Old Rockpile. Overfield kept telling Carnevale how impressed he was with the fact that nobody was able to make solid contact with Jones's pitches. The right-handed reliever appeared in 23 games for the Bisons and was 5–2 with 7 saves and a 2.04 earned-run average before being called back up to Cleveland to stay. Jones has made the American League all-star team for the last three years, recording more than 30 saves each season. Last season he saved 43 games and was rewarded with a 1991 contract worth $2 million. "Overfield was right," Carnevale says. "He's a great pitcher."

"When I went to Buffalo, I knew it was make-or-break time," says Jones, who now relies most heavily on a fastball and a change-up.

If I didn't do well, I wouldn't stand a chance with Cleveland, because they wouldn't have any interest in me anymore. But just because Cleveland didn't like the way I pitched those first three weeks of the season didn't mean I could never pitch again. I figured some other team would be interested in me.

So I went to Buffalo with the attitude of "I'm just going to show them that they've made a mistake, and they didn't give me the one more opportunity I needed." It ended up coming down to that. I really believe that if I had just one more opportunity I might have done a little better.

I had a tough start that year with Cleveland, but it was nothing major. It was an attitude thing in the way I was approaching my outings. I'd go out on the mound and see Dave Winfield or Don Mattingly and I'd kind of forget what I was trying to do. I had more on my mind than just throwing strikes. I'd think, "This is Dave Winfield; how am I going to get Dave Winfield out?" When they sent me to Buffalo, I told myself, "I'm just going to throw strikes and get people out and let things happen the way they will and not worry about the things I can't control."

For me, that was the biggest adjustment, and it was a mental adjustment. The mental foul-up had caused me to change my approach to the hitters, and that affected my mechanics. I was pitching very tentatively; I wasn't following through, and that was something completely different for me.

Once I got to Buffalo, I realized I could only control so much of the game. When you try to do more than you can, that's when you get in trouble. Buffalo was a big step for me, because that was one point in time when I had to make the mental adjustment; that was my last chance. . . .

I enjoyed Buffalo. We lived about a block away from a place in Grand Island that sold chicken wings. I learned to love Buffalo wings. War Memorial was a tough park, but it didn't bother me. You can't use a park as an excuse. I've always been a ground-ball pitcher, and the infield has always been the same distance from home plate in War Memorial or any place else.

When I got sent back down to Buffalo in 1987, it was disappointing, and it bothered me, but what can you do? You come to a point where you have to understand that the big-league team you're with isn't the only team in baseball. So you go back down to the minors to give yourself an opportunity.

There are stories all over the minor leagues about guys who have bounced around from team to team, and they still keep playing. Why? Because somebody is going to take a chance on them, and then you never know what might happen. I waited a long time, but when I came back from Buffalo, I made it in the major leagues.

JAY BELL

In the spring of 1989, Jay Bell found himself back in Buffalo, running out of opportunities to prove himself. There were doubts about his range at shortstop and his ability to hit.

Bell's first trip to Buffalo came in 1987, when he walked into War Memorial Stadium as a prime prospect with the Cleveland Indians. "That old stadium had a lot of character," Bell recalls. "Some players didn't like it, but I thought it was great. It was so big; I had never been in a park with 40,000 seats."

That season, he hit 17 homers and batted .260 with the Bisons. As the 1988 season began, he was with the Indians. But he hit only .218 in 73 games and was sent down to Colorado Springs in Triple-A. In March 1989 Bell was traded to Pittsburgh and opened the season in the majors by going 1 for 20.

The doubts grew, and Bell heard the whispers that he didn't

have enough range to play short and couldn't handle big-league pitching. "That's how it is in this game," he says. "You always have to prove yourself. And people won't believe in you until you do."

Bell's second tour of duty in Buffalo proved to be crucial—not so much for enhancing his physical skill, but for allowing him to mature as a pro ball player.

"When I came back to Buffalo, I really believed I was on the verge of emerging as a complete player," he says. "I knew I had to work on my defense and my hitting. That was when I learned how to concentrate and use the ability I had."

Bell erased the doubts in June, when he hit .347 and knocked in 27 runs in 27 games. He was called up by the Pirates in July, after hitting .285 for Buffalo with 10 homers and 54 RBIs.

Bell sparked the Pirates to a strong second-half finish and hit .258. In 1990, he played a key role in the Pirates' battle for the National League East title. His fielding improved, and his batting average was .254 to go with 7 homers and 52 runs batted in. Jay Bell, who didn't turn twenty-five until after the 1990 season, had finally arrived.

Amid his newfound success, his thoughts drift back to Buffalo:

> I spent two seasons in Buffalo under very different circumstances. When I was with the Indians, I was still learning to play baseball and trying to get to the big leagues. The second time I came back, I had to hone my skills to get back to the big leagues.
>
> It was discouraging to go back down to the minor leagues. But I knew I was close to becoming a good ball player, and I figured Buffalo was a good town to play in. I've got to say that Buffalo was my favorite minor-league town. They just have an outstanding organization, and you couldn't ask for a better owner than Bob Rich. There's nobody in baseball who's better to play for than Bob Rich.
>
> I went there with the idea of doing my best and getting back up. For six years, people said I couldn't play shortstop in the big leagues. Well, I played shortstop in Buffalo, and then I came up here and did the same thing.

Now, I think I've proved my point. You don't develop into a winning player overnight; you learn that in the minor leagues, and I learned it in Buffalo.

Bell also was enchanted by Pilot Field: "It's a beautiful place to play baseball. You look at that park and that field, and you realize just what this game is all about."

Part Four

11

WHERE DREAMS CAN COME TRUE

It was October 15, 1988, a Saturday night. Barry Levinson, director of such films as *The Natural* and *Good Morning, Vietnam* and destined to win an Academy Award for *Rain Man,* was in the living room of his home in the Bel Air section of Los Angeles watching game one of the World Series. The Dodgers, decimated by injuries, were in L.A. playing the heavily favored Oakland A's. The home team's fate appeared sealed from the very start because, as NBC sportscaster Vin Scully told a national audience, season-long hero Kirk Gibson was so badly hurt that he wasn't expected to play. The gimpy outfielder was feeling pain in his right knee, and he also was suffering from a pulled left hamstring. Gibson couldn't run; in fact, he could barely walk. He was limping and unable to take batting practice. In the clubhouse, he received pain-killing injections for the knee, which he kept wrapped in ice. Since he wasn't able to go to the dugout, Gibson could barely hear the roar of the overflow crowd at Dodger Stadium. Like Levinson, who was just ten miles away, Gibson was watching the game on TV. But then he took the ice pack off.

Levinson had watched as Oakland's awesome relief pitcher Dennis Eckersley retired the first two batters in the bottom of the ninth inning, with his team leading, 4–3. Levinson had seen Eckersley mow down hitters before, including those of his favorite team, the Baltimore Orioles. "Oh, well," Levinson thought to himself, "the Dodgers are dead."

At the start of the ninth, unknown to Scully, Levinson, or anyone else in the more than 18.5 million households tuned in to the telecast, Gibson had asked a bat boy to go get Tommy Lasorda, the Dodgers' manager. Lasorda rushed to the clubhouse, where Gibson told the manager that he would be available to hit for the pitcher, who was due up after the eighth batter in the lineup, Alfredo Griffin. Lasorda looked at Gibson's legs, shook his head, and smiled. In the clubhouse, Gibson had been practicing his swing, gaining determination with each stroke of the bat. Gibson's heart was aching more than his legs. He desperately wanted to get into this game.

Lasorda jauntily trotted back to the dugout. There were two outs when Lasorda sent Mike Davis to the plate to pinch-hit for Griffin. Kneeling in the on-deck circle was light-hitting infielder Dave Anderson. Eckersley, well aware that Anderson was the next scheduled batter, decided to pitch carefully to Davis, who had power, but he lost him: Davis walked.

The stage was set: Bottom of the ninth. Two outs. Dodgers down by a run.

Lasorda now made a dramatic choice: a left-handed batter—Kirk Gibson.

Gibson limped to the plate. The crowd went wild, its noise rising to an eardrum-threatening level. Across America, viewers were doing double-takes. At home, Barry Levinson sat up in his chair. He couldn't believe it—they were robbing this plot from his movie. Was this Kirk Gibson? Robert Redford? Roy Hobbs? All three?

It seemed like a flashback to the climactic scene of *The Natural:* Redford, as Hobbs, bleeding and limping, coming up to the plate in the last of the ninth with the league championship on the line and hitting the game-winning home run. All that was missing was some of Randy Newman's soundtrack music.

"No," Levinson thought, "this is real life; it just couldn't happen."

Could it?

Eckersley, a right-hander who arguably was the most effective relief pitcher in baseball, had too much on his mind to think of fiction; he wanted to get out of this game as soon as possible. So he was going to serve Gibson a steady diet of fastballs. Gibson lunged at one of them and missed. He fouled off a pitch and gamely protected the plate. Everyone could see that Gibson was in pain, but Eckersley couldn't afford any sympathy. Here was an opponent who had batted nearly .300 with 25 home runs during the regular season, credentials that helped him become National League Most Valuable Player. Eckersley then tried to cross Gibson up with a slider. Gibson took it, and Davis stole second base. Now, all Gibson needed was a single to knock in the tying run. The count was full: three and two.

Eckersley knew Gibson was expecting a fastball. Ron Hassey, the Oakland catcher, decided to call for another slider, aimed low and at the outside corner. Gibson stood at the plate, wincing from the aches in his right knee. Levinson sat on the edge of his easy chair, his eyes transfixed by the TV images enacting a baseball drama as gut-wrenching as one from any movie. Eckersley made the pitch. Then, as in *The Natural,* everything seemed to move in slow motion. The slider was just a bit high, Gibson dug in, and then made his swing. It was flawless. The bat met the ball, sending it soaring through the smogbound sky above Chavez Ravine, like a rocket heading to the stars. Eckersley turned emphatically, staring at the flight of the ball in rigid disbelief. Gibson dropped his bat and stepped toward first base, watching the ball's wondrous arc. Finally, the ball disappeared five rows into the right-field bleachers. The fans screamed in delirious celebration as Gibson continued to limp around the bases, pumping his right fist. When he touched home plate, Gibson was mobbed by teammates after finishing the slowest home-run hobble in history. Eckersley, head bowed, stormed from the mound. The Dodgers had won the game 5–4, and—led by Buffalo-born pitcher Orel Hershiser—would go on to win the series in five games.

In more than forty years of radio play-by-play, Hall of Fame broadcaster Jack Buck had seen it all, but Gibson's imitation of Hobbs inspired him to exclaim to his 50 million listeners on CBS that "I don't believe what I just saw!"

Levinson was stunned. "I can't believe it—it really happened," he thought as he watched Gibson gingerly circle the bases. After the game, when Gibson went to his locker, someone had taped a name on it: ROY HOBBS. The next day, sportscasts nationwide played a videotape of the home run, using music and scenes from *The Natural.* Levinson was thrilled. "They used our setup from the movie, and I got a kick out of that," he says. To Barry Levinson, the home run by Kirk Gibson reinforced the meaning of the movie. "Gibson's home run was what *The Natural* was all about: history, mythology, and baseball. When I watched him trot around the bases, I kept thinking of Robert Redford in War Memorial Stadium. It was just like being in Buffalo."

A few months later, Kirk Gibson himself was in Buffalo, accepting Dunlop's national award as the year's outstanding professional athlete. It was only for one night, but Roy Hobbs was back in town.

PETER UEBERROTH, THEN the commissioner of baseball, had certainly been prophetic during the winter meetings several months before Pilot Field opened when he said, "One of the best baseball experiences in America will be in Buffalo with its new stadium."

If anything, that proved to be an understatement. Where for twenty years or so the city, its rigorous weather, and its Old Rockpile had been targets for scathing coast-to-coast ridicule by newspaper columnists, magazine writers, and comics right up to Johnny Carson, the arrival of Pilot Field seemed to transform Buffalo's loser image to one of having risen above adversity to achieve something special.

A former Yale first baseman named George Bush donned a Bisons cap and toured Pilot Field in 1988 during a campaign swing in Buffalo and told Bob Rich that Pilot Field was a "wonderful ballpark."

No one was more enthusiastic than national talk-show host Larry King, who unabashedly said, "I love Buffalo."

King was a baseball traditionalist, having grown up on the streets of Brooklyn, where he played in the shadows of Ebbets Field with a neighborhood pal who was a future Hall of Famer: Sandy Koufax. He knew the game, its people, its places—and he was nothing short of captivated by Buffalo's ballpark: "Pilot Field is the nicest baseball stadium I've ever been in; Pilot Field is what a baseball stadium is all about. . . . I like the charm of the place. It's a brand-new baseball stadium that feels like it has been there all these years. It's a very warm stadium . . . that feels like a baseball place. I can't picture a football game ever being played at Pilot Field."

Typical of the reactions to Buffalo's glistening new ballpark

Robert E. Rich, Sr., *(sitting)* and his son Bob Rich, Jr. *(Buffalo Bisons)*

Sluggers from the
Bisons' past:
Ollie Carnegie
(left) and Luke
Easter. *(Joseph
M. Overfield)*

Buffalo's "Marse" Joe
McCarthy with Joe
DiMaggio. *(Buffalo
Bisons)*

Left to right:
Ralph Hubbell,
Warren Spahn,
and Vince
McNamara.
(Chris Grupp)

Don
Labbruzzo
(center)
holding
Buffalo
Baseball Hall
of Fame
plaque,
during his
1987
induction.
*(Buffalo
Bisons)*

Don Colpoys
(left) and Bob
Rich, Jr., in War
Memorial
Stadium, soon
after Rich bought
the team. *(Ronald
J. Colleran,* The
Buffalo News*)*

Wilford Brimley *(left)* and Robert Redford during the filming of *The Natural* in War Memorial. Buffalo resident Kevin Lester sits between them. (*Kevin Lester*)

Jon Dandes, a vice president of the Buffalo Bisons.

Bob Rich, Jr., Mindy Rich, and Bill Gisel making plans in Rich's office. (*Buffalo Bisons*)

Pilot Field, 1988. *(Joe Traver)*

Mindy Rich, Bob Rich, Jr., Governor Mario Cuomo and Mayor Jimmy Griffin on Opening Day in Pilot Field, 1988: the first game at the new park. *(Joe Traver)*

Pilot Field from the inside. *(Buffalo Bisons)*

The Earl of Bud in Pilot Field.
(Buffalo Bisons)

Mike Billoni on "Bison One" walkie-talkie during a cold April night game. *(Buffalo Bisons)*

The Buffalo Baseball Hall of Fame Committee, in front of the Hall of Fame Exhibit in Pilot Field. *Left to right:* George Daddario, Joe Overfield, Cy Williams, Gerri Kozlowski (secretary), Vince McNamara, Joe Alli, Ralph Hubbell, Cy Kritzer, Pete Weber, Anthony Violanti. *(James P. McCoy)*

Bob Rich, Jr. and Bisons' Manager Terry Collins. *(Joe Traver)*

Cy Williams *(left)* and Erie County Executive Dennis Gorski take in a game. *(Joe Traver)*

Robert E. Rich, Sr., with grandson Barney on his lap: the next generation of Buffalo baseball dreams. *(Joe Traver)*

were those of New York Yankees shortstop-turned-broadcaster Tony Kubek, who called it "great," and ABC sportscaster Al Michaels, who described it as "beautiful."

Pilot Field, said sportscaster Chris Berman of ESPN, "is a state-of-the-art facility. . . . It reminds me of a mini–Royals Stadium in Kansas City. It's got that old-time feel that baseball fans love; they're close to the action, and every seat is a good one. It's a family place. Honest, until I came to Buffalo, I couldn't believe how nice it really is; it's nestled right in the heart of downtown. It's opened my eyes, and I'm impressed. Let me tell you, Pilot Field is the real thing."

The print media were no less impressed. *Sports Illustrated* magazine, which in the late sixties derisively portrayed War Memorial Stadium as the worst place in America to play a major sport, was now praising Pilot Field's design, calling it one of the best examples of a modern baseball stadium anywhere: "Buffalo's new ballpark is so modern it's traditional."

And among the echoes were these:

- *New York Times:* "The house that Rich built . . . [is] the linchpin of Buffalo's expansion dream and the jewel of a resurgent downtown."

- *Washington Post:* "Pilot Field . . . is a $43 million architectural gem."

- *The Sporting News:* "The park is an oasis that has blended the best features of old and new baseball architecture."

- *Christian Science Monitor:* "A wonderfully inviting new stadium with all the latest amenities as well as the charm of the best-loved older ballparks."

- *San Francisco Examiner:* "The enormous popularity of Pilot Field is Exhibit A in their campaign to bring a major-league expansion team to Buffalo and rub out its image as the buckle on the Northeast Rust Belt."

Perceptions had changed.

Moreover, reality had changed. Amazingly, Jimmy Griffin,

Bob Rich, Jr., and their followers had managed to achieve something almost unheard-of in the world of baseball opinion: unanimity.

There was no looking back now. Buffalo had a mission to accomplish.

. . . .

THE CHALLENGE CONFRONTING Buffalo and the Bisons was boiled down to a catch phrase: "putting up the numbers." In the fearsome competition to acquire an expansion franchise, they had to demonstrate to Major League Baseball that the fan support for the game was so overwhelming that they couldn't be denied. Which is what they proceeded to do.

In 1988, the Bisons' first year at Pilot Field, they had twenty-one sellouts in seventy-two dates, drawing a total of 1,186,651 fans to set an all-time single-season attendance record for a minor-league franchise. That year, they even outdrew three clubs in the majors: Atlanta, Seattle, and the Chicago White Sox. It was nearly two and a half times more people than the Bisons had ever attracted to War Memorial Stadium and nearly three times more than had ever come to Offermann. The population of the city proper was much lower than in those days, but the level of support for baseball was never higher.

"I know Buffalo, and I know our people; I'm one of them," Bob Rich says.

> I know how much sports mean to people here, and I know how tough it was for all of us in the last fifteen to twenty years.
>
> I've watched the hurt in Buffalo as the city went through the pain of going from a blue-collar town to a banking and service community. I've seen firsthand the frustration of losing big industries.
>
> I've watched children become disillusioned and young people leave here. We've lost too many young people. But things are changing for the better in Buffalo, and Pilot Field is literally a symbol of hope for everyone.

The demand for tickets hit such a peak that Rich put a ceiling of 9,000 on season-ticket sales so that there always would be at least 10,500 seats available for fans on a game-by-game basis.

For the long-suffering baseball fans of Buffalo, young and old and every age in between, this was like living a dream.

"The building of Pilot Field has done more for Buffalo's image and Buffalo's pride than any event in my memory," says Joe Overfield, the team's historian, who saw his first professional baseball game at old Bison Stadium in 1925. "And what a thrill it is to go there and see the game played as it should be, under the sun and the stars and on real grass."

The feeling is shared, too, by those who have spent a lifetime seeing Buffalo sports from the inside.

"It's just a wonderful feeling to sit with your friends and watch a baseball game in Pilot Field; it's a park that was made for the people," says George Daddario, one of the best schoolboy athletes in Buffalo history while at Kensington High and a former pro baseball player and front-office man with both the Bisons and the NBA's ill-fated Buffalo Braves. "I think the people in Buffalo have shown how much they love baseball in a place like that."

For the baby-boomers who didn't desert Buffalo in its darkest hours, Pilot Field not only means a renewal of pride but an overdue sense of vindication. "This is the kind of baseball park you'd always dreamed they would build one day in Buffalo," says fortysomething John Keller, a lifelong fan from South Buffalo. "I mean, I come and this place is so beautiful, I still can't believe it. It's one of those rare times in Buffalo when they did everything right, and they put it right in the middle of downtown. It means so much to this city."

Much of Pilot Field's magnetism has to do with its atmosphere—festive and picniclike, conjuring up an old Pittsburgh Pirates motto: "We are family."

"The new stadium changed everything in Buffalo," says Carlos Ledezma, who was the trainer of the risen-from-the-dead Bisons back in 1979. "In the old days, people used to laugh and joke about baseball in Buffalo, but now everyone believes it has a chance for the big leagues. You come to this park, and you know it can happen."

Ron Krauza, the team's clubhouse supervisor, shares that feeling. In the late fifties and early sixties, he was a bat boy for the Bisons. "Those were great days for baseball," he recalls. "Offermann Stadium was beautiful, but so is Pilot Field. And every time you come here, you know that someday this park and this city will be in the major leagues."

THE SUCCESS OF the first season in the new ballpark carried over to the 1989 season and continued to bring national recognition to the team's prime movers.

Bob Rich, who had earned distinction as American Association Executive of the Year for 1986, received that honor again in 1988 in addition to being named *Sporting News* Minor League Executive of the Year.

In a unique double for a husband-and-wife team in professional baseball, Mindy Rich was named Rawlings Female Minor League Executive of the Year. She also was in the local spotlight as one of the *Buffalo News* Citizens of the Year, an accolade previously earned by both Bob Rich, Jr., and his father.

Mike Billoni, his creative juices flowing no less powerfully than in the Old Rockpile days, when it seemed as if it was Bob Rich and him against the world, was to win the 1989 Lee MacPhail Trophy for promotional excellence in minor-league baseball, the first Bisons general manager to receive the award in thirty years, when Don Labbruzzo was the recipient.

Although his name couldn't be found inscribed on any national trophy, Jimmy Griffin had the satisfaction of knowing that he had been an essential force in reaching a goal that so many people had thought was beyond Buffalo's grasp.

"In the last fifteen years, I've seen Buffalo go from the edge of despair to the strongest part of the state," said Mario Cuomo. "Buffalo is just beginning to realize its potential. Watch what happens when the Canadian free-trade agreement really starts booming and people become more aware of Buffalo. The world is just coming to understand what a great place it is to live."

But even the great and the near-great get bloody noses.

While the addition of Pilot Field has meant an economic impact of more than $20 million a year, the community around it has continued to grapple—sometimes unsuccessfully—in an effort not to lose what it already has.

Buffalo's locally owned retailing chains, which had once flourished, were fast becoming extinct.

Fisher-Price Toys closed two of its plants in the suburbs and laid off about half of its work force—more than 1,700 people. The banking business, its meteoric rise made possible by the regulatory relaxation of the early eighties, came hurtling back to earth with stunning suddenness. The most notable casualty was far-flung but overextended Empire of America Federal Savings Bank, its tower a downtown fixture, which was taken over and dismantled by the federal government, leaving its stockholders, including Mayor Jimmy Griffin, holding the bag.

In the political arena, Griffin was still in conflict with the news media, albeit less intensely. There was a federal investigation into alleged corruption by the head of the Parks Department, but Griffin endured. Not only did he win his first Democratic primary in four tries, he won a three-way general election in 1989 with 70 percent of the vote and steamrolled to a record fourth term. "He has been lucky," says veteran Democratic pol Joe Crangle, "but he's been able to take advantage of his luck." Griffin's political allies say the man makes his own luck, and there was talk that he might run for county executive.

Jimmy Griffin, sixty years old as he began his fourth term, still lives in South Buffalo, where he plays catch with his teenage son, Thomas, just as Jimmy's own father, Rocko, had done with him. The mayor has season tickets to Pilot Field, where he sits with his brother, Tommy, on the first-base side; Jimmy's son is one of the team's bat boys. "It's great going to a ball game in downtown Buffalo at a stadium like this," Jimmy Griffin says with pride. "This is what it's all about, and I never doubted our people would support baseball. We're going to the big leagues in Pilot Field."

ALMOST OVERNIGHT, PERCEPTIONS of Buffalo's position in the baseball universe were changing, and nowhere was this more evident than among the people who know the game best.

"Bob Rich is a good man," said Fay Vincent, commissioner of baseball. "He's done a first-rate job with baseball in Buffalo. It's a wonderful franchise, they run it beautifully, and it's a very impressive program."

Douglas Danforth, chairman and chief executive officer of the

Pittsburgh Pirates and head of the National League Expansion Committee, said Rich has "brought a commitment to baseball, and he believes in the game. He's demonstrated that with the new stadium and the organization they have built in Buffalo."

"Since they moved into the new ballpark, Buffalo has been one of the great success stories," said Roland Hemond, general manager of the Baltimore Orioles. "It has all the features of a first-class major-league ballpark."

"Pilot Field is a ballpark, not a stadium," said Corey Busch, San Francisco Giants vice president, emphasizing that Buffalo's approach proves that "you can build a ballpark in an urban environment and make it work physically and aesthetically as well."

After Pilot Field's record-shattering attendance of nearly 1.2 million in 1988, the question arose of whether the novelty might wear off. Louisville, which had drawn 1,052,438 fans to watch its Triple-A Redbirds in 1983, was the only other minor-league city to have ever drawn a million or more fans. Before 1988, the most Buffalo had ever drawn for baseball was less than half a million. Yet in 1989, helped in no small measure by the energetic and innovative ticket-selling strategies of executive sales director Jim Mack, the Bisons' attendance reached 1,132,183, and in 1990 it was 1,174,358, for an average of more than 1,164,000 for its first three years.

Buffalo was "putting up the numbers" like no other minor-league city in history.

The Bisons' move to Pilot Field coincided with the switch of their working agreement from the Cleveland Indians to the Pittsburgh Pirates. "In Pittsburgh, we wanted to put our Triple-A players in a major-league environment, and Pilot Field was the place," said Syd Thrift, who then was general manager of the Pirates. "It's a tremendous facility, and everything about it is big-league."

In 1988 the Bisons, managed by the crusty, tobacco-chewing Rocky Bridges, had finished third in the Eastern Division of the American Association, and their 72–70 record was competitive enough to keep the fans cheering. But at times, the crowds seemed to be enjoying the ballpark ambiance even more than the baseball. That began to change in 1989, when Terry Collins was named manager for the Bisons' second season at Pilot Field.

Collins had managed in the Los Angeles Dodgers' organization for eight years. Not known as a diplomat, he was wont to speak his mind in behalf of his players and his minor-league club. That caused some problems for him with the front office and led to his leaving the Dodgers. But Bob Rich thought that Collins' fiery independence was just what the Bisons needed, and he persuaded the Pirates to sign him for Buffalo.

It was an inspired choice. Collins, an exacting manager, generated exciting baseball, with emphasis on the steal, the hit-and-run, and taking the extra base. Despite a paucity of power (fifty-seven home runs), the 1989 Bisons finished second in the American Association East with an 80–62 record, best for a Buffalo team since 1959.

Bob Rich liked what he saw because, like any good businessman, Collins made the most of his material.

"I don't think we had the best talent in the league, but every night, we took the field believing we could beat the other guy," said Collins. "Pilot Field is a big park, and when you play here, you can't wait for things to happen. We had to depend on pitching and running to make runs. Everybody was willing to do anything to help the team. That's the kind of club we had."

Collins and his sidekick, pitching coach Jackie Brown, despite a disconcerting 110 roster moves by the parent Pittsburgh club, led the 1990 Bisons to a first-place tie with Nashville in the Eastern Division with an 85–61 record. Brown, who in Buffalo guided the careers of such future big-league pitchers as Dave Johnson, Bob Patterson, Stan Belinda, and Bill Landrum, had a special link to the Bisons' last moment of glory. In 1961, the first season in War Memorial Stadium, his brother Paul had pitched a one-hitter against Louisville to complete a four-game sweep of the Junior World Series—Buffalo's only professional baseball championship since 1906.

In 1990 Buffalo had another shot at postseason glory, but the Bisons lost a pulse-pounding, eighteen-inning playoff game 4–3 at Pilot Field, leaving Collins in tears and his bitterly disappointed team out of the final playoffs. "But I'm proud of these guys," said Collins, red-eyed but already looking forward to next year.

The game had lasted five hours and eight minutes, finishing at twenty-seven minutes past midnight, prompting an emotionally drained Pete Weber, the "voice of the Bisons" since 1983, to say,

"It was the most exciting game I've ever seen. All the frustrations, joys, and agony of this season were wrapped up in those eighteen innings of baseball."

Mike Billoni said Collins had "made it special" for Buffalo fans in 1990, and *Baseball America* voted him the top managerial prospect in the minor leagues.

In each of Pilot Field's first three seasons, Buffalo was host to the annual Old Timers Baseball Classic, attracting such immortals as Hank Aaron, Ernie Banks, Lou Brock, Bob Feller, Sandy Koufax, Brooks Robinson, and even the great DiMaggio himself.

As dazzled as the fans of Buffalo were by their proximity to those baseball legends, the legends themselves were dazzled by Pilot Field. The praise was unanimous, typified by the words of Warren Spahn: "The first time I saw it, with all those steeples, it reminded me of the place where they have the Kentucky Derby. Then I went inside, and I'll tell you, that park is perfect for baseball. It's like stepping back in time. . . . I don't know how they did it, but it turned out great."

The effect of Pilot Field was magical, sometimes mystical. On Friday nights, it even went ballistic. Then, as well as for the Fourth of July and for Fan Appreciation Night, fireworks exploded in the downtown sky, not only after the game, but every time the Bisons exploded with a big scoring play. At times, it was eerily reminiscent of cinematographer Caleb Deschanel's pyrotechnic extravaganza in the finale of *The Natural*—only fitting, because Buffalo's new image reflected that scene. As far as baseball was concerned, the city was now referring to itself as "The Natural for Expansion."

NEARLY THIRTY YEARS earlier, Buffalo's beloved Offermann Stadium had been torn down to make way for a junior high school. Now, much-maligned War Memorial Stadium was being demolished and replaced by a neighborhood recreation complex. But the Old Rockpile had served its purpose.

"I'll always remember War Memorial Stadium," Barry Levinson says, knowing full well that the future of Buffalo baseball—and, in many respects, Buffalo itself—lies with Pilot Field: "That's good for Buffalo, because Buffalo is a city in love with sports."

While Pilot Field had nothing in common with the Old Rockpile other than being in the same city, it brought back many memories of Offermann Stadium, particularly among former players whose careers had brought them there.

"Pilot Field is a special place, just like Offermann Stadium," says former major-league pitcher Jim Bunning, now a congressman from Kentucky, who was a Bison in 1953 and 1955. "It's a beautiful park and adds something to the game."

"I just hope baseball people understand that this is the kind of ballpark fans want, not the ones with domes and 70,000 seats; we've got too many of them," says Dallas Green, who went on to become both a big-league manager and general manager after having pitched for the Bisons in their last two seasons at Offermann. "Baseball was meant to be played in daylight, in an open stadium, in front of full houses, and on green grass. The people in Buffalo have shown they certainly can support major-league baseball."

Among those who were on the visiting side when they played at Offermann were Tommy Lasorda and Chuck Tanner, both of whom eventually managed World Series champions.

Lasorda, whose career took him to Los Angeles, says Pilot Field is "a great facility, and I think Buffalo would be a tremendous place to put a major-league baseball team."

"Pilot Field is a big-league ballpark," says Tanner, who achieved his greatest success in Pittsburgh. "Everything about it is big-league: the press box, the dugouts, the dressing rooms, the field. But what I like most about it is the feeling you get in that place. It reminds me of Ebbets Field in Brooklyn: The fans are close, the place is always packed, and it's a great environment for baseball. It's a fans' ballpark built for the fans. There's no dome here, and that's fine. Pilot Field has grass and dirt, and that's what baseball is all about."

Such words were especially gratifying to Bob Rich, who remembers that the situation was pretty bleak just a handful of years ago.

"I remember going to War Memorial Stadium when we first bought the team and sitting there with 250 people," Rich says.

I thought it was pathetic, but I never lost hope.
I figured we knew Buffalo, and we knew what a great

sports town it is. . . . I'm not that dumb. Like everybody else in Buffalo, I knew that baseball in the right environment would make it big in this city.

And that's one of the reasons we got involved with this: to see a stadium come about downtown. It's good for Buffalo, but it's also good for my family, my neighbors, and my community.

The reaction of his neighbors and his community was summarized with simple eloquence at Pilot Field by a fan holding a hand-lettered sign that said

THANK YOU
BOB RICH

THE DEEPEST EMOTIONS stirred by Pilot Field were in the people whose lives had been part of Buffalo baseball the longest.

"Joe would have loved Pilot Field," the dean of Buffalo sportscasters, eighty-year-old Ralph Hubbell, said in 1990 of his best friend, Joe McCarthy. "It's the kind of place baseball people cherish."

Pete Calieri, whose request for a W-2 form in 1979 had started Buffalo's baseball comeback, but whose career as an umpire had been cut short by injury, felt that Pilot Field was almost too good to be true: "God, it's such a beautiful place! I have to pinch myself every time I come here. I mean, I sit here and I think back to that day in 1979 and that phone call about my taxes; it makes me feel great. Sure, I miss baseball, but I still get a kick to think I played a part in bringing it back to Buffalo. That's something I can tell my grandchildren. Geez, I love this stadium!"

Don Colpoys, the first general manager of the Bisons when pro baseball came back to Buffalo in 1979, absolutely beams while beholding the new ballpark: "This is a baseball place. This is where the game was meant to be played, and it's a hell of a lot of fun to come here for a game."

At Pilot Field much sentimentality is elicited by the sight of Joe Alli and Don Labbruzzo, the two men, now retired, who had left so many tears in a New York hotel room two decades earlier, when the Bisons' franchise went down the drain.

"It is a beautiful park," Alli says. "If we would have had this park back then, we would have never lost our team."

Labbruzzo, who had used so much of his own money—and even borrowed on his life insurance and lost the equity in his home to the IRS—during those frenetically desperate days when he tried to save the Bisons by himself, finally had the opportunity to be reflective. Having recovered from a stroke, he could now sit back and allow himself to be soothed by Pilot Field:

> It's funny, I always told the people in Buffalo that if you build a fifteen-thousand-seat stadium downtown, you would pack the place. I was right. Thank God for Jimmy Griffin and Bob Rich. If those guys and this stadium had been around twenty years ago, Buffalo would already have a major-league club. I'm thrilled to death about Pilot Field. You can't imagine how good I feel in this ballpark. I only wish it could have been there when I was in Buffalo.

It was here now, though, first and foremost for the young: for Kevin Hodge's generation and those that will follow. Hodge, now in his early twenties, had been a bat boy when the Bisons were born again in 1979. These days, he works in the Rich Products bakery and takes care of the Pilot Field clubhouse. "This is a wonderful setting for baseball," he says with awe. "It makes you love the game even more."

Mindy Rich's reaction to Pilot Field is that "it's a repose. You can sit and get lost within yourself or take in the sights, sounds, and smells of the ballpark. . . . I also think the ballpark helps us to realize the shared dream of major-league baseball."

The people of Buffalo were now looking to her and her husband to make that ultimate dream come true.

12

BOTTOM OF THE NINTH

The streets are clogged with yellow cabs and people that never seem to stop swirling in chaos and congestion. At this stage of Buffalo's crusade to become part of major-league baseball, Bob and Mindy Rich are sure of at least one thing: They aren't in Cleveland anymore. Although that meeting occurred only three months ago, it seems longer. This time, there is no Buster Bison mascot to lend moral support. And there are no busloads of aroused fans from back home chanting, "Let's go, Buffalo." There aren't even any swarming reporters; they're ensconced at an ad hoc media headquarters in the Halloran House hotel four blocks away. Today—Tuesday, September 18, 1990—the caretakers of Buffalo's baseball hopes find themselves in New York City. It's a cool and breezy 68 degrees at just after three in the afternoon as bright sunshine dances with a bluish glow off the aluminum and glass of the fifty-nine-story Citicorp Center at 53rd Street and Lexington Avenue in midtown Manhattan, where Bob and Mindy Rich enter an elevator. There is an air of nervous anticipation as they and two other members of their group—Erie County Executive Dennis Gorski and national media analyst John Mansell, Jr.—start riding toward the forty-ninth floor. Once there, they walk down a corridor to a waiting room at the law offices of Wilkie, Farr & Gallagher, where within minutes they will have their pivotal encounter with the National League Expansion Committee. Buffalo has been waiting years for this.

The four of them are dressed almost as a team. Bob Rich, Gorski, and Mansell are in dark suits, white shirts, and power ties. Mindy Rich wears a black suit and gray blouse. Their appearance sends a clear message: We mean business. The four of them had arrived the day before and have spent most of the last twenty-four hours in the Hill & Knowlton public relations offices on Lexington Avenue, rehearsing a presentation that must be letter-perfect.

Their mood is purposeful yet somewhat uneasy, akin to that among applicants for a first job. As they sip coffee, their conversation is light, if a bit forced, as they wait for the last member of their group—a former professional baseball player—to arrive.

Notable by his absence is Jimmy Griffin. Several months earlier, while the expansion timetable was still unclear, Buffalo's mayor had planned a trip to Ireland with his wife, Marge, to visit the home of their ancestors. For two weeks, since learning that the two events would conflict, Griffin had been anguished, but the loyalties to his wife and to their homeland couldn't be denied. Nothing else could have kept him from helping deliver Buffalo's biggest major-league pitch. "This is the toughest decision I've made and one of the biggest disappointments of my political career," said the man who brought professional baseball back to his city in 1979. "I promised Marge I would go, and I'm going." But the mayor isn't totally absent on this pivotal day, says Bob Rich: "We feel Jimmy is here in spirit."

Pinch-hitting for his political adversary as a representative of local government is Dennis Gorski, although the second-year county executive doesn't see his role in quite that way. In August, the county had committed about $26 million toward the proposed expansion of Pilot Field, to be financed through the sale of bonds by the Erie County Industrial Development Agency and a percentage of the county's hotel bed tax. That amount reflected 52 percent of what was needed for an upper deck to increase the stadium's capacity from 20,900 to 41,530 for big-league ball.

"I feel there is a regional responsibility for county government to help finance this project," Gorski said. "The stadium may be in Buffalo, but a major-league team in Pilot Field would benefit everyone in the metropolitan area."

Dennis Gorski, forty-six, who decades earlier had been a scrappy catcher at South Buffalo's Bishop Timon High School, had anted up for the county and was now a major player in the most important baseball competition in Buffalo history. This was *his* shot at the big leagues. And as the highest-ranking representative of the county's taxpayers, he says, "I have a right to be here."

UNLIKE JIMMY GRIFFIN'S, or Bob Rich's, or Mario Cuomo's, Dennis Gorski's father was a politician—Chester C. Gorski, who for nearly four decades had been one of the most influential political figures in Western New York. He served one term in the House of Representatives and spent fourteen years as president of Buffalo's Common Council. Chet Gorski, who died in 1975, was a dyed-in-the-wool Democrat, an absolute party loyalist, fully absorbed in his job, sometimes at the expense of time for his family, including his two children, Dennis and older brother Jerome. "My father was a consummate politician," Dennis Gorski says. "My only regret is that I didn't spend more time with my father."

All four of Dennis Gorski's grandparents came to America from Eastern Poland near the turn of the century. His father and his mother, Helen, reared their children in a neighborhood called Kaisertown on Buffalo's East Side. Young Dennis began building his baseball reputation at Our Lady of Czestochowa grammar school on Clinton Street. None of the other kids wanted to take the physical beating of playing catcher, so Dennis volunteered. Although he was continually banged up, he enjoyed catching because he felt a sense of control and liked the idea of being in on every play.

His father's demanding political and governmental schedules precluded much sharing in Dennis's baseball exploits, but one particularly memorable day the two did spend together was in Pittsburgh, where they went to see the St. Louis Cardinals play the Pirates at Forbes Field. None other than Stan "The Man" Musial came over to talk with the boy and his father before the game and left an indelible imprint. "Stan Musial was a hero to every Polish kid in America," Dennis Gorski recalls, "and to have a chance to talk to him was one of the greatest thrills in my life."

The boy's hometown thrills were provided by the Bisons, and he couldn't spend enough time at Offermann Stadium. To him, the player who stood head and shoulders above the rest—even above the exalted Luke Easter—was a burly catcher named Ray Noble, whose last name rhymed with his first and who had a total of forty-one home runs and 134 RBIs in the seasons of 1957 and 1958. "He was this big [five feet eleven inches, 220 pounds] Cuban guy, and I was in awe of him," Gorski says of Noble, who was a member of the famed 1951 Giants team that beat the Dodgers for the National League pennant on Bobby Thomson's "shot heard round the world." Noble, who was thirty-eight by the time he arrived in Buffalo, "was a good catcher," Gorski says, "and he could hit home runs. . . . One day, they let the kids on the field to talk to the players. I ran up to Noble. He was talking about catching, but he had a thick Spanish accent. I couldn't understand him, and I was disappointed, but he was still my favorite player."

Gorski's first big decision as a teenager was to enroll at Bishop Timon High, then a baseball power in the Buffalo Catholic League. Brimming with self-confidence, he wrote on his catcher's mitt: "the best." During his freshman season, seven of Coach Mel Palano's nine starters at Timon earned all-league honors, including outfielder Frank Cipriani, a future major-leaguer with the Kansas City Athletics. Gorski had big-league aspirations of his own, but there wasn't much call for five-foot ten-inch, 155-pound catchers with weak throwing arms. Still, he did everything he could to attract the attention of local baseball people, most notably Cy Williams, Buffalo's best-known major-league talent scout. Gorski played amateur ball and could hit, but the big-league size and arm just weren't there. "I always hoped Cy Williams would take some interest in signing me," he says, "but he never did." (Years later, Gorski would laugh at the irony of his brother Jerome, a future State Supreme Court Justice, marrying Janet Williams—Cy's daughter.)

By the time Dennis Gorski was sixteen, Offermann Stadium was being torn down. "I had such affection for the place, because it was such a big part of my childhood," he says wistfully. "I remember one day when they were tearing it down, I took a ride over there." On that late fall afternoon in 1960, Gorski stepped onto the old field and was overcome by a sense of melancholy as he slowly surveyed this baseball graveyard: "I walked on the field and just looked around. I felt terrible; it was like a part of my life was being destroyed. The stands along the left-field line were torn down—just a pile of wood, steel, and concrete. Offermann was such a special place, and now here it was, being smashed to bits. I thought baseball in Buffalo would never be the same." As was the case with most local fans, it didn't take Gorski long to lose interest in the Bisons after they moved to War Memorial Stadium in 1961: "I'd go to games there, but it was different. It just wasn't made for baseball."

It wouldn't take long, either, to realize that he just wasn't made for baseball, at least as a pro. So he furthered his education at Le Moyne College, earning a degree in English literature but uncertain about a career. He graduated in 1966, at the height of the Vietnam War, and the sense of duty instilled by his father compelled him to do his part. He enlisted in the Marines and served from 1967 to 1969 in Vietnam, where he was a captain in combat.

After returning home as a decorated veteran, Dennis Gorski was ready to extend the family's legacy of public service. He began his political career by winning a seat in the Erie County Legislature in 1972. Two years later, he was elected to the New York State Assembly, where he spent the next thirteen years.

In the early seventies, Gorski's friendship with Bob Rich blossomed. Gorski was a strong supporter of the Riches in their battle with the Bills' out-of-town ownership to affix the family name to the new pro football stadium in Orchard Park. He also helped Bob Rich get appointed to the state's sports advisory board. He and Rich were teammates on handball teams in the Empire State Games during the early seventies, earning silver and bronze medals. By the mid-1980s, though, the two men had drifted apart, personally and politically.

In 1987, Gorski won a tough primary to earn the Democratic nomination for county executive, an office that had been held by Republicans since its inception twenty-seven years earlier. His father had run in that first county executive's race in 1960 and lost by a close margin. Now, the son would take his own case to the people. Long ago, the father had realized what a tenacious competitor his son was and nicknamed him "Tiger." That tenacity, sometimes mistaken for humorlessness, was never more evident than in the 1987 campaign, when his opponent was two-term incumbent Ed Rutkowski.

Rutkowski had long enjoyed a high public profile in the Buffalo area. He had been a jack-of-all-trades—even a last-resort quarterback—after coming from Notre Dame to play for the Bills. He had gone on to serve as an analyst for Bills radio broadcasts and was a longtime friend and political ally of then-Congressman Jack Kemp, who had been the Bills' quarterback in their glory years. Griffin, a nominal Democrat, was backing Republican Rutkowski for county executive in 1987. This rankled Gorski, an earnest party man. In addition, Bob Rich was serving as Rutkowski's campaign treasurer. Nevertheless, Gorski won the election with 62 percent of the vote to become the first Democratic county executive in the history of Erie County.

Three months after Dennis Gorski took office, Pilot Field opened. But Gorski's euphoria was, to a large extent, spoiled by political tension. On Opening Day, he helped cut the ribbon for the new ballpark, but he wasn't invited onto the field for the ceremonies. The county had played a relatively minor role in the construction of Pilot Field, so on one of his city's most glorious days, Dennis Gorski was virtually an invisible man.

Time didn't seem to heal the wounds, either. On Opening Day 1990, for instance, Gorski was invited to the pregame parade but not to the on-the-field ceremony. So he passed up both the game and the parade, spending the time instead at a party to celebrate the Polish-American tradition of Dyngus Day.

Just a few months later, though, Gorski was the point man for the county's commitment of $26 million toward readying Pilot Field for major-league baseball—the largest share from any level of government. In another of the countless examples of baseball unifying the community, Dennis Gorski and Bob Rich saw their fellowship renewed.

"I think this thing has brought Bob and me back together," Gorski says. "It has been a restoration of an old friendship." For this father of five and his wife, Mary Jo, Pilot Field "symbolizes the resurgence of the Buffalo metropolitan area. It's such a beautiful park; it's got the spirit of Offermann Stadium, and I thought I'd never find that anywhere again. I take my boys there, and it's just like when I was a kid. We go early and watch batting practice and infield practice. Somehow, you never outgrow this game. You know something? I truly love baseball; I always have."

"Dennis," says Bob Rich, "has done an excellent job for baseball."

"I don't know if it can resolve every conflict," Gorski says, "but baseball is a reflection of this community. To put it simply, baseball has brought people together in our community. We all share the same dream."

ON THE FORTY-NINTH FLOOR of the Citicorp Center, in the same place where five years earlier Buffalo had tried to get a collective foot in Major League Baseball's door, the three pursuers of a city's dream have been waiting with their carefully selected media analyst for the arrival of the fifth member of their group: the governor of New York.

At ten minutes before the appointed hour of four, Mario Cuomo enters, far into a day not only of running the nation's second-largest state but of campaigning for a third term. The generally frenetic pace of Cuomo's schedule has not permitted him to rehearse his remarks in behalf of Buffalo baseball; for the most part, he will be reading from index cards prepared for him. On a day in which he's booked solid, this isn't even the final stop; right after this, he's to go to the Halloran House for a baseball news conference and then hurry to an appointment on Wall Street. Having had almost no time for lunch, the governor is hungry and tired.

The decision that Cuomo should be part of the Buffalo group for this vital presentation had been a calculated risk; the presence of an outspoken politician can cut both ways in conclaves with the power brokers of baseball. "We thought about that," Cuomo had said. "I said to Bob and Mindy, 'I'm not sure exactly what role you should have me play. How do they feel about politicians? If it's better for me to stay away, I will . . . but if you think it's right for me to talk, I will. . . . Under some circumstances, your political identification with politicians could be a negative. I don't know how baseball people feel about it.'"

But Bob and Mindy Rich harbored no doubts. "Other governors are going to be there from competing cities," they had told Cuomo. "We'd like you to be there."

Actually, says Cuomo, "I'm glad I'm here. It's important for the owners to know to what extent government will contribute to stadium expansion. . . . They want to see it on the record; they want to know the money will be there."

So with Buffalo's baseball future at stake, Mario Cuomo is here—physically drained, overdue for a meal and with nowhere near the preparation he would like. But the waiting room is free of worry. Who better than Joe DiMaggio to be batting for you in the bottom of the ninth?

IT'S FOUR O'CLOCK. Zero hour.

The Buffalo contingent slowly walks down the hallway to the meeting room.

The meeting is scheduled to last forty-five minutes, which has been the length for other presentations on this day by three ownership groups from Miami and one each from Sacramento and Denver. The presentation by Denver, considered Buffalo's chief rival, has just finished as the Buffalo group enters. Colorado Governor Roy Romer is leaving the room and waves hello to Cuomo. He then looks at the Buffalo group, smiles and says, "Good luck."

Cuomo has brought along Vincent Tese, the state's economic development director. After they, Gorski, and media analyst Mansell are in the room, the only ones still to enter are Bob and Mindy Rich. Just before they go inside, Bob Rich kisses his wife on the cheek. "Mindy," he says softly, "here it is; this is what we've been waiting for." She smiles and squeezes his hand. Bob Rich will say later that he feels like a figure skater about to take the ice in the Olympics. Now, it's time for the big jump—the triple axel—to dazzle the judges. After nearly eight years of practice, he's ready for it. He takes a long look at Mindy and thinks with pride about how his wife has worked herself to the point of exhaustion in preparation for this day. She has been indefatigable and unrelenting; just a few weeks ago, on Labor Day, Mindy, in a sweat suit, and he, in walking shorts and a T-shirt, had left a picnic in Canada to head back to Rich Products headquarters to work on the presentation. For the greater part of a year, there hasn't even been time to enjoy holidays. They have been driving themselves so hard, and this, now, is their moment.

Preceding the Buffalo group into the room were the six National League representatives: Douglas Danforth, chairman of both the Bisons' parent club, the Pittsburgh Pirates, and the league's Expansion Committee. With him are fellow committee members Fred Wilpon, owner of the New York Mets, and John McMullen, head man of the Houston Astros. Assisting them are Louis Hoynes, Jr., attorney for the National League; Phyllis Collins, league vice president, and Tom Ostertag, general counsel for Commissioner Fay Vincent. Curiously, Bill White, president of the league and a member of the committee, isn't here.

The meeting room, carpeted in dark blue, is crammed with reference materials and gadgets. A huge, light-oak table takes up most of the center. At one end of that table is a smaller one, creating an ell shape. There are no windows, and in each corner of the room is a wooden booth with a telephone. At one end of the wall behind the committee members is a bar. At the other end are two videocassette recorders on top of a television. Nearby is an easel that holds a large chart, now covered. Next to the easel is a screen for showing slides, and there is a slide projector at one end of the large table. Lighting from round fixtures hanging from the ceiling reflects subtly off the textured, ivory-colored walls.

Cuomo, who is to speak first, becomes the focus of attention. The first person to greet him is Danforth. "Don't forget, Governor, you once signed a contract with the Pirates," Danforth says as he and Cuomo shake hands. Wilpon, who grew up in Brooklyn with Sandy Koufax and Larry King, stands next to Danforth. When Wilpon hears Danforth joking with Cuomo about Pittsburgh, he can't resist a bit of needling. "Hey, Governor," Wilpon says, "how can a guy from Queens be pulling so hard for Buffalo?"

Cuomo laughs and points to his watch: "Fred, the people of Buffalo gave me this watch ten years ago, before I was governor, and I've worn it ever since. It is evidence of my eternal commitment to that area."

Danforth greets the Riches and says, "Too bad you didn't pull out that eighteen-inning playoff game against Nashville."

"We tried our best," says Bob Rich. "That was a killer."

Mindy Rich nods. "I'd rather not talk about it," she says with a laugh.

McMullen asks about Jimmy Griffin. "He had to go to Ireland," Bob Rich responds.

"Give him my best regards," McMullen says, "and tell him it's okay. No Irishman worth his salt can turn down a trip to the Old Sod."

They all then take their seats, which are on opposite sides of the large table. Cuomo, his reputation for eloquence preceding him, begins the presentation by talking about Buffalo's economic resurgence. "At the moment," he says, "this is the strongest economic area of the state. Buffalo, with free trade, with a new burst of vitality, is attracting investments from all over . . . [and has] the lowest unemployment rate in the state. Buffalo has a baseball team and a football team that draw capacity crowds."

Cuomo, glancing at his three-by-five cards, emphasizes that "these are *real* baseball fans. . . . These people in Buffalo like being out at the game where it can rain on your head. I also like the idea there is no roof on this field and that there's real grass." Cuomo and Tese both recite economic statistics to support Buffalo's case, and the governor reiterates his support for the expansion of Pilot Field to accommodate a big-league team.

Now, it is Gorski's turn.

"Unemployment in the Erie-Niagara Frontier is 4.6 percent, lower than the state and national average," he says, adding that the free-trade agreement with Canada is expected to create 50,000 new jobs for the region. He says that real-estate values are up by nearly 20 percent in the last three years, in contrast to other areas of the state, where those values have dropped. Gorski says sales-tax revenues in Erie County have risen by 6.7 percent, while the average rise in the state has been 3 percent. He mentions that *Fortune* magazine has declared Buffalo one of the top five growth communities in the country. Gorski points out that tourism is an $850 million industry in the region, with 7.5 million visitors each summer coming to nearby Niagara Falls during the baseball season. Then he talks about financing stadium expansion: "There is virtual unanimity of support of a financing package to put an upper deck on Pilot Field. It is not dependent on a referendum, not dependent on the whim of a county legislature or the state legislature. The plan is in place, and as soon as Buffalo gets a team, it will be put into action. That's all there is to it."

About twenty minutes into the Buffalo presentation, the floor is opened to questions for Cuomo and Gorski. The committee appears a bit in awe of Cuomo, a consummate ad-libber, and all the queries are aimed at Gorski.

"When were you elected, and how long do you plan to stay in office?" Danforth asks.

Gorski smiles. "I came into office in 1988, and I intend to be there a long time. But even if I'm not, there is virtual unanimous support to expand Pilot Field, and for baseball in Buffalo."

After a few other questions, the public officials are finished with their part of the presentation. Cuomo and Gorski get up and shake hands with the committee members. During the encounter, Gorski says to Danforth: "Good luck with the Pirates' game tonight."

Wilpon, standing standing next to them, interjects, "Hey, what about the Mets?"

Gorski, laughing nervously, replies, "I didn't mean anything by it, and I certainly wish you and the Mets the best of luck."

Wilpon laughs.

Cuomo smiles.

"Let's go, Dennis," the governor says, and the two politicians leave the room. They've done their jobs.

FOR ALL PRACTICAL PURPOSES, this is John Mansell's game to win or lose for Buffalo. In this era of billion-dollar deals for the rights to televise professional sports, the conventional wisdom is that the size of Buffalo's media market is simply too small. It is now up to Mansell, a hired gun with no personal ties to Buffalo, to shoot holes in that conventional wisdom.

Bob and Mindy Rich have selected him for maximum impact. The thirty-eight-year-old lawyer from Fairfax, Virginia, works for Kagan Media Appraisals and is an editor of the publication *Media Sports Business,* the recognized authority on sports media marketing. Most important, Mansell is an insider. His firm has done marketing work for Major League Baseball, and his credibility is unquestioned. "He wasn't some guy we just pulled off the street," Bob Rich has said. "The owners have worked with him, and they know and respect his opinion." The dark-haired Mansell, about five feet eight inches, and of average build, projects a studious attitude that's accented by thick glasses. The man speaks softly but carries a big portfolio—in this instance, a brown leather briefcase packed with charts, graphs, and fact sheets.

Mansell's data form the centerpiece of the entire presentation; the strategy is to market Buffalo as a regional franchise, encompassing not only western and central New York State but also northern Pennsylvania and southern Ontario. A native of Detroit, Mansell has been a lifelong Tigers fan, and his face lights up with the mention of the 1968 World Series and bygone heroes such as Al Kaline, Mickey Lolich, and Willie Horton. This season, his rooting interest is in Cecil Fielder's quest for fifty home runs. "What a great year he's having!" Mansell will say later in casual conversation. "I check the papers every day to see if he hit another home run." Fielder eventually would hit 51 for the Tigers, and on this day, Mansell is stepping up to the plate for Buffalo, for a big-league team of the future called the Bisons. He rises from his chair and comes out swinging.

"I'm here to dispel some misconceptions about the size and strength of the upstate New York market," he tells Danforth, McMullen, Wilpon, and the others, pointing out immediately that within a seventy-five-mile radius, Buffalo has a higher television penetration, including over-the-air and cable, than rival candidates such as Tampa–St. Petersburg, Denver, and Phoenix. Buffalo has 1.05 million TV households, or 64.6 percent penetration, he asserts, compared with 58.9 percent penetration for Tampa–St. Pete, 52.3 for Denver, and 43.7 for Phoenix.

Furthermore, he says, the advantage increases at a radius of 150 miles. "If you look at the reach of other candidates over a 150-mile radius," Mansell says, "Buffalo (2.2 million) turns out to be the size, in TV households, of Phoenix (1.2 million) and Denver (1 million) put together. In terms of cable subscribers, there are 1.22 million within a 150-mile radius of Buffalo. That's three times as many as in Denver (452,000) and twice as many as in Phoenix (580,000)."

Only Tampa–St. Pete (1.48 million) has higher numbers among Buffalo rivals. Buffalo's seventy-five-mile TV-penetration rate of 64.6 percent, Mansell says, is higher than in three current big-league markets: Cincinnati, 64.0 percent, Minneapolis–St. Paul, 46.8 percent, and St. Louis, 46.4 percent. At the 150-mile radius, he says, Buffalo increases that advantage over those cities.

Mansell reiterates that Buffalo's four commercial television stations reach 1.05 million households. For a major-league team, a Buffalo station would act as flagship for a regional over-the-air network that could include such communities as Binghamton, Elmira, Rochester, Syracuse, Utica, and Watertown. "Sports networks play a very important role in the television revenue of a given market," Mansell says. "And in upstate New York, there are 800,000 subscribers to the Niagara Frontier Sports Network. Denver has a 700,000 regional sports network and Phoenix 230,000."

Population? It was time for Mansell to take another healthy cut. He tells the committee that there are 2.8 million residents within a seventy-five-mile radius of downtown Buffalo, more than Kansas City's 2.2 million and comparable to big-league cities such as St. Louis, Minneapolis–St. Paul, and San Diego. In a 125-mile radius, Buffalo has 3.7 million residents from which to draw. That, he says, is more than the population of the entire state of Colorado, 3.3 million, or Arizona, 3.6 million. Even when using only a seventy-five-mile radius, he says, a study by the KPMG Peat Marwick research firm projected an average attendance of 1.9 million for Buffalo with a big-league team.

As Mansell is talking, Bob Rich is operating a slide projector to display the statistics. But the pressure of the moment is evident. Every so often, he clicks too rapidly or too slowly. "Let me say one thing," Rich says with an exasperated smile. "This is the last presentation at which I use the clicker on a slide carousel."

Everyone laughs. The pressure is eased. After answering some questions, Mansell leaves the room, and Bob Rich walks up to the chart on the easel. On it are listed the six primary criteria established by Major League Baseball for an expansion franchise: government support, media-market size, location, experienced management, ownership, and stadium. When Cuomo and Gorski had concluded their remarks, Rich uncovered the chart, picked up a strawberry-scented marking pen, and put a big, bright-red check mark next to the first criterion. Now, with particular relish, he checks off the second. As far as he's concerned, the myth of Buffalo as a small-market city had just been demolished by John Mansell.

A relatively late-developing perception considered damaging to Buffalo's chances is geography. After it became clear that Major League Baseball intended to add only two teams in the nineties, the notion developed that there would be one from the East and one from the West—presumably from virgin territory—and that Florida would get the one from the East. Buffalo's proximity to Toronto, Cleveland, and Pittsburgh also raised the issue of whether the region already had enough franchises and whether one more would impinge on any of the others.

It is Mindy Rich's turn to tackle head-on the nettlesome question of location.

"Our franchise should have no negative impact on adjacent major-league markets," she tells the committee, adding that Toronto is on its way to setting a major-league attendance record of nearly 3.9 million while the Bisons went over a million for the third straight season. She mentions a recent survey of the eight-county region of Western New York showing that 4.2 percent of respondents are Blue Jays fans. The same survey shows that 1.4 percent of the respondents are Pirates fans and 1.9 percent are Indians fans. She stresses that the fans in the survey said they are hungry for a local big-league team and that 74.3 percent of them said they would attend big-league games locally, while just 13.7 percent said they had attended big-league games elsewhere in the last two years.

Bob Rich rises again and checks off the third criterion: location.

The next category on the chart is experienced management. Bob and Mindy Rich explain how Buffalo has operated Double-A and Triple-A franchises during the last eight years and that the Bisons have enjoyed unprecedented marketing success at the minor-league level, with group sales, promotions, concerts, advertising partnerships with major corporations, youth baseball clinics, baseball seminars, hot-stove luncheons, a speakers' bureau, and the extraordinary, fan-friendly atmosphere at Pilot Field. The Riches remind the committee that Buffalo is the first minor-league city to draw a million or more fans more than once—and that it has done so for three consecutive years. In 213 dates at Pilot Field, average attendance was 16,400—for a ballpark with a capacity of 20,500—including forty-one sellouts. They point out that more than 16,000 fans already have placed down payments to reserve season tickets for a major-league team in Buffalo, to go along with 9,000 existing season-ticket holders for Triple-A ball. The torrent of favorable facts is all but overwhelming, and Bob Rich once again walks to the chart and puts a big, red check mark next to the fourth criterion: management.

Four blocks away, Cuomo is extolling Buffalo's fans to members of the new media covering the expansion race and reminds one reporter skeptical of Buffalo's weather that in 1990 there was a grand total of three rainouts at Pilot Field.

For Bob and Mindy Rich, the next item on the agenda for the committee is perhaps their greatest strength: stability of ownership.

Everyone in the room realizes that the most powerful point in Buffalo's favor is the Rich family itself; its community roots run deep, its long-term commitment is unquestionable, its resources are formidable, and its perseverance has been nothing short of amazing. In May, veteran *New York Times* reporter Murray Chass had written in *Sport* magazine about the fifteen baseball people every fan should know. Chass had placed Bob Rich fourth on the list, labeling him "The Expansionist."

But even The Expansionist couldn't go it alone at a time when Major League Baseball was charging $95 million just to get into the game. Bob Rich would head an ownership group that included Mindy, his father, and his brother, David. No problem there. Yet it was equally important that the other investors likewise have reputations as heavy hitters.

Their names had been a closely kept secret until two weeks before this presentation, and one name had jumped out at seasoned observers as not only surprising but perhaps decisive: Jeremy M. Jacobs.

The Jacobs name had been prominent in the sports world since not long after the family business was founded in 1915 by Marvin Jacobs, Jeremy's uncle, along with his father, Louis, and uncle Charles. Their father was a Jewish tailor who emigrated from Poland to lower Manhattan at the turn of the century and tried to climb out of grinding poverty by moving to Cedar Street on Buffalo's lower East Side. Max Jacobs's three sons were to be the founders of Sportservice, which began by selling candy and peanuts at burlesque houses and grew into an astonishingly lucrative worldwide food-service and sports concessions empire that by the eighties was generating annual gross revenues well in excess of a billion dollars.

Louis Jacobs wore the hats of vendor, office worker, and concessions partner at Buffalo Baseball Park, a relationship that "began prior to 1920," writes historian Joe Overfield, and "from that day forward, Bison fans always bought their peanuts, popcorn, Coney Island red hots, beer, pop and scorecards from the Jacobses." The three brothers were part of a group that helped build Offermann Stadium, and they eventually gained control both of the ballpark and the baseball franchise. They shrewdly helped finance baseball figures such as Connie Mack and Bill Veeck, as well as major-league teams and ballparks. Their significance was such that when the three brothers died within nineteen months of one another in the late sixties, Overfield writes, "*The Sporting News* proposed that the brothers be given a special niche in the Hall of Fame for their contributions to baseball, saying: 'The Jacobses meant the difference between staying afloat and sinking for many clubs. They put their money on the line.'"

Now, as the nineties began, Jeremy Jacobs, the principal heir, who had begun in the family business as an ordinary, unprivileged, learn-from-scratch concessionaire at Offermann Stadium, was putting *his* money on the line. Sportservice had evolved into Emprise, Sportsystems, and now a conglomerate called Delaware North Companies, with holdings that included racetracks, and the Boston Garden; Jacobs himself owns the NHL's Boston Bruins.

Jeremy Jacobs, now fifty and the father of six, has been chairman and chief executive officer of Delaware North since 1980 and also is chairman of Goldome Bank. With a fortune estimated at $550 million or more, he is far and away the wealthiest person in the Buffalo area. "I know my father taught me the desire to keep our family business at the forefront of the sports world," this intensely private man had told *Western New York* magazine in July, and despite the vast scope of that business, Jeremy Jacobs has kept its home the same: downtown Buffalo. And in this case, what was good for Buffalo would be especially good for Delaware North; it would manage the concessions once Pilot Field became a big-league ballpark.

By coincidence, Louis Jacobs had groomed his youngest son for the top job by giving him responsibility for the Canadian arm of Sportservice, much as Robert Rich, Sr., had done with son Bob at Rich Products. There had never been a closeness between the two families, but now they were being drawn together by a fusion of two forces so compelling as to be irresistible: Buffalo and baseball.

In terms of influence and financial clout, the only other Buffalo family considered to be in the same league with those of Jacobs and Rich are the Knoxes, the culturally distinguished inheritors of the F. W. Woolworth Company retailing fortune and the prime movers behind the renowned Albright-Knox Art Gallery and the NHL's Buffalo Sabres. Bob Rich proudly tells the committee that members of the Knox family, including Marine Midland Bank chairman Northrup Knox, are part of his investment group, too.

Of the eleven additional investors in Rich's group, seven are from outside the Buffalo area (one from southern Ontario), including Luis A. Gomez, Jr., a San Juan, Puerto Rico, insurance executive who owned the Puerto Rican Baseball League's Mayaquez Indians for fifteen years; and a prominent African-American businessman, Robert W. Jones, president of Robert W. Jones & Associates, of New York City, the state's largest minority real estate appraisal, consulting, and development firm, a man who decades ago rooted for Jackie Robinson.

Among the Buffalo names, one stirs particular poignancy: Robert Swados, an attorney with close ties to the Knoxes who is vice chairman and counsel of the Sabres and serves as secretary of the NHL. Twenty-two years ago, it was Swados who had come to Chicago to spearhead Buffalo's bid for a big-league franchise, only to see it end in bitter disappointment when the National League chose Montreal instead. This time, things are different. "We didn't have a stadium like Pilot Field," Swados says, "and we didn't have an owner like Bob Rich."

Bob Rich walks back to the easel.

Ownership: *check.*

Now, for his finale, Bob Rich is ready for some showmanship. He will bring one of his investors into the room, by videotape, for the climactic category: stadium.

Bob Rich turns on a VCR. On the screen appears the familiar image of one of his out-of-town investors, Larry King.

"I remember the first time I laid eyes on Pilot Field," King says. "It reminded me of all the things I love about baseball: The fun, the excitement, the feelings you get from this park—an intimacy, a closeness to the action—are really what baseball's all about. What they've done here in Buffalo is blend the best of baseball tradition with the luxury and comfort of a modern stadium. . . ."

There is no mistaking the second image, either: Pilot Field, jam-packed with exuberant fans. There are interviews with fans of all ages and even chats with some old-time ball players, including Buffalo-born Warren Spahn. King goes on to say that Pilot Field is "a symbol, not only of Buffalo's surging economy, but of the baseball heritage of this proud city." He concludes the four-minute video by saying, "When you consider the criteria, when you consider the facts, one thing is clear: Buffalo is The Natural for Expansion."

Bob Rich goes to the easel for the sixth time.

He makes one last bold stroke in bright red.

Stadium: *check!*

"These were your criteria," Bob Rich confidently tells the committee, "and I think we've met them."

The formal presentation is over. The committee praises the Buffalo group for its thoroughness and, at the end of the first of three days of presentations from the ten prospective cities, appreciates that Bob Rich has kept within the time limit. It is now time for a little inside baseball—the assiduously guarded business side. The meeting continues for about forty-five minutes, doubling the allotted time. This is the committee's choice, but Bob and Mindy Rich have no complaints.

After having started at four, it is now five-thirty. Finally, there are no more questions. As Bob and Mindy Rich leave the room to link up again with Gorski and Mansell, there is an unspoken sentiment: Thank you, Jimmy Griffin, wherever you are.

AFTER ANOTHER FORTY-NINE-STORY elevator ride, Bob and Mindy Rich, Gorski, and Mansell are back on the streets of midtown Manhattan. They are awaited by the reporters at the Halloran House four blocks away. Or is it four miles? The journey to the front porch of major-league baseball had been a long haul indeed. There was nothing more the people of Buffalo could do; it was out of their hands now. Speaking not only for herself but for the three people walking with her, Mindy Rich exhales and says, "You know, I'm just exhausted. I just want this thing to be over."

It isn't, though. Almost as if on autopilot, the four of them trudge through the phalanxes of rush-hour commuters en route to East 49th Street and Lexington Avenue, where Bisons General Manager Mike Billoni is nervously pacing outside the Halloran House. He seems lost without a walkie-talkie; in fact, he keeps putting his hand to his ear as if he's using one. "Geez," he says to himself, "I've got to get my walkie-talkie back."

Mike Buczkowski, the Bisons' director of public relations, is at a deli grabbing a quick roast beef sandwich. While eating, he notices that two cabs collide, although not seriously. Buczkowski thinks nothing of it until one of the cabbies takes a large red wrench and proceeds to smash the windshield of the other cab. Buczkowski practically falls off his chair. "What's wrong?" asks a woman sitting nearby. "Did you see that?" Buczkowski says in a startled voice. "That was nothing," the woman replies. "This is *New York;* it happens all the time."

The reporters and camera people assembled around Billoni are getting a bit impatient as the evening sky turns into twilight. One of them is red-haired, *Eyewitness News* cameraman Mickey Osterreicher from Buffalo's ABC affiliate, WKBW-TV. He had worked with Billoni and Joe Alli at the *Courier-Express* as a photographer until the paper died in 1982. Any moment now, his thumb will be pressing the lens button to start his ENG machinery and record the Buffalo group's return from the long-anticipated presentation. Unlike the still-startled Buczkowski and most of the others from Buffalo, Osterreicher feels right at home. "I was born in the Bronx in 1952, after Mickey Mantle just came to town," he says. "I was named after Mantle." Now, he acknowledges, there are new loyalties: "It would be great for Buffalo to get a big-league team. It's just so exciting to be here today and be a part of it."

A nearby presence is the "voice of the Bisons," Pete Weber, carrying on a tradition of Buffalo baseball broadcasting that includes play-by-play men such as Roger Baker, Ralph Hubbell, Bill Mazer, Phil Soisson, Van Miller, and Stan Barron. Similar to the way Bob Rich and Mindy Roth had found each other, Pete Weber proposed to his future bride, Claudia, at a baseball game, and this moment is one of profound emotion. "This day," says Pete Weber, "has been a long time coming."

At about ten minutes to six, Bob and Mindy Rich, Gorski, and Mansell arrive at the front door. There is a media rush. "How did it go, Bob?" a reporter yells. "Great!" Rich says with a smile as he continues walking at a brisk pace. "It's always nice when baseball people get to talk to other baseball people."

Just as Mario Cuomo had held court at the Halloran House about ninety minutes earlier, Bob and Mindy Rich, Dennis Gorski, and John Mansell now hold their own news conference. Bob Rich hasn't had much to say publicly since August, when he expressed interest in buying the Montreal Expos if owner Charles Bronfman couldn't meet his September deadline for finding a Canadian buyer. The Canadian government and private interests had intervened at the eleventh hour, and it appeared that the Expos would remain in Montreal. That door was apparently closed, so Buffalo had only one way to get in: expansion.

For most of the next hour, Bob and Mindy Rich, Gorski, and Mansell talk with the media. Most of the discussion centers on how Buffalo stacks up against the other nine contending cities: Denver, Miami, Tampa–St. Pete, Orlando, Phoenix, Washington, Sacramento, Nashville, and Vancouver. One of the Florida cities, most likely Tampa–St. Pete, was considered a cinch. That left seven cities besides Buffalo in the hunt for the one remaining franchise, with Denver thought to have the inside track because of geography, but Buffalo right alongside as perhaps the most deserving candidate among the ten. Could this possibly mean that Buffalo was being set up for another fall—that it would again be Heartbreak City? Was Jerome Holtzman correct back in Cleveland when he called the whole process a "charade" and concluded that Denver and Tampa–St. Pete were locks?

The word-of-mouth emanating from the national media was beginning to indicate otherwise. Political commentator, best-selling author, and baseball maven George F. Will was calling Buffalo the favorite, because of Bob Rich's ownership and Pilot Field. NBC sportscaster Bob Costas, too, said Buffalo was an "excellent" choice for one of the two expansion clubs. "If baseball is going to adhere to its own guidelines," Paul Hagen of the *Philadelphia Daily News* wrote in *Baseball America*, "Buffalo has to get a team." And today, the day of Buffalo's presentation, widely respected writer Peter Gammons says flat-out on ESPN that Buffalo had a "tremendous" shot at one of the franchises. Why? "Ownership . . . Bob Rich."

Before the gathering of reporters at the Halloran House, however, Bob Rich emphasizes that it's much too early to celebrate. "There's nothing more we can do now but wait," he says, referring to the expansion timetable that calls for a "short list" of finalists by December and then, sometime between March and September of 1991, the committee's recommendation of two cities to the twenty-six major-league owners, who in turn will vote whether to approve. "It's all going to come down to those twenty-six owners in one room on that day," Bob Rich says. "They're the ones who will make the decision. Today, we showed that we met all the criteria and reaffirmed what a wonderful sports town Buffalo is; now, it's up to baseball. . . .

"We've paid our dues."

At about seven, the news conference ends. From an official standpoint, this longest—and longest-awaited—of days is finally done.

OUTSIDE THE HOTEL, darkness.

After Bob Rich and Dennis Gorski do some phone interviews with radio stations back home, it's time for the Buffalo group to decompress. A party of eight—the Riches, Gorski, Mansell, Billoni, Buczkowski, Peter Fleischer of Hill & Knowlton, and Gabrielle "Gaby" DeRose, director of corporate communications for Rich Products—takes cabs about a dozen blocks to Felidia, a two-star northeastern Italian restaurant in the 200 block of East 58th Street. This place is posh, to say the least, and the homemade pastas include Istrian-style fuzi, which can be completed by delicacies such as quail, rabbit, pigeon, or deer. The likes of Paul Newman, Anthony Quinn, Alan Alda, and Loretta Swit have been known to dine here, and its ambitious cuisine has made it one of Bob and Mindy Rich's favorites. The downstairs is crowded and noisy on this night, so the party of eight seeks refuge alone amid the greenery along the white walls at the rear of the balcony. They sit on high-backed chairs with tapestry cushions at a long rectangular table covered with white linen. A good meal—and peace and quiet—are long overdue.

This airy and rustic brick-walled restaurant is run by an immigrant family, the Bastianiches, and Bob Rich is taking the opportunity to thank not only the members of this group, but, symbolically, the many other members of the Bisons' extended family, whether they be as nearby as Buffalo or as far away as Ireland. "Today, we made the triple axel," Bob Rich says, using a figure-skating metaphor that everyone understands. Now, minus his red marker with the strawberry scent but raising a glass of red wine with a robust bouquet, he offers a toast to one and all.

Most of the conversation is lighthearted; not too much baseball talk. At this time and in this place, there are years' worth of unwinding to do.

About eleven o'clock, the eight say their farewells for tonight and go their separate ways. There will be much to remember about this experience. Now, though, it is time to head home.

"You know something? None of this would have happened if the fans—the people of Buffalo—didn't come out in the numbers and support baseball," Gorski says later. "When you come right down to it, that's why we're here—because those people love baseball."

LESS THAN A half-hour past midnight, the large, white corporate jet is nearing the end of its fifty-minute flight from New York, beginning its descent through the black September sky toward the flickering lights of the city. Hello again, Buffalo! The last time a major-league baseball franchise had been within reach of the people down there was twenty-two years ago. And so much has happened since. Bob Rich, hollow-eyed and bone-tired, can't help but reflect for a moment on that pain and disillusionment of 1968. Could history, cruel as it so often is, repeat itself? No, he says, "we're going to make it this time."

Mindy Rich, sitting next to her husband, acknowledges in a soft voice that even at this late date, it's still just a dream. "But what's nice about it now," she says, "is that we're not building the dream on dreams. We're building the dream on what's real."

13

INSIDE BASEBALL

The flight home from New York gave no hint of what would be clear soon afterward: The sky was falling. Baseball was on the brink of civil war, and Bob Rich—with a foot in both camps—was caught in the middle.

At stake was the eighty-seven-year alliance between Major League Baseball and its minor-league affiliates. The 170 teams in the minors had drawn more than 25 million fans in 1990, nearly one-third of baseball's total attendance, and the value of franchises had soared. Some were worth millions. The majors wanted not only a greater share of that prosperity, but greater control. If they didn't get it, they would start a separate minor-league system of their own. Minor-league owners, many of them operating the baseball equivalent of mom-and-pop stores, saw this as a threat to their very survival. They saw themselves in a no-win situation resulting from something Major League Baseball had allowed to get out of hand: greed.

The timing couldn't have been worse for Bob Rich, who owned three teams in the minors but desperately wanted to give his city one in the majors. Throughout October and early November, Rich was besieged by long-distance phone calls from minor-league owners asking him to take a side—their side. He offered moral support but was hesitant to speak out publicly as he left in late November for the annual minor-league meetings in Los Angeles. "We established a strategy early on, that we would stay out of this one," Rich said. "This was a fight we didn't want, because, hopefully, there would be some resolutions, and we didn't want to run the risk of alienating major-league ownership."

To make matters worse for Rich, the minor-league owners were personalizing much of their outrage toward Baseball Commissioner Fay Vincent, the most powerful figure in the game.

"There's no doubt that all this is coming from Vincent," said fifteen-year baseball man Jack Tracz, who owns parts of two Single-A teams, Hamilton and Prince William, and was assistant general manager of the Bisons when baseball came back to Buffalo in 1979. "They want to control us, and now they can. When Vincent came in, everybody thought he was a good man who wanted to carry on Bart Giamatti's legacy. Now, we can all see he has no inclination to do that. I can't figure out the major leagues. They pay millions to mediocre players, they pay millions for collusion, and they fight with umpires. They can't win one, so now they're coming after the minors—the little people."

"This commissioner is trying to dismantle the minor leagues," said Miles Wolff, publisher of *Baseball America* and president of the Single-A Durham Bulls, whose fictional counterparts were immortalized in the film *Bull Durham*. "He forgets he's supposed to be the commissioner of all of baseball and look after the best interests of everyone, including the minor leagues."

Typical of the minor-league owners feeling the pressure was Sam Nader, who runs Oneonta's rookie team in the Single-A New York–Penn League. Nader has been running the club for nearly twenty-five years in Oneonta, which has a population of about 15,000. One season, he made $81; another time, he lost about $100. He wasn't in it for the money, he said, but could ill afford a new agreement with the majors that would cost his club about $25,000. Although that might sound like peanuts to major-league owners who shell out millions for utility infielders, it could put Nader out of the baseball business. "The only trouble with baseball is the people who run it," Nader said, adding that Vincent has "demonstrated by his actions that he is not a friend of minor-league baseball."

Publicly, the only counterattack to the anti–Vincent onslaught came from Bill Murray, director of operations in the commissioner's office and chief negotiator for the majors. He denied that Vincent or the majors were trying to control the minors. "We never were looking for complete control," he said. "We asked that the commissioner step in when guidelines are not enforced." Vincent's involvement, though, was coming under public scrutiny. In August, Vincent reportedly had sent a letter to the twenty-six major-league clubs telling them not to renew contracts with their minor-league affiliates until negotiations were concluded. On August 15, fifty-six contracts between major- and minor-league clubs expired. There also was a memo ordering the majors not to make payments to the minors for territorial television broadcast rights but, instead, to send the money to the commissioner's office. Another memo warned major-league teams of fines if they negotiated individually with those in the minors. Vincent's response was that he did not recall every communication from his office but that he would not call the reports erroneous.

Vincent told *Baseball America* that "the major-league owners are saying, 'Here are these minor-league franchises that are selling at very high levels. And one of the reasons the franchises are so valuable is that we, the major-league teams, are spending five, six million dollars apiece supporting that operation. And we're willing to carry the brunt, but we think that economic allocation should be revised.' "

By November, the battle was being waged in negotiations for the Player Development Contract between the major leagues and the National Association of Professional Baseball Clubs that was to expire in January. The major leagues were demanding a 5 percent share of minor-league ticket revenue from each team. The minors would also be responsible for more expenses, such as travel and equipment costs. The majors also wanted to control aspects of minor-league operations such as stadium design, number of games scheduled, and sales or shifts of franchises. If they didn't get it their way, the majors were threatening to put their own developmental teams in existing minor-league cities, or keep their minor-league players at training complexes in Florida and Arizona and have them play against one another.

The minor-league owners saw this as a monopoly run amok. Their fury prompted some of them to contact members of Congress in the hope that hearings could be opened on whether Major League Baseball should continue to enjoy its antitrust exemption.

Major League Baseball's power play against its minor-league brethren didn't sit well with many sports columnists, either. George Vecsey of *The New York Times,* for instance, wrote that "baseball has been trying to squeeze the minors to help pay its collusion penalty and to help support major-league owners' habit of spending millions of dollars on Walt Terrell, Bud Black, and Danny Jackson." Thomas Boswell of the *Washington Post* commented that "the owners are putting the hardball squeeze on 170 minor-league franchise owners, trying to rip the last nickel away from these small-time, small-town operators."

It didn't take Bob Rich long to realize that these were issues on which he couldn't remain publicly silent, even at the risk of falling into disfavor with the elders of baseball who would determine the fate of his expansion bid. "We literally got to a point where Mindy and I looked at each other and said, 'Hey, we can't stay out of this anymore. It's too important.'"

Rich's three franchises were estimated to be worth $15 million, but his emergence as a high-profile spokesman for his struggling minor-league associates was motivated by values far deeper than any financial stake. "We've been in minor-league baseball for eight years and built up a lot of friendships, not just with the people in our leagues, but with people all over the country; from teams in the Pioneer League to the Southern League," he said. "What the major leagues were suggesting could not only cripple a lot of the smaller franchises, but drive some teams out of business and force them to sell. Listen, I'm not talking about Buffalo; we're doing great, we can afford to pay. But it's the other teams, especially in the small towns, that this will hurt most of all. Those little guys, like Sam Nader, are the heart of this business."

Nader, unlike Rich, has no major-league aspirations. He just wants to run a Single-A team, but he found much to admire in his fellow owner: "I think Bob is sincerely concerned about the minor leagues and baseball, and that's why he did what he did. We all knew it wasn't easy for him, but he is a man of principle. He jeopardized his position with the major leagues to stick up for us. Let me tell you something: That takes guts."

Rich made sure that everyone knew where he stood. "I have to stand up for the sport, the industry and what I believe in," he told the Associated Press. To *USA Today*, he said, "The major leagues have to do everything possible to keep the minor leagues alive, and right now, they're not. It's a shame." If the majors abandoned the minor leagues, Rich said, he would sign his own players and run an independent team in Buffalo.

By mid-December, the minor leagues averted disaster by agreeing—barely—to a seven-year contract with the majors. It was hard to swallow, but it was better than being choked to death.

Minor-league officials said it would cost them $5 million annually, and they lost much of their control to the majors and to the commissioner's office. Dan Lunetta, general manager of Rochester, seemed to express the consensus when he told the *Democrat & Chronicle* that "the choice is, do you take a bad deal or don't you take a deal at all?" Lunetta said Rochester might have lost its franchise without the agreement, which he estimated would mean an additional $50,000 annual cost to his Red Wings, who in 1989 had lost $227,000.

Owners praised Bob Rich for standing with them. Miles Wolff said Rich "gave us strength when we needed it. You learn a lot about people in that kind of situation. Bob had good reason not to speak out, but he did. It's hard to find that kind of integrity in baseball these days."

Bob Rich was well aware, however, that some of baseball's power brokers might look upon his actions in a different light, and he addressed that possibility head-on: "If baseball uses this against me—standing up for our town and the towns we're in; and for minor-league baseball, which is so sadly mismatched against the major leagues—then I can tell you clearly that I don't want any part of that club. I say that categorically, and I've said that to some of the major-league people, too. I've told them, 'I hope you understand our intent, but if you don't, then you don't want me as an owner.'"

The $95 million question remained: What kind of new owner *did* Major League Baseball want? Big bucks and big TV audiences were becoming such dominant elements of the expansion picture that, for the first time, there were rumblings that both of the National League expansion franchises would be awarded to that most lucrative of untapped markets: South Florida.

Baseball had changed since Peter Ueberroth had announced the expansion criteria and A. Bartlett Giamatti, as National League president, had referred to Buffalo as the only city going about seeking an expansion team in the right way.

When Giamatti, the romantic, succeeded Ueberroth, the marketer, in the spring of 1989, no one could have suspected that his term as baseball commissioner would last only five months. The man running baseball was now Fay Vincent, whose specialty was corporate hardball. It was anyone's guess how much Bob Rich's reputation as a baseball traditionalist would ultimately count with

Vincent. What was on the record, though, was something Vincent had told Williams College's Class of 1990:

"Economics usually crowds out ethics in the crunch."

IN SEPTEMBER 1989, a heart attack killed Bart Giamatti. He was fifty-one. Left forever unanswered was the question of what long-term impact this lover of Renaissance and medieval literature, this baseball purist would have on the game he cherished, a game that had turned into such a big business.

Eight days before he died, Giamatti had banned Cincinnati Reds Manager Pete Rose from the game for life amid a scandal that included accusations of illegal gambling on sports and filing false income-tax returns. Rose, baseball's all-time leader in hits, later was tried in federal court and sent to prison. "I will be told I'm an idealist," Giamatti said on the day he banned Rose. "I hope so. I will continue to locate ideals I hold for myself and for my country in the national game."

Giamatti had invoked the commissioner's statutory right to act "in the best interests of baseball," a power that now belonged to the man who had been his deputy and was quickly chosen as his successor, Fay Vincent.

The two New Englanders, who had been born less than two months apart in the spring of 1938, became friends in the late 1970s. Both had strong ties to Yale; Giamatti was an undergraduate and a professor there before serving as the university's president from 1978 to 1986, and it was there that Vincent earned a law degree. They shared a passion for literature, and they both enjoyed baseball, although in different ways.

Their tastes in teams told a lot about the two men. Giamatti, from Boston, was a permanent passenger on the roller coaster of those eternal heartbreakers, the hometown Red Sox. Vincent, who grew up in New Haven, Connecticut, preferred the predictably efficient, almost clinical New York Yankees, who steamrolled to unparalleled success in the 1940s and 1950s. Casey Stengel's Yankees were the closest baseball came to a sure thing.

"I think Bart's passion for the Red Sox was almost superhuman," Vincent was quoted as saying after he became commissioner. "My passion for the Yankees isn't like that. When you work in baseball and you have this position, baseball changes. It's not like an afternoon in the ballpark in the sunshine. There's a reality to it you can't escape."

Francis Thomas Vincent Jr. was the son of a former Yale football captain who worked for the telephone company. The father kept close to sports as a professional football referee and an amateur baseball umpire, and the son was an offensive lineman on his high school football team. The son also was a brilliant student. After graduation, he spent one summer working in a Texas oil field owned by future President George Bush, an older brother of one of his high school pals, William H. T. "Bucky" Bush. Being well-connected came naturally to the strapping young man, whose next stop was Williams College.

In 1956, when Vincent was a freshman at Williams, one of his roommates locked him in their dormitory room as a prank. Vincent climbed out a window but slipped off a ledge and fell four stories to the ground. He was temporarily paralyzed from the waist down and, to this day, walks with a cane.

Vincent graduated Phi Beta Kappa from Williams and, after earning a law degree at Yale, was a lawyer in New York and Washington before being named associate director of the Securities and Exchange Commission's Division of Corporate Finance. His annual salary there was about $47,000 when, in 1978, he received a far more attractive job offer: from Hollywood. Herbert Allen, Jr., a fellow Williams College graduate who was chairman of Columbia Pictures, wanted him to become chief executive officer of the movie studio, which had been rocked by the David Begelman financial scandal and was under federal investigation.

The fact that Vincent knew nothing about the movie business was considered a plus by Allen. "Nobody knows him. Nobody can lay a glove on him," Allen was quoted as saying in *Indecent Exposure: A True Story of Hollywood and Wall Street*, David McClintick's book on the scandal. "We need a healer in this situation. "We need a Judge Landis."

Like Kenesaw Mountain Landis (baseball's first commissioner) had done in the wake of the Black Sox scandal nearly sixty years earlier, Vincent did what was necessary to root out corruption and restore Columbia's image of being aboveboard and—above all—profitable. He was well aware that he was swimming with sharks, and acted accordingly, which often meant ruthlessly. Vincent cleaned house, triggering what McClintick described as "ugly scenes, loud denunciations, screaming telephone conversations, tears, and sleepless nights."

Whether his job called for repulsing a hostile takeover attempt or firing a powerful colleague, Vincent didn't flinch. Blood on the floor came with the territory. With hit films such as *Kramer vs. Kramer, Gandhi, The Big Chill,* and *Tootsie,* Columbia's bottom line was brightening; *The Natural,* too, was a Columbia release. Herb Allen was pleased. Vincent's salary jumped to six figures when he joined Columbia, and he was soon on his way to his first million. When the Coca-Cola Company bought Columbia in 1982, Allen and Vincent "made a killing," according to McClintick. After the sale, Vincent headed Coke's entertainment division, and by the time he left six years later, he reportedly had company stock valued at more than $20 million. No one could doubt that Fay Vincent understood high finance.

Giamatti and Vincent had met in 1978 at a small, private dinner in the home of a mutual friend in Princeton, New Jersey, where the other guest was *Jaws* author Peter Benchley, whose book *The Deep* had been turned into a film by Columbia a year earlier. Eight years later, Giamatti, who from time to time had mused about one day heading the American League, became president of the National League. After a little more than two years in that job, he succeeded Ueberroth as baseball commissioner on April 1, 1989, and asked Vincent to be his deputy. Vincent, a father of three and delighted at the opportunity to work for both a friend and game he found so dear, accepted. Giamatti valued Vincent's legal and business acumen, entrusting him right away with the Rose investigation. Giamatti took office with a theme of "stability and unity," represented by a seven-point agenda that included National League expansion and improving relations between the major leagues and the minors. But five months later, he was dead.

On September 13, Vincent was appointed commissioner, and 34 days later, faced the task of shepherding baseball through an American tragedy—the San Francisco Bay Area earthquake, which struck moments before Game 3 of the World Series was to begin. Despite pressure to cancel the rest of the Series, Vincent made the decision that it should resume, and after an eleven-day delay, it did.

In retrospect, the Northern California disaster was seen by

some as a portent of the tremors that would emanate from base-ball's fault lines during the first full year of the Vincent regime.

As with most anyone thrust into a leadership role after a sudden death, the man now sitting at the biggest desk on the seventeenth floor of 350 Park Avenue was granted a honeymoon of sorts by re-porters and columnists. In public, Vincent has a disarming, almost avuncular way about him. Although physically imposing at 6-feet-3 and 240 pounds, he speaks softly, deliberately, cordially. Below a receding hairline, his oval face is large yet unthreatening, almost gen-tle, accented by glasses that give him a bookish look. He enjoys the finer things—opera and expensive cigars, for instance—but in big-league ballparks or at spring training, he's likely to be found leaning on his cane or sitting in a golf cart, wearing a sun hat and chatting with managers, players, reporters or fans. During one summer night in 1990, Vincent sat with Joe DiMaggio for a game in Baltimore. "He talked with me for three hours," Vincent said. "I asked him who was the hardest pitcher to hit, could he hit the knuckleball, how about Bobby Feller, what was Joe McCarthy like, why didn't he hit .400?" That was Fay Vincent at the ballpark: the easygoing fan.

But it was obvious to anyone paying attention to off-the-field developments in baseball during 1990 that when the mahogany doors closed, Fay Vincent wasn't at all reluctant to exert whatever muscle was necessary to remind everyone who was boss.

In his first spring as commissioner, he took no action to prevent the owners from locking out the players from training camps for more than a month during a labor dispute. As a result, more than half the exhibition schedule wasn't played, disappointing fans who planned their vacations around spring training and costing the econ-omies of Florida and Arizona tens of millions of dollars. The first week of regular-season games had to be rescheduled.

The four-month investigation that in July led Vincent to banish Yankees owner George Steinbrenner from the day-to-day baseball operations of the team was generally thought to have achieved a desirable result. However, questions soon arose about baseball's conduct in the matter—whether the enforcement was selective and whether transcripts were altered while exploring Steinbrenner's al-leged payment of $40,000 to admitted gambler Howard Spira for information damaging to Yankees outfielder Dave Winfield. *Sports Illustrated* criticized the commissioner's office for not investigating

Spira's links to Winfield. "Baseball did not do itself proud in the Steinbrenner case," said the magazine, which described the investigation as "a tale of contradictions and double standards."

Vincent, who also found himself being faulted by National League President Bill White for not supporting him soon enough in a dispute with umpires, drew the most fire for his part in Major League Baseball's intensive efforts to exact more tribute from the minors.

"Fay Vincent may have talked hours of baseball this summer while sitting in his golf cart at every major-league stadium, but he is also a tough lawyer who dealt severely with underlings at both Coca-Cola and Columbia Pictures," wrote Bob Ryan of the *Boston Globe*, the dominant paper in Vincent's native New England. "He may have evoked the memory of his good friend Bart Giamatti time and again during these sessions, but he . . . is no Bart Giamatti when it comes to recognizing what's in the best interests of the real baseball man and the real baseball fan."

While discontent was bubbling in the background, the spotlight at Major League Baseball's winter meetings was on the frenzied bidding for free agents—more than $150 million for about two dozen who, for the most part, were considered mediocre players. The vast majority of them were being signed by National League teams, who were already beginning to spend the $190 million that would be coming from expansion.

"The amount of money being paid is staggering; it blows your mind," said Lou Gorman, general manager of the Boston Red Sox. Dal Maxvill, general manager of the St. Louis Cardinals, called the free-agent spending spree "complete insanity."

Was this any way to run the national pastime?

Bob Rich was beginning to wonder.

"It breaks your heart," Bart Giamatti once wrote of baseball. "It's designed to break your heart."

Would that be Buffalo's fate?

Again?

ONE OF BART GIAMATTI'S greatest fears had been that television's increasing influence over the game would start turning ballparks into nothing more than glorified broadcast studios, where the measure of a team's appeal and ultimate value was not how much the people were enjoying it from stadium seats but how many of them were watching it from living room sofas. The first embodiment of this was in Atlanta, where Ted Turner's Braves were identified far more with his superstation than with the ballpark in which they played.

Giamatti once said a ballpark is "the last pure place where Americans can dream," and Bob Rich shared that view. The evidence of this was Pilot Field, a modern version of Giamatti's Fenway Park. Or of Ebbets Field. Or of Wrigley.

But the signals that Fay Vincent was sending were not so clear. Vincent, who was a senior at Williams when Rich was a freshman, had told the Class of 1990, for instance, that it should "believe that everything should be governed by the highest ethic but act as though this conviction were not widely shared."

There was a message there, but Bob Rich wasn't quite sure of its full implications. What he did know was that he and his city had followed Major League Baseball's expansion criteria to a T. But somehow, between June and December of 1990, the perception of Buffalo's chances in the race for expansion had fallen from front-runner to long shot.

"When we went to Cleveland for that meeting, I thought we finally knew where the finish line was," Rich said. "Now, we still don't know.

"We categorically demonstrated we didn't have any deficiencies. When we got into this hunt, we knew that Buffalo would have to be better by all dimensions, because of the perceptions of this city, its economy, its weather, its location and its TV market. We accepted that challenge, and we knew . . . there were those who said that baseball has never wanted and never will want Buffalo in the major leagues. I will not concede that this is true, but I will certainly agree that we knew all along that we had to be better."

Better, yes, but by what standard? The economics of baseball were changing, dramatically. And almost daily.

"When I got into baseball, it was still a sport," said Charles Bronfman, who was selling his Montreal Expos. "You could make a few bucks and lose a few bucks, but basically, it was a sport. Today it's a big business. It's a tough business, and there's too much enmity."

One symbol of baseball's new economics was that Miami had suddenly leapfrogged to prominence as a candidate for an expansion franchise, so much so that the National League was giving ever-stronger consideration to placing both new teams in South Florida.

Television had a lot to do with that possibility. Miami was the nation's fourteenth-largest TV market, and Tampa–St. Petersburg was seventeenth. Miami had no suitable ballpark; its football stadium would have to be renovated. It had no proven minor-league attendance. Its proposed ownership had no baseball experience. But what it did have was money—plenty of it. One source close to the National League surmised that Miami's ascent—and perhaps Buffalo's descent—had begun in September, when a newcomer, Fort Lauderdale's H. Wayne Huizenga, owner of the four-year-old Blockbuster Video chain and co-founder of Waste Management Incorporated, walked in to make his presentation to the expansion committee in New York, dropped a $95 million check on the table and said, "Let's talk."

"I guess we're ultimately going to see how important the criteria are," Rich said. "We have built our case around the criteria. Now, we're going to find out whether the criteria prevail or whether, in fact, it may become an auction."

To observe baseball's current attitude toward auctions, there was no need to look any further than the winter meetings in Chicago, where—even though each owner was smarting from a nearly $11 million arbitration penalty for collusion—the spending for free agents was somewhere between reckless and absurd. Arguably the most notable example was thirty-two-year-old pitcher Matt Young, who—despite a record of 8–18 for 1990 and 51–78 (with a 4.25 ERA) for his career—went from Seattle to Boston with a three-year deal for more than $6 million. Not only were Jose Canseco and Darryl Strawberry earning an average of more than $4 million a year, but at the $3 million level, the number of players was more than two dozen—and counting. Before 1990, no player was at $3 million. Membership in the $2 million club more than tripled from 29 players at the start of 1990 to nearly 100 as 1991 began.

It was reaching the point that a $1 million salary was hardly worth mentioning. Major League Baseball reported that in just the last year, the average salary had risen by 20.2 percent—from $497,254 to $597,537. Oakland would become the first team in history with a $30 million payroll, and the Mets and Giants were not far behind. Player contracts signed from October to December leaped to an average of $1.9 million—an increase of 90 percent.

Could teams outside the very largest markets continue to absorb such costs?

"It's a source of great concern," said Milwaukee Brewers President Bud Selig. "It's frightening everyone in the game."

Charles Bronfman, after two decades as owner of the Expos, had become fed up. "Expenses may soon choke many of us," he told his fellow owners. "Players' salaries at the major-league level have lost not only all sense of proportion, but all sense of reason."

Judging from their actions, baseball's owners didn't seem to be paying much attention to their departing colleague. Bob Rich made note of baseball's autumn of upheaval in a published letter in which he noted that "the cost of free-agent signings has gone through the roof in just the last few weeks. The number of mediocre players earning $1 million is at an all-time high—with no end in sight."

On paper, though, Major League Baseball hardly seemed to be setting itself up for a fall. Rather, these appeared to be glorious times. Early in December, the Associated Press reported that the major leagues had increased their operating profits by 75 percent in 1989, to a record $214.5 million, for a per-team average of about $8.3 million. But this was misleading. What the figures didn't show is that most of the profits came from big-market cities such as New York, Chicago, Toronto, and Los Angeles. Those high rollers were raking in most of the local TV revenue, led by the Yankees' reported $50 million a year. *The Sporting News* reported that 35 percent of all local TV revenue—estimated at $250 million by *Broadcast Magazine*—went to four clubs: the Yankees, Mets, Dodgers and Phillies. Yet small-market teams such as Pittsburgh, Seattle and Cleveland—lucky to get $5 million in local TV money—were struggling to make ends meet. Major-league owners were saying that in 1989, one-third of the clubs actually lost money. Vincent said that in 1990, five to ten clubs ended up in the red.

For some teams, winning did not ensure economic rewards, either. Pittsburgh drew more than 2 million fans, won the National League East title and yet reportedly lost money, even though the Pirates' average salary of about $590,000 was fifteenth among major-league clubs and their total payroll of $15.5 million ranked seventeenth. When the season ended, the team lost free agents Sid Bream, Wally Backman, Ted Power and R.J. Reynolds, and it spent $10.5 million to keep pitcher Zane Smith, who in his career has had

17 fewer victories than losses. The Pirates' payroll had skyrocketed, from $6.5 million in 1988 to an expected $22 million in 1991—more than 300 percent in a little over three years.

Escalating salaries wasn't the only economic headache. Instability of the franchises in Montreal, Kansas City, and Houston led to their being put up for sale, although Kansas City was taken off the market because the bids had been too low. The San Francisco Giants declared their intention to leave Candlestick Park and find a new home. Since 1980, fifteen of the twenty-six major-league franchises had changed ownership. Gone were the staunch, family-oriented patriarchs in the mold of Tom Yawkey and Phil Wrigley who had lived the game for so long. In their place was a new breed of corporate owners. They wanted significant returns on their investments. Fast. And whether their teams and their homes were in the same city was of secondary concern.

Of ever-increasing importance was the television market. The bigger it was, the better. "If you don't have a revenue base locally, including local media that's powerful, you're not going to be able to do it," Fay Vincent told *Baseball America.* "And nobody wants to have sort of two tiers, the major cities that win all the time and then the small cities that provide the competition. That's not what baseball is all about, and thank God it hasn't happened."

At least not yet. Actually, a small-market team, Cincinnati, won the 1990 World Series—in a sweep.

But in reality, baseball's grand, old one-floor plan was indeed beginning to resemble a split-level. *The Wall Street Journal* reported that big-market teams such as the Yankees, Mets and Dodgers reaped $110 million each in revenues for 1990, while the Seattle Mariners took in only about $32 million. While the Yankees got close to $41 million in local broadcast revenue, the Kansas City Royals' total was $5 million and Seattle $1.5 million. "You deal with realities," Vincent said. "In the optimum would be teams wherever there are a substantial number of people who would like to have them, but in the real world, that can't work. You're just not going to have a team in Hartford."

Forget Hartford, there were already teams in Cleveland, Pittsburgh, Seattle and Arlington, Texas, that appeared headed for financial ruin while their big-market friends were fattening their bank accounts thanks to a revenue flow from a cash cow called television.

Television. Its grip on the game had never been tighter. The ballpark experience had lost none of its magic, but its significance was being overshadowed by the size of the TV market. As 1990 came to a close, however, there was strong evidence that television had finally overreached. Ratings and advertising revenue had plunged precipitously. CBS's billion-dollar contract for four years had gone through its first season by losing $55 million, causing the network to set aside an additional $115 million to help cover future losses now estimated at $300 million. ESPN, the cable sports network, reportedly lost $53 million in the first year of its four-year, $400 million baseball deal. In December, CBS went to baseball, hat in hand, and asked for money back. The response was hardly surprising. Baseball turned the network down flat; it was willing to give television just about everything it wanted—except money.

Could this have been the first evidence of backlash by the faithful? Perhaps. But whether or not the public was feeling manipulated, it certainly was feeling confused. It had been used to getting a Saturday afternoon Game of the Week throughout the season—something NBC had been providing for nearly forty years—but now was being offered such games only sporadically. CBS had outbid NBC for network rights to big-league games by an astounding $400 million yet was giving the fans less. Furthermore, CBS had muscled out ABC, which had been telecasting big-league games since 1976, primarily on Monday nights but also on some Thursday nights and Sunday afternoons; so the less was far less. This was the new economics?

Maybe it was just a matter of television's having tampered with one baseball treasure too many. It had long since taken away the World Series from the school-age crowd. No longer would kids find it necessary to smuggle pocket radios into school or sprint home in time to watch a Bill Mazeroski hit a historic home run or a Don Larsen pitch a perfect game. There was no more sneaking a peak at a portable TV in the workplace or sitting at home with the whole family to watch Game 7. With Series games almost exclusively in prime time, the first pitch comes at about twenty minutes after eight in the East, pretty close to bedtime for many of the future Hank Aarons or Warren Spahns—or Mario Cuomos. To live through the unforgettable heroics of a Kirk Gibson, you'd need to stay up well past eleven, but if the hero is a Carlton Fisk, you'd need to keep your eyes open beyond half past midnight. For most youngsters and for countless working people, the message was unmistakable: Program the VCR, folks, and postpone your thrills a day.

Indeed, the game was changing—primarily in increments, but sometimes with a rush. More than ever, it meant different things to different people.

There was no doubt whatsoever that Fay Vincent was at the controls now, and 1991 would be the year when he would have a lot to say about whether the best interests of baseball and the best interests of Buffalo were one and the same.

BY EARLY 1991, more than five years after he had first gone to New York to confer with baseball's hierarchy, Bob Rich was dealing with only two certainties concerning National League expansion: Buffalo had made the short list, and it had done absolutely everything it had been asked. And then some.

Yet there was the feeling that the dream might be slipping away.

An old phrase from television, *due to circumstances beyond our control,* had come to mind as Buffalo's baseball dreamers found themselves at the mercy of volatile economic forces—the nation's first in eight years, recession disarray among financial institutions, world crisis in the oil-rich Persian Gulf, budget fiascoes in government, and runaway inflation in the game they had loved for so long. It seemed like a nightmare. In view of modern Major League Baseball's seemingly insatiable financial appetite, maybe Buffalo simply just couldn't afford it anymore.

"We said from the beginning that this has to make business sense," Bob Rich said. "It must make economic sense not just for us, but also for the city, the county and our fans."

And it was approaching the point where it might not.

The $95 million entry fee, despite causing more than a few gasps, wasn't prohibitive for Buffalo, although expansion applicants across the board had expected the amount to be more on the order of $70 million to $80 million. Even when adjusted for inflation, the $95 million entry fee was nearly double the NHL's asking price in its most recent expansion, more than two and a half times the NFL's, nearly triple the NBA's and more than *six times* what Major League Baseball itself asked of Toronto, whose $7 million entry fee in 1977 was the equivalent of about $15.4 million in 1990. What's more, the

1990 sale of the San Diego Padres had been for $75 million, and that included not only a full big-league roster, but a farm system already in place.

That wasn't all. Initial operating costs, including a brand-new farm system, would be an additional $30 million. And if that weren't enough, there was a double whammy waiting for the two expansionists regarding television revenue. In a departure from past practice, Major League Baseball announced not long before the expansion presentations were made that it was going to deny the new franchises any of the national TV money—about $14 million each—until their second year on the field. That would be 1994, the first year of a new network contract that—in the aftermath of the CBS debacle—would undoubtedly be for much less money.

Did this make any sense?

And there was no forgetting the impact of the new economics on player salaries. How much higher would *those* be allowed to go?

"If the major leagues are looking for a guy who just says baseball at any price," said Bob Rich, "then it's probably not me or Buffalo they are looking for."

Local government had already been highly supportive, particularly regarding Pilot Field, but there was a point beyond which it wouldn't go, either: the use of general tax revenues to subsidize a franchise. After all, major-league baseball is a private business—one that ought to be in the black, not in a black hole—and no one was more aware of that than Bob Rich. He was anything but a fast-buck artist; his family and its business had been stalwarts in the community for nearly half a century. His stake in this was more than anyone else's.

"We told the National League in our presentation that the Rich family as general partners would invest no less than 25 percent," he said, which meant no less than $23.75 million of the entry fee alone. "We said that was meant to be a minimum amount, the least we would invest."

Each of the prospective limited partners, who by December numbered at least fourteen, would invest up to $10 million, Rich said, and there was a possibility of more partners coming aboard in 1991. The money was in place to bring a team to Buffalo, Rich said, and the hope remained that there could be a way to make it work permanently.

"The city has done so much for the Bisons and baseball; we can't do any more," said Mayor Jimmy Griffin, without whom none of this would have been possible. ". . . Costs have gone crazy. I don't think the average person realizes what is happening."

Major League Baseball, meanwhile, was faced with another incipient civil war, one that had the potential of going all the way to a "best interests" decision by Fay Vincent. The National League owners were aglow at the prospect of dividing up the $190 million in entry fees from the two expansion franchises but aghast upon learning that their American League counterparts wanted a piece of the action—perhaps half of it. The word *blackmail* was being whispered, given the implied threat that the American Leaguers wouldn't provide the votes needed for National League expansion if they didn't get some of the dough.

"People can request anything they want," National League President Bill White was quoted as saying at the winter meetings. "Jesse James requested money, too."

Such was the state of Major League Baseball as it entered its 116th year.

THE SHORT LIST was announced in mid-December, and there was uncertainty until the last moment.

Three days before the list was announced, a letter to the editor from Bob and Mindy Rich was published in *The Buffalo News*. In it, they expressed concern about the city's big-league prospects because "the economics of baseball have changed considerably in the past few months since we made our formal presentation to the National League."

The letter was widely perceived as meaning that the Riches and their community wouldn't be able to afford big-league ball; in actuality the issue was whether the major leagues had priced themselves out of the Buffalo market—and perhaps out of the markets of mid-size cities across America.

It wasn't the dream that had changed; it was the reality. Nevertheless, the letter was a public-relations disaster. The Riches had fallen victim to their own success, bearers of uninterrupted good tidings who suddenly delivered a message of less than great expectations. Feelings were hurt, and the resulting media firestorm came dangerously close to incinerating the dream all by itself.

The timing couldn't have been worse. In its Sunday Sports section two days before the short list was announced, *The New York Times* published a condensed Associated Press report on the letter with an erroneous but near-fatal headline: "Bowing Out in Buffalo."

Seeing this, members of the National League expansion committee urgently called Bob Rich to ask whether it was ture. Of course not, Rich assured them; he was in the race to stay. But had they not called, Rich said, Buffalo very well might not have even made the list. Yet only hours before the announcement, Mindy Rich said, "I had heard rumors that we weren't going to be on the short list. I usually don't believe rumors, but this time, I was worried. Then the announcement came, and we were thrilled. Now, we have to dig in for the rest of the fight."

Besides Buffalo, the cities on the short list were Tampa–St. Petersburg, Miami, Washington, Denver and Orlando. All they could do now was wait, presumably for an announcement by at the latest September.

The negative reaction to this letter, as well as the doubts that had arisen amid the disillusioning brawl between the majors and the minors, had taken an emotional toll on Bob Rich. But when the short list was released, the hint of a glaze was gone from his eyes, and the full fire was back.

"I'm not surprised, because Buffalo deserves this more than any other city on the list," he said. ". . .Our dream is very much alive."

Of the six cities on the short list, *New York Times* columnist George Vecsey wrote, "Buffalo is the best." But there was increasing worry among Buffalonians that the best still might not be good enough.

As important as the expansion race was, Rich couldn't let it be a preoccupation. April wasn't that far away, and there was the business of providing his ninth season of Bisons baseball. He had built the most successful minor-league franchise in baseball history, and he was confident that attendance would exceed a million for the fourth time in as many years at Pilot Field. For Buffalo, which had grown accustomed to being cast as an underdog, it had been a miracle to even reach this point.

"I wouldn't have changed anything in any way," he said. "I have no regrets. . . . A lot of people have told me, 'I love Pilot

Field. I like being able to buy a ticket and a hot dog at a reasonable price.' People have said, 'Well, if you don't get to the majors, will you sell the team?' I don't think I'd do that any more than I'd expect that the real fans would stop coming to games."

Curiously, there was much talk among insiders that Major League Baseball wanted Bob Rich but not his city, or his TV market, whichever the case might be. Many calls have come from major-league teams who want him as an investor. "The major leagues like Bob's name, his money, his business, and his national reputation," said a source close to Major League Baseball. "The major leagues want Bob Rich; whether they want Buffalo is another story. If Bob lived anywhere but Buffalo, he'd probably get a franchise."

The National League had considered offering Rich part-ownership of an expansion franchise, but not in Buffalo, according to a New York source close to the league. Rich would not comment, but those who know him best are certain that he would never operate a big-league team outside his city unless there was a guarantee that he could soon bring it to Buffalo.

In fact, Rich said, during the summer of 1990, he had discussed buying any of the three teams, with an eye toward relocation in Buffalo. Two purchase offers were made, one for $100 million, he said, but to no avail. For the foreseeable future, at least, there appeared to be only one hope: expansion.

But National League expansion will leave more prospective cities disappointed than satisfied, so there even have been murmurings of a third major league, presumably with a moderate-size network TV contract. "It's a long shot," said one player agent, "but you get a guy like Bob Rich, and he would give it credibility. He's the kind of guy who could make this thing go."

Bob Rich expresses no interest in such a league, however; it wouldn't be true to the dream. "No one is more committed to bringing major-league baseball to this city than I am," he says, fully intending to continue sailing against the wind in his quest to "give the game back to the fans. . . the people who love the game."

Like the people in Buffalo.

SNAPSHOT—EVERYMAN

Look in Section 100, Row M, Seat 6, right behind home plate at Pilot Field, and you will find him. He sits close to the dominating influence of his life: a baseball diamond. He wears a white porkpie hat, sport shirt open at the collar and slacks; it is the casual uniform of a big-league baseball scout, a job he held for nearly forty-three years. Each game—and he never misses a single one—dozens of people stop by to share ballpark fellowship, sometimes more on the order of paying homage, and the resulting conviviality is much the same as you would find at a picnic or a wedding reception. For Edwin "Cy" Williams, who in the summer of 1991 celebrates his seventy-seventh birthday, there is no longer any work attached to baseball; now, it's pure pleasure.

"Whenever I come here," he says of Pilot Field," I just enjoy looking out at that field. It brings back so many memories. . . . I enjoy these games as much as I did when I was a youngster," and that enjoyment is magnified immeasurably by the ballpark his city's team now calls home.

You know, I've been in just about every major-league ball-park, and there's nothing like Pilot Field. The architecture is wonderful. Sometimes, late at night, I drive by there just to see it with the lights on. It gives downtown a whole new look—everything is so bright.

I can't explain about everything that has happened to baseball in Buffalo over the past seven years. To me, even at my age, it's exhilarating. I travel all over the city, and everywhere I go, people are talking baseball. This game can break your heart, but it's a wonderful game, and it means so much to a city like Buffalo.

I relish what baseball has done for Buffalo, and as a baseball person, it makes me proud. There's a relationship in this community between baseball and the people that is very special. It means so much, and this is the way we always knew it could be. Now, it's happening—and it's a dream come true.

For Cy Williams, the dream began when Babe Ruth was just beginning his big-league career with the Boston Red Sox and when Woodrow Wilson was in the White House. Williams and Joe Di-Maggio were born exactly four months apart. The Williams family lived on Perry Street, in the Hydraulic section on the outskirts of South Buffalo's First Ward, in a neighborhood of well-worn buildings, smokestacks, and railroad tracks. As a kid, he played pickup games of baseball on grassless lots and acquired the nickname Cy as a nod to Fred "Cy" Williams, who played nineteen years in the majors for the Cubs and Phillies. To this day, few people are even aware that his given name is Edwin.

Baseball held so much appeal because of its timelessness. "Little boys can play baseball, and old men can play baseball," he says. "It's a game you play to have fun; that's what real baseball is all about."

When young Cy Williams went to Bison Stadium, he cheered hardest for a couple of Irishmen—Billy Kelly, a first baseman, and Jimmy Walsh, an outfielder—who in the memorable season of 1925 combined to hit well over .300 with forty-eight home runs and 247 RBIs for their fourth-place club.

As an adolescent, Williams earned a reputation as a special ball player on the green fields of Cazenovia Park, a welcome relief from his cramped, grimy neighborhood. And it was right there, on a South Buffalo ball field, that his life would change forever.

One day, he was playing third base, but instead of watching the batter, his eyes were fixed on an adjacent diamond, where there was a girls' softball game in progress. The shortstop was a teenager, like Cy, and she was attractive. Moreover, she looked very much at home on a baseball diamond; she could hit, run, and field. But what impressed him the most were her looks. Heavens, she was pretty! Cy watched as a ball eluded the young lady and rolled toward his diamond. This was the opportunity he had been waiting for; she came running after the ball, and, at the last instant, he bent down and picked it up. Then, as he tossed it to her, he flashed a smile and said in an uncharacteristically husky voice, "Here you are, sweetie." She smiled back and said, "Why, thank you."

Edwin "Cy" Williams and Madelaine "Babe" Currey had now met—on a baseball field. He was eighteen; she was sixteen. Three years later, in August of 1935, they were married in Holy Family Church.

The preceding March, Williams, a third baseman, was signed to a professional contract by scout Johnny Mokan of the St. Louis Cardinals. At a salary of $75 a month, Cy played three seasons in the lower minors at Salisbury, South Carolina; Oswego, New York; Zanesville, Ohio; Cornwall, Ontario, and Albany, New York. Despite swinging a potent bat, he never came close to making the big leagues. His career really came to a halt on a field in Salisbury, when he suffered an injury to ligaments above his left knee while making a slide. The injury lingered for about a year and reduced his mobility. By 1937, married and the father of a son, Williams left the game for a better-paying job in the steel plant. Then came other jobs, as a construction worker, a security guard, a car salesman, a railroad worker, and even as a gravedigger. Work was hard to come by; this was the Depression.

Williams was one of an army of young laborers who helped build War Memorial Stadium in the mid-1930s. He was barely twenty and glad to have a job. "You got fifteen dollars a week, and that was good money," he recalls, noting that he spent most of those workdays lugging heavy concrete blocks. "It was exhausting work. There were so many people [nearly 1,300] working on that stadium, you thought you were building the pyramids of Egypt."

Baseball, though, was in Cy Williams's blood, and he longed for a way to get back in the game. The opportunity came in 1946, when Wish Egan, chief scout and director of player personnel for the Detroit Tigers, asked him whether he would be interested in scouting the New York–Pennsylvania League. The salary was only $3,000 a year, but Cy jumped at the opportunity. "By that time,"

Babe Williams recalls, "we both knew that baseball was something he loved, and he would have to find some way to be part of the game to be happy." Two years later, Cy's old friend from South Buffalo, Vince McNamara, became president of the league, and for the next thirty-seven years, the two kindred spirits delighted in a unique camaraderie that was as deep as it was long.

For the entire fifties, sixties, and seventies, and most of the eighties, Cy Williams spent his time on the road, away from his family for eight months out of every twelve. The new locales, strange faces, and cheap motels became part of his routine. There was, however, one place he always felt at home: near a baseball field, watching kids play. He had an innate ability to evaluate baseball talent; his method went far beyond the customary, to the very heart of a young ball player. Williams looked for the qualities you couldn't quantify: desire, hustle, and love for the game.

Babe, meanwhile, was at home in South Buffalo, in a house they purchased across the street from Cazenovia Park. There she reared six children—Bob, Janet, Jim, Tom, Ed, and Maureen— while Cy wandered eastern America's backroads, searching for future big-league stars. In his career, he personally scouted or signed nearly fifty future major-leaguers, including Al Kaline, Willie Horton, Joe Sparma, Pat Dobson, John Hiller, Dave LaPoint, and Dick McAuliffe.

Cy Williams has as many friends as anyone in baseball. One day in 1960, he ran into Tommy Lasorda, who was embarking on a scouting career after nearly fifteen years as a minor-league pitcher. Lasorda had walked up to a high school baseball diamond in Butler, Pennsylvania, where he noticed Williams in his trademark porkpie hat, watching players and scribbling in a notebook.

Lasorda struck up a conversation. Williams said that he was from Buffalo and that he had seen Lasorda pitch many times for Montreal against the Bisons in the International League.

"Tell me, Cy, what did you think of me?"

"Tommy, you had a great curveball, and you were a hell of a battler."

"C'mon, Cy, don't be nice; tell me what you really think."

"Honest, Tommy, you were a good-looking pitcher."

"Then how come I didn't make it in the majors?"

"Tommy, even scouts don't have all the answers."

Lasorda became close to Williams in those days. Williams covered primarily the Northeast and Canada for the Tigers, while Lasorda was a Los Angeles Dodgers scout in a six-state region, in the East.

The two men often shared a ride in Williams's car through the dusty, out-of-the-way towns that are part of a scout's itinerary. For Lasorda, trying to judge seventeen-year-old high school baseball prospects proved to be daunting.

"Holy cripes, Cy," he once told Williams, "these kids don't look big or strong enough to be professional baseball players."

"Tommy," Williams said, "you've got to project how they're going to mature, and how they're going to grow. You've got to visualize what a kid will look like at twenty-four."

"I don't know, Cy," Lasorda said. "Let's get back in the car, find a nice restaurant, and eat some Italian food."

Williams laughed and said, "Tommy, if you're going to be a scout, you've got to hit the road, work all the time, and keep looking at kids."

"Cy," Lasorda told him, "I think I'd rather be on the field."

Sixteen years later, after eight seasons and four pennants as a minor-league manager and four seasons as a coach in Los Angeles, Tommy Lasorda was named skipper of his beloved Dodgers. Bleeding Dodger blue all the way, he became one of the most successful managers in the big leagues, with fifteen years of service and more than 1,100 victories, including four National League pennants and two World Series crowns.

"Cy is still a very dear friend of mine," Lasorda says. "We spent so much time together when I was scouting, and we've kept in touch over the years. He's probably as a nice a man as you will ever meet.

"I hung around Cy because he taught me a lot, not just about scouting, but about life. He's a very knowledgeable man, and he understands what's important—in baseball and in life. He knows this game as well as anybody."

Johnny Pesky, a former shortstop who was a teammate of Ted Williams's at Boston and later managed the Red Sox, remains appreciative of Cy Williams for helping him learn his job as a minor-league manager in the Tigers' system after he retired as a player in 1956.

"He had a tremendous influence on my life," says Pesky, now in his seventies and the manager of Pawtucket, a Triple-A opponent of Buffalo's in the American Association. "Cy's one of the reasons I made it as a manager. I'm like a kid brother when I look up to him. He taught me so much about working with kids and staying in baseball.

"Cy's one of the wonderful men in baseball. He's not a loudmouth, and he's very dedicated to the game. But to me, what's more important is that he is a great friend."

Cy Williams spent twenty-nine years scouting for the Tigers and nearly fourteen years with the Major League Scouting Bureau. In Detroit, his boss was Jim Campbell, now chairman of the Tigers. "I'll tell you something: Cy Williams is one of the best scouts who ever worked for the Tigers," Campbell says. "He worked hard, and he'd cover every corner of that New York, Pennsylvania, Ohio, and Northeast area. Cy would look everywhere for kids who could play baseball."

Williams also was concerned about those kids after they signed. During spring training in 1967, Cy caused an uproar in the Tigers' organization when he told Detroit newspaper columnist Joe Falls about the old, wooden quarters in which young players were being housed in Lakeland, Florida. "One spark and the whole place could go up in flames," Williams told Falls. After the story appeared, Cy was chewed out by the Tigers' top brass. But soon afterward, new housing was built. "I got in a lot of trouble over that one," Williams says.

The Tigers, though, were appreciative of his contributions as a scout. In 1968, after Detroit won the World Series, the club gave Williams a bonus, enabling him to buy a new Cadillac. They also gave him a specially engraved diamond ring as one of six scouts who had been with the organization for more than twenty years. Each season, Detroit would bring him down to Florida to coach young players. "He really knows the game, and that's why we had him working with kids in spring training," Campbell says. "He's a class guy, and he made a great contribution to the Tigers."

Scouting in five decades, Cy Williams scrutinized thousands of ball players, but one stands above the rest:

"Joe DiMaggio was the best all-around player I've ever seen. He could do everything—hit, hit with power, run, throw. And he was a tremendous influence in the clubhouse. He didn't say much, but he was a guy all the other players looked up to."

Williams was also close to DiMaggio's first manager, Joe McCarthy. "I used to visit Joe all the time," he says. "He was a great manager, and he loved Buffalo." At Marse Joe's funeral, Cy was a pallbearer.

Cy's dedication to the game has long since become part of Buffalo's folklore. It was so intense, in fact, that it once even exasperated Babe, the love of his life, whose own passion for baseball wasn't much less than his. Cy had been away on a long road trip, and Babe was determined to make his return special. She had a steak in the oven, and the six children were scrubbed and dressed up, waiting at the dinner table. Cy walked in the door, kissed his wife, and a minute later, the phone rang. He spent most of the next hour talking baseball.

This was too much, even for a true-blue baseball wife such as Babe. She grabbed one of the kids' baseball gloves, put it on a plate, stomped out to the dinner table and put it right in front of her husband. "There!" she snapped. "You talk baseball, sleep baseball—now, go ahead and eat it!"

The baseball bloodline continued in the Williams family. His son Bob was a minor-league shortstop until an elbow injury ended his career in the Tigers' organization. "My dad was my biggest booster; he taught me everything I know," says Bob Williams, now a Buffalo police officer who runs the Police Athletic League program at Cazenovia Park, in the shadow of his parents' home. "He never pushed me into baseball, and he was always there when I needed him."

Cy's grandson Bobby, whose father is Bob Williams, pitched professionally for five seasons in the Baltimore Orioles' organization before quitting in 1990. "Cy was a big influence on me when I was growing up; he came to every game I pitched," says Bobby, now in his mid-twenties and a history student at the University at Buffalo. "I remember when I was a little kid, I'd go into his house and there'd be a ball game on television, and Cy would be talking baseball."

Bobby recalls that when his grandfather celebrated his seventieth birthday, he took a baseball glove of his own along when the two of them walked to Cazenovia Park. "He said, 'Let's play catch. Someday you can tell your kids that your grandfather played ball with you on his seventieth birthday.' Cy's always been in great shape.

"One time, I went out with him on a scouting trip. We were staying in this little motel, and I woke up when I heard this funny sound about seven in the morning. It turned out to be Cy, doing sit-ups on his bed."

Anyone who doesn't know Cy Williams would guess that he's perhaps in his fifties, not approaching his eighties. His perfectly combed hair is still jet-black, and there isn't a hint of wear and tear to his debonair, spit-and-polish image. At a svelte five feet ten inches, and 170 pounds (only five pounds over his playing weight from the thirties), he power-walks nearly four miles a day, golfs, and still seems more suited to taking a turn at third base than posing for a picture with his eleven grown grandchildren.

"That son of a gun never ages," Johnny Pesky says. "I can't figure it out; he's been in this game a long time, but he never gets any older."

One would think that being a longtime baseball fan in Buffalo would have accelerated the aging process. Cy Williams still remembers those dark days in the seventies, after Buffalo had lost its baseball franchise. "It was a low ebb for the city and for me; I felt as down as I could be," he says. "Something was missing in Buffalo without baseball, and there was a void in my life. But you know something? Deep down, I never lost hope that the game would return, because the people who live in Buffalo never lost their love for baseball."

The game did return, and now, most of all, the unflagging dream of seeing Buffalo with its own major-league team is what keeps Cy Williams young.

The opening of Pilot Field in 1988 coincided perfectly with the closing of Cy Williams's long career as a baseball scout, and there was never any doubt about what he now would be doing with his time.

"Pilot Field has become home for him," his grandson Bobby says. "He loves it there; in a way, he feels responsible for seeing that everything in the park is all right."

"He loves the atmosphere and being right in the middle of it," says Cy's son Bob. "When you come right down to it, that's his life."

Longtime historian Joe Overfield puts it this way:

"If anybody exemplifies Buffalo baseball, it's Cy Williams."

Mr. Baseball.

Considering the hopes and the dreams he has personified for so long, Cy Williams could easily be called something else, too: Mr. Buffalo.

ON THE MUGGY NIGHT of September 1, 1988, a Thursday, the Buffalo sky was black, and the stars were shining. Summer was ending, and autumn loomed on the horizon. But on this night, no one wanted to leave Pilot Field. It was the last game of the stadium's first year, and the Bisons had pulled out a dramatic 2–1 victory over Nashville in their last at-bat. Minutes after the winning run scored, there was a magnificent fireworks display. Afterward, the sellout crowd stood and sang an emotional, especially joyous rendition of "God Bless America." Standing in front of Seat 6, Row M, Section 100, Cy Williams was one of 19,500 voices in the chorale. When the singing stopped, the scene seemed frozen in time. The people—Cy Williams prominent among them—lingered at their seats, trying to make the moment last. Cy directed his gaze at the newborn baseball diamond, whose grass seemed such a gorgeous shade of green in the bright outfield lights. "I haven't felt this way about a baseball park since I was a kid," Cy Williams said with a gentle South Buffalo twang, his eyes atwinkle. "Sometimes, I just wish the season would never end."

ABOUT THE AUTHOR

ANTHONY VIOLANTI is a former sports writer and current feature writer at *The Buffalo News*. He has been at the paper for 13 years and has won awards for his sports and feature writing. His work has been published in *The Sporting News* and *Football Digest*. Violanti is currently cohost of a radio sports talk show in Buffalo. Violanti did play-by-play and color announcing for radio coverage of the University of Buffalo football team and was color announcer for the Buffalo Bisons cable-TV broadcasts in 1985. He is one of eight charter members of the Buffalo Baseball Hall of Fame Committee. He covered the Bisons for four seasons, 1979–1982, for *The Buffalo News* and has also covered major league games. Violanti, who graduated from Daemen College, lives in Buffalo with his wife, Andrea, and daughter, Heather.

FIRST EXIT - michigan - right
PAST 5/MD
THRUWAY

GO TO
OHIO
ST
STAY RT

RT
OHIO